LOVE HURTS

MOTORWAYS, MADNESS AND LEEDS UNITED

love hurts

Motorways, Madness and Leeds United

Neil Jeffries and Fraser Marr

MAINSTREAM
PUBLISHING

EDINBURGH AND LONDON

First published in Great Britain in 1997
MAINSTREAM PUBLISHING COMPANY (EDINBURGH) LTD
7 Albany Street
Edinburgh EH1 3UG

ISBN 1 85158 921 X

A catalogue record for this book is available from the British Library

Typeset in Garamond
Printed and bound in Great Britain by Butler and Tanner Ltd

To Alice Cheverton and Mackenzie Marr.
And to the Leeds United youth team
1996–97. New life and new hope.

Dedicated to the memory of
Brian Robert Jeffries

CONTENTS

Acknowledgements

I've told it like I've seen it but I wouldn't have seen it the same way without the greatest football supporters in the world, the followers of Leeds United. To all of them I owe a massive debt and I am proud to be one of their number even though I cannot know them all.

I would especially like to thank the supporting cast who drift in and out of this tale in various disguises. I list you here in alphabetical order but you know how important you were: John Aizlewood; Phil Alexander; Paul Bowen and Big Steve; Ian Bratt and Niki Clarke; Derek Cattani; Wahid Chaker; Mark Crossley; Jeff Dawson; Hamish Dewar; Mark Dormon; Terry Edson; Paul and Steven Elliott; Michelle Gardiner; Duncan Grant; Tony Greenwood; Jim Hague; Helen Hamshaw and family; Kay Hayes and family; Nick Hornby; Rhys Hughes; Derek Johnston; Tracey Keenan; Mark and Billy Kulke; Dave Ling; Andy Linton; Tony Luff; Joe Mackett; Lee Marr; Mike at Hamiltons; Giala Murray; Derek Muse; Ian Nathan; Huw Owen; Richard Perry; Andy Rowley; Andy Russell; Xavier Russell; Garth Sumpter; Jason Thomas; Phil Thomas; Trevor, Barbara and Howard Varns; John Walsh; Don Watson; Steven Whalley; the amazing David Wilson . . . and not forgetting Dave Shack and family, without whom I might still have a life.

I should also like to thank: Bill Campbell, Cathy Mineards, Andrew Laycock and everyone at Mainstream; nearly everyone in the Premiership (and elsewhere); Alan Roberts, Bob Baldwin, Andrea Ledger and Tony at Elland Road; and all the playing and coaching staff at Leeds United AFC (especially the youth team) – I hope that although you couldn't endorse this, you might at least understand it. No hard feelings, Carlton . . .

Introduction

Excited and anxious I await my dream
To escape, applaud and embrace my team
Opening day I can always trust
It's just for this high that I crazily lust
Return of our hero does brighten the days
Just briefly my troubles get lost in the haze
The grace from the field arouses the crowd
Reflects on the days when I was quite proud . . .

Opening dialogue from *The Fan*, directed by Tony Scott, based on the book by Peter Abrahams, screenplay by Phoef Sutton © 1996 Mandalay Entertainment. Words spoken by Robert De Niro as Gil Renard.

It's not often a Leeds United fan gets to follow Billy Bremner down the Elland Road players' tunnel and out on to the pitch. But I just did. Well, I didn't actually go on to the pitch itself. But I did let one of my size tens tread casually on the perimeter of that majestic green field. And Billy Bremner didn't know I was following him. Oh, and I guess I should admit that there was no match on and Bremner was dressed casually and holding the hand of his grandson. But I have walked down the Elland Road tunnel in the footsteps of Billy Bremner, and no one can ever take that away from me.

Billy Bremner was captain of the legendary Leeds side of the late '60s and early '70s. Small of stature but big of heart, his fiery determination inspired the team and everyone who supported them. Although Bremner isn't my all-time footballing hero – that is Allan Clarke, Leeds' number eight from 1969 to 1977 and scorer of the 53rd-minute diving header that beat Arsenal in the 1972 Centenary FA Cup final – he is, indirectly, the reason I'm here. With my size ten on the edge of the pitch. Grinning like a buffoon.

But that's a bit of history. Today the year is 1996, the date is 9 August. And while Billy Bremner laughs and jokes with the ground staff getting Elland Road ready for the new season, I am being led to a place just between the new dugouts, recently christened by the backsides of Spain, Bulgaria, France and Romania in Euro 96. I am here with my friend The Photographer, with whom I spend more Saturdays than is strictly healthy. His wife accuses us of having an affair. Sometimes I wonder if she really is joking. Our guide is Bob Baldwin, the club's commercial manager, who has just given us a quick tour of the West Stand and is now pointing to the two upturned blue plastic seats that our season tickets allow us to call our own for the next nine months.

But the seats are directly behind the dugout, so when manager Howard Wilkinson stands up (to berate Carlton Palmer, celebrate a goal, or – more likely – usher on substitute Rod Wallace as a replacement for a limping Tony Yeboah), The Photographer and I will be able to see bugger all. Baldwin sympathises with our plight and assures us we'll be able to change positions if we're not happy.

'Just go see the girls in the East Stand ticket office. No problem.'

We follow Baldwin back down the tunnel and through into the reception area, gazing once again at the deep-lacquered wooden panel bearing the names of all the players capped while playing for Leeds United, listed chronologically in gold paint under the name of the country they represented. Bremner's name is there under Scotland, Clarke's is under England and Yeboah's is in the right-hand corner, the sole representative of Ghana. The board is a beautiful thing and it's crazy, but at this stage in the season's proceedings, if this book all goes to hell and I get barred from the ground then at least I've got this far. And been led out by Billy Bremner.

Bob Baldwin shakes our hands, smiles and says goodbye. Walking back to my car we look at each other and shake our heads in disbelief at what we've just seen and done. Baldwin listened politely and intently to our plans for this book. We've stressed I'm a fan writing an honest season's diary and The Photographer is a fan too, hoping to bring to matches cameras he normally uses only in his day-job to record what we see. Baldwin seems convinced that we're not moles from some renegade fanzine or, worse still, Manchester United fans planning a hatchet job.

His office was like a den, packed with old pennants, videos, handbooks and photos and dominated by baffling shots of a handful of the *Coronation Street* cast dressed in last season's kit leading some bemused-looking Leeds players out of the tunnel. He has been suspicious, perhaps, of my southern accent, but appears relieved when I recall 1970's 1–0 FA Cup semi-final second replay defeat of Man United as the moment that led me here (the goal scored by Billy Bremner). He is far more impressed by The Photographer's subtly understated, and therefore expertly delivered, tale of how he was 'only a toddler' when his grandfather introduced him to Don Revie, thereby preventing him from becoming a Hull City supporter and instead giving him a real purpose in life.

About the last thing Baldwin said to us in his office was that he would raise our requests for 'special access' at the next manager's meeting. But then he showed us that deep-lacquered wooden panel and took us into the tunnel, and there was Billy Bremner . . .

Chapter One

Pre-Season

Wednesday, 7 August: ten days to go

At this stage of the summer, time seems to slow to a crawl. Like a watched pot, the fixture list never seems likely to come to the boiling point of opening day, no matter how many times you look at it. As August comes around and the gap between tabloid speculation and matchday perspiration closes, time can be measured in days, even hours, but some of the minutes seem to take forever. Especially those listening to Clubcall.

Forewarned by The Photographer that the news on Leeds United's Clubcall is depressing, and depressingly long, I can't bring myself to ring until it's almost time to leave work. Sure enough, within seconds, I am depressed.

It's been a bad summer to be a Leeds fan. It started well enough, with a £16 million takeover deal by 'media and leisure' group Caspian announced on 2 July. The very next day manager Howard Wilkinson bought Charlton Athletic's highly rated 19-year-old midfielder Lee Bowyer for £2.6 million. But then a threatened injunction from a 'rebel director' opposed to the takeover meant Wilkinson has had his hands tied in the transfer market. Okay, he signed Liverpool's Ian Rush (on a free) in May but has chiefly only shed players now past their sell-by dates, plus Gary Speed, for whom Everton generously paid £3.4 million in June. The lack of fresh blood was miserable enough, but the 23 July announcement that captain Gary McAllister was to join Coventry City was too depressing for words. The only light on the horizon at that point was that his £3 million fee finally allowed Leeds to buy a new goalkeeper, Crystal Palace's Nigel Martyn, for £2.25 million. But still the new squad looks weaker than last season's.

On Clubcall, Wilkinson is complaining that signing new players now they have become part of some other club's pre-season plans is all but impossible. And much worse, Ghanaian goal ace Tony Yeboah, easily the club's most gifted player, is proclaiming himself a cripple.

Yeboah has been injured since last March and is to have an operation tomorrow. On the way home all hopes for more of his 'beautiful goals' begin to evaporate as I stand on a main-line train which is packed, thanks to another tube strike. Through a forest of armpits I catch a glimpse of Highbury as the train rattles into Finsbury Park. For a nanosecond this excites me, then I look away in case anybody is watching and thinks I support Arsenal.

Yeboah's fears about his fitness are repeated, in almost identical words, on Ceefax and Teletext. I firmly believe that the people at Teletext get their stories by reading Ceefax. Although it may be the other way around. I make a mental note to watch when a big story breaks to get to the bottom of this mystery. Then make another mental note to forget all about the first one.

Leeds are playing at Huddersfield tonight in a pre-season friendly. I will have to check the score on Ceefax. But as ITV have highlights of Rangers vs. Vladikavkaz on at 10.40, I decide to resist discovering that score and sulk a little more about Yeboah. After seeing Rangers come from behind to win 3–1, with Brian Laudrup playing the proverbial blinder, I bite the bullet and tune to Ceefax page 302. The bad news is on page 313. Leeds were held to a goalless draw.

Saturday, 10 August: away to Grimsby Town

While everyone queues to watch the big new movie *Independence Day*, the first item on the main news is about boffins confirming that there is, or was, life on Mars. My naturally tidy mind files this piece of information away, ranking it second in significance to the Ceefax report that Tony Yeboah's knee operation has gone well – but even so, the Ghanaian goal machine is likely to be out for two months or more and so the team are without their most prolific goalscorer for the start of their most significant season in years. But at least that spares him a trip to Grimsby for a pre-season friendly.

*   *   *

I fully expect to die in a car crash. It's not that I'm a bad driver, or even one with a death wish, it's just that driving is the most dangerous thing I do and I do it a lot. Living in London, I have to if I want to watch Leeds United. And so not because of any morbid foreboding or suicidal tendency, I believe that, statistically, I am most likely to die driving my car either to or from a Leeds United match.

I often think about this and wonder, with what I admit is an unhealthy degree of perversity, whether the newspaper reports (if any) will make mention of the fact that I was *en route* to or from a Leeds game. I'll probably be wearing a team shirt so chances are they might. If I had to choose, I'd want the reports to read something like: 'Jeffries was travelling home from watching his boyhood heroes Leeds United beat Manchester United 3–1 at Elland Road . . .' That would be nice. Obviously it would be of scant condolence to my family. And had it happened, say, on Christmas Eve 1996 when that score was actually true, then no amount of statistically accurate obituaries would have cheered up the festive season for my surviving relatives.

This morning is not a good day to die. The papers wouldn't get much mileage out of this one. 'Jeffries was on his way home from Grimsby for a pre-season friendly . . .' Or worse, '. . . on his way *to* . . .' That would be terrible. Where's the glory in that? Would St Peter welcome me with a handshake, a slap on the back and say, 'Tough break, son, do you want to know the result?'? So through the light yet endless rain in north London, I make my way to the A1 with caution.

I don't like the A1. It wants to be a motorway but never quite manages. It keeps stopping to let roundabouts interfere with its best intentions and keeps going to places that I don't want to drive through, let alone get out and visit. Far better is the M1, my favourite road in the whole world. It starts near my home and only goes to Leeds. And back. So compared to it, the A1 is rubbish.

Today, about 25 miles north of my home the A1 becomes clogged with coaches full of people making their way to Knebworth to see Oasis, and I am forced to spend 30 minutes covering five miles. Radio 5 tells me that 125,000 people will go to Knebworth today. Presumably there would have been more, but Leeds are playing at Grimsby in a pre-season friendly, a testimonial for John McDermott.

Although it's the first pre-season friendly I've been able to get to, it's the last one Leeds are playing. I've missed them beat Irish team Shelbourne 2–0 in Dublin. I've missed all their games on the short tour of Germany. And I missed that doubtless less-than-spectacular goalless draw at Huddersfield in midweek. I'm travelling alone today as The Photographer is having his hair cut, or something, and I'm thinking how this might establish my credibility with you, dear reader. I obviously have to be pretty keen (or stupid) to drive 179 miles, alone, to watch a fixture like this. To further boost my cred, I'd rather hoped it would rain all day, just as it was in London when I set off, but unfortunately all the likely dramatic nuances of that scenario have evaporated come Knebworth, and according to the weather forecast the whole country is bathed in warm sunshine. And so instead of the steady tattoo of windscreen wipers my head is occupied with thoughts of Ian Rush. Why did we sign him?

Is he any good any more? And was it really very clever of him to tell the *Sun* this morning that he thinks the Premiership this season will be a three, not a two, horse race: Manchester United, Newcastle United and . . . Liverpool. (Or, as he pronounces it, 'Li'poo'.) No chance for Leeds, then? No, obviously not. In their heart of hearts, Leeds fans know this already, of course. But they certainly don't need to be told by the new captain Ian Rush, the star whom in Tony Yeboah's enforced absence they are being coaxed into treating as a hero. I don't need to be told it either, certainly not when I'm about to drive 179 miles to Grimsby . . .

I've never been to Grimsby before and, cup competitions aside, hope very much that I'll never need to go again. Although after Knebworth the journey is quite painless and the countryside approaching the town is almost pleasant. Even Grimsby's satellite borough of Cleethorpes seems more like a nice place to visit than a place whose name sounds like an Olde English term for haemorrhoids. I motor through it, along the main street, and spy the floodlight towers. I turn right, park and, as it's only ten to two, take a walk to the end of the street, over the railway bridge and on to the beach to look at the Humber. I take a photo of some crudely handpainted 'Leeds United FC' graffiti and feel very silly doing so because a family of four stand clear of the shot while I focus. Then, because the sea wall seems to be infested with dog shit and small black flies, I give up on the Humber and make my way to the ground.

When I walk into Blundell Park at two o'clock, the crowd is so sparse I wonder if a football match is to be played here at all this afternoon. I take some more photos just because it looks like a nice place to sit for a while, what with that nice green field and all these empty seats. Then two strange things happen. First, a steward tells me with the utmost politeness that I'm not really supposed to take photographs, even though it doesn't bother him personally. He even indicates the relevant regulation, apologetically, on the clipboard he carries. Next, at the refreshment kiosk, the lady tells me, with the utmost politeness, that the hot dogs aren't much more than warm yet and I'd be better off with a sausage roll, which is cheaper at just 65 pence. Once more, the very idea that there might be a football match here today seems farcical. These people are too nice to work at a football ground; I must be in the wrong place. Impressed by their generosity of spirit I buy a cup of tea as well as a sausage roll and then pay £2 for a rather unimpressive programme, trusting that John McDermott must indeed be worthy of my support if he's spent his entire ten-year career playing right-back for Grimsby.

When the Leeds players come out for a warm-up I feel a strange upsurge of pride mixed with a sense of confusion. Who are all these guys? Why do most of them look younger than a police recruit? And are any of them half as good as the former club captain Gary McAllister, recently sold to Coventry City? As well as Yeboah, injuries mean that also missing today are veteran left-back Tony Dorigo, young Irish international right-back Gary Kelly, hard-working but goal-shy striker Brian 'Deano' Deane and the, er, occasionally reliable centre-back John Pemberton.

With around 20 minutes to kick-off the Osmond Stand is at last starting to fill with Leeds fans, many of whom, like me, are struggling to recognise players sporting new summer haircuts. Tigerish young midfielder Mark Ford has had a crop which has gone right down to the wood and will, as the guy beside me comments, get him booked just for looking like a thug. Last season Ford was a notorious hot-head, and although his trim might cool his follicles, it's hardly going to improve his image with referees. Leeds' other midfield hot-head, new signing Lee Bowyer, has a similar skinhead cut that makes him look identical. Helpfully, he wears white cycling shorts under his yellow strip to help me distinguish him from Ford.

Most impressive in the warm-up is new keeper Nigel Martyn. He catches a few girlie knock-ups from 20-year-old midfield reserve Jason Blunt, then doesn't bat an eyelid as everyone in shooting distance begins blitzing him with shots that would have knocked last season's keeper, John Lukic, since free-transferred back to Arsenal, out of his boots. A quick head count reveals that Leeds have brought 18 players here today, and there's one that looks like Ian Rush. But of course, it *is* Ian Rush.

The players this season are wearing new gear made by Puma and bearing the logo of new main sponsor Packard Bell. It says a lot about the anti-Manchester United mentality of Leeds fans that in front of me one declares he won't buy the new shirt 'because it has red on it'. He's referring to the hair on the head that forms part of the Packard Bell logo which is, I have persuaded myself, more of a fluorescent orange. But I don't like it either. It doesn't take a rocket scientist to recognise that the whole shirt would have looked better if all logos were reproduced in a nice blue. But it looks like the fans are stuck with this for two years and there will surely be other, more serious, things to get upset about before then.

At five to three the two sides reappear and line up in a guard of honour as McDermott trots on to applause from all around the ground. This is unexpected, as the travelling Leeds support has a notoriously partisan and unsympathetic element. This element is very funny if you stand alongside it, but very embarrassing when it's reported in the press. The nicety is short-lived, however, because as McDermott applauds our end of the ground for the respect it has just shown, that notoriously partisan and unsympathetic element chants back, right on cue.

'Who the fuck? Who the fuck? Who the fucking hell are you?'

This is, I'm certain, very funny. If a tad disrespectful. After this there is a superbly observed minute's silence for a recently deceased servant of Grimsby Town, and then the match begins.

Immediately, Leeds look shaky. Either Howard Wilkinson already knows his best team and is using this match as a gentle run-out for the second string or he hasn't got a clue and is still desperate to find out. He's not the only one. And just when it looks like the highlight of the first half is going to be the baiting of the woefully silent home support with the cry of 'You only sing when you're fishing', up steps Carlton Palmer with a moment of madness to get caught in possession 30 yards in front of his own goal. Martyn races forward to close down the advancing Grimsby forward as Palmer chases helplessly in pursuit. The forward chips Martyn magnificently and, knowing he is beaten, our expensive new keeper turns and walks back towards his goal to pick the ball out of the net. Except it hits the bar and bounces back into his arms. Leeds leave the field to a half-hearted chorus of boos and it's like nothing has changed at all since the record-equalling string of six consecutive defeats at the end of last season.

The second half sees some token changes of personnel but no real improvement, yet somehow a later substitute, the 20-year-old defender Rob Bowman, rises to head an opening goal. The relief is enormous but still Leeds are sluggish going forward. Then Rush, who has been two or three yards off the pace all afternoon, slips a ball through to Rod Wallace, hitherto two or three seasons off the pace, who jinks and swerves and finally has no alternative but to score past the Grimsby keeper. It's almost a shame, because if anyone deserved to score today it was Leeds' mysterious young number ten, who runs his heart out and is finally identified by word of mouth from three people who have seen him play for the youth team as Lee Matthews. As the dull match winds to its pointless conclusion a deluge of substitutions see all 18 of those kitted out get a go, followed when Ford limps off after everyone else has come on, by a portly gentleman wearing number 20 who isn't some secret close-season signing from Old Etonians but coach and former Welsh international David Williams. He's not bad but this game has gone far enough, and when the whistle goes, so does everyone else.

Driving away, I identify that Leeds' major weakness, as obvious as a fart in a spacesuit, is that the team has no midfield general to replace McAllister. I'm still pondering this when the mobile phone rings and it's my friend The Wolves Fan telling me the shock news that Leeds have signed Lee Sharpe from Manchester United for £4.5 million. The obvious reaction is, how will fans who don't like a bit of red in the sponsor's logo react to an 'ex-rag' playing in a white shirt? Well, I hope. He is, after all, from that old school known as 'midfield' and prefers playing on the left, Leeds' specialist area of weakness since this summer also saw the offloading of Gary Speed to Everton. Suddenly, in front of me, looms Lincoln Cathedral and I realise I have lost track of the A46. Heading away from the cathedral and following signs to Sleaford, it occurs to me that Sharpe might just be the guiding light that steers Leeds – if not an idiot like me – back on course . . .

Monday, 12 August: six days to go

Clubcall says Leeds' recalcitrant Swedish international striker Tomas Brolin has opted not to return for pre-season training and is rumoured to be playing beach volleyball in his home country instead. Brolin is therefore in breach of contract (which insists he reports for training rather than forbids him from playing beach volleyball) and Howard Wilkinson sounds in a foul mood when the Clubcall interviewer speculates about his future with Leeds.

'Frankly, I've got more important things to think about,' spits the manager, apparently into a car phone.

Wednesday, 14 August: four days to go

The start of the season is no good without tickets. Getting tickets last season was The Man From Birmingham's specialist subject. His abilities in this area were second to none. They all came from the club, too. He never once had to deal with some character with a smile like a werewolf and a handful of fivers. No, The Man From Birmingham had class. He somehow made a block booking for the Coca-Cola Cup final and came up with 14 seats.

And so, when he explained he would get everyone tickets for Derby, none of us gave it a second thought. Even during the fortnight leading up to the match, when he failed to return any of my calls and left his mobile in the custody of his mother, I failed to consider the possibility that he could let us down. Then one morning, with just four days to go, it turned out he had.

During the summer Leeds had scrapped their controversial membership scheme – you had to have paid £10 for the credit-card-style ID card if you wanted to buy a ticket for an away match, and even at Elland Road you could only take one non-card-carrying guest. The system worked fine, I thought. The card was a statement of loyalty and said more about you than mere cash ever could. It said you were Leeds and proud of it, and when you'd had a few and became more proud of it, the card was always there to be flashed at people who never seemed to be quite as impressed by it as you had hoped. But this season, to get first refusal on the limited allocation of away game tickets you needed to be a season-ticket holder, and even though I am, by the time The Man From Birmingham admits he failed us, all tickets in the away block have been sold. Cut TMFB in half and he'll bleed white, yellow and blue but he isn't a season-ticket holder, and even he couldn't beat the new system.

The Photographer called everyone he knew but drew a blank. I do the same and The Biggest Yorkshireman In London comes up with the simple suggestion that I try Derby County itself. It has clearly been a long summer, as the idea would never have occurred to me. But the plan has its drawbacks. Leeds beat Derby County in both cup competitions last season and the atmosphere each time was ugly. The fans there still hated us from back in the '70s – because our team was better than theirs, presumably. But whatever the reason, it means that if we get tickets from Derby we will almost certainly be surrounded by people who do not like us at all. They might like us so little that they report us to stewards and have us ejected. They might like us even less and thump us . . .

*   *   *

None of this seems important as I borrow a *Rothman's Yearbook* from another part of the building I work in and note the Derby County phone number.

The phone rings three times and then an answerphone message clicks in to inform me that no one at the East Midlands Christian Fellowship is currently available to take my call. Strange that, but cross referencing with Directory Enquiries reveals that *Rothman's* is four digits out and so I dial again. Busy. After a mere 16 redials a very nice lady announces there are still tickets available and puts me through to the ticket office. After what seems like 16 minutes she comes back on the line to apologise for the delay, explaining that they are very busy today. Tragically not busy enough to sell out the first home game of the season four days in advance, I think to myself, but decide against mentioning this when a young man's voice finally answers in the ticket office.

I'm an honest kind of guy, but telling him I was a Leeds fan was, in retrospect, rather too honest and not a little stupid. He explains, quite politely, that he is therefore unable to sell me any tickets. He then asks a question that gives my feelings of stupidity a better perspective.

'Could you please tell me your name so I can make a note of it in case you call back later and tell me you are a Derby fan?'

I hang up and, figuring even he won't be so stupid as to not recognise my voice if I try again, call The Photographer and enlist his help. He calls the number, claims to support Derby, and is promptly asked to name a stand. He hangs up and calls me back.

This is serious. I understand, of course, that Derby's motives are entirely honourable. Tempers get heated enough as it is without mixing two potentially volatile sets of supporters. I personally am unlikely ever to knock anything tougher than the crust off one of the Baseball Ground's pies, but my slow-witted friend in the ticket office doesn't know this – and so must try to prevent me from getting in. But if he wants to play games, so can I. I run up four flights of stairs and borrow Brian Inglis's *Football Grounds of England*. Mr Inglis has omitted to include a ground plan, but by studying one photograph and reading his text I am able to draw a map of the ground. With this in front of me, along with photocopies of *Rothman's* and a note bearing the names of County's last three 'big' signings (one of whom, striker Ashley Ward from Norwich, is injured and unlikely to play, as I intend to mention, given the chance), I prepare to bluff my way through. It takes ages to get through again until the same voice answers. But he doesn't recognise my voice and I feel very confident. Too late I notice that the *Rothman's* was two seasons old and the last match I was going to say I'd been to is now ancient history. But I remain calm and await my starter for ten.

'Where would you like to sit?'

'The Toyota Stand.'

'That's sold out, I'm afraid,' comes the reply with just a hint of malice. Perhaps he *has* recognised my voice.

'We've got some restricted view in the Osmaston Stand,' he offers.

Oh dear. That looks like the home end. I ask if he has anything in the ABC stand. This clinches it. Now known as the Main Stand, only an old Derby fan would still call it the ABC. It is sold out, too, so I say the Osmaston will do nicely.

'How many tickets would you like?'

'Four, if possible.' I start to sweat.

'Where are you travelling from?'

'We'll be coming up from London; I'll collect on the day.' This seems unlikely, but I know my credit card details will confirm my address and I don't want to trust the post. Unfortunately I'm unable to blow my cover by asking where the collection point is, but at least we're in.

I punch the air as I hang up and then regret that he didn't ask me to name any players. Or even the colour of the ABC stand roof . . .

Chapter Two

August

Saturday, 17 August: away to Derby County

For the five people sitting around the table in this remote country pub somewhere near Birmingham, the air of expectancy that precedes the start of the season is about as thin as the team's chance of winning the Premiership. No one here has any bets hanging on this season's performance. No one dares make any positive predictions. With almost half the Leeds side of this afternoon playing together competitively for the first time no one dares.

Sitting around five plates of above-average pub grub, The Photographer, The Biggest Yorkshireman In London, The Man From Birmingham (I don't like to ask where his ticket came from), The Copper and myself make vague attempts to look on the bright side. New England manager Glenn Hoddle has spoken to Howard Wilkinson about the nation's shortage of good left-sided midfield players and Lee Sharpe's name came up. Much is being made in the press about Sharpe's intentions to revive his England career and while this seems a little fanciful, it does give us some grounds for hope. On paper, Leeds don't look significantly worse than last season. But, given that we finished 13th and would surely have been relegated if the disastrous closing form had begun just three games earlier, this is no great cause for optimism. A fretful silence settles over the table until The Biggest Yorkshireman In London, who has been gazing at the blackboard menu, swears bizarrely.

'Fucking hell, pineapple upside-down cake!'

No one is quite sure how to react and so it is some relief when he explains he had a dream about it last night. 'Perhaps it was an omen,' he suggests, helpfully, and orders two portions and five forks. I'm not generally superstitious, but over the last three seasons I have convinced myself that not shaving on a matchday, wearing certain socks, underwear and replica shirts, and leaving off my wristwatch is lucky – but then I tried all of them together at Hillsborough last season and Leeds got beaten 6–2. Then again, Leeds' sterling start to last season ended inexplicably the first match that The Photographer didn't wear the Ghana shirt he bought in honour of Tony Yeboah. These days, I only try to avoid shaving on the morning of a matchday, as if the glimpse of my three-o'clock shadow, out of the corner of their eye, would be likely to make Cantona, Shearer et al. have an off-day. But when the pineapple upside-down cake arrives we all tuck in and leave for the final leg to Derby feeling just that little bit more confident . . .

*   *   *

It's amazing, really. We have, in effect, had three months to reach the Baseball Ground but we still arrive late. The sun beats down as we jog around the uninviting industrial estate which is the ground's hinterland feeling panic and exhaustion rather than hope and elation. At the ground, about a dozen pretty girls wearing Sky TV T-shirts and black ski-pants are handing out plastic bowler hats like the Snickers ones so popular at Euro 96. These bear the logos of the *Sun* and Sky TV and are colour-coded black and white for Derby fans and white for us. Unfortunately, the commercial logos are coloured red and so very few Leeds fans will touch them with a bargepole.

The painfully slow-moving ticket-collection queue sees to it that the first ten minutes of the match, and the season, are only heard from behind C Stand. The noise from within is enough to convince us that Leeds have started badly and Derby are horribly close to scoring. When we finally reach our seats we are in the second row and are relieved to see that we are only yards from the Leeds fans to our left and that the ugliest of the Derby followers are in C Stand, rather further to our right. These are the people who punched and pulled the shirt of Gary Kelly as he lent against the barrier to take a throw-in during last season's FA Cup tie. They are a particularly unpleasant throwback to the '70s and seem determined to spend the afternoon announcing that, to the tune of 'Football's Coming Home', 'Yorkshire's full of shit', in between reminding all who may have forgotten that they all hate Leeds and Leeds and Leeds. The player they really hate, however, is Brian Deane. He is booed every time he touches the ball because it was his clumsy challenges that saw Gary Rowett sent off and Stimac injured in that cup game, which Leeds won 4–2 after being 2–0 down.

Leeds fans, though, are far more interested in Lee Sharpe, whom Wilkinson has positioned as left wing-back. His ball control and mazy runs are a revelation and so is his appearance. He has grown his hair long and looks a bit like actor Sean Bean. Thankfully playing rather better than Bean in the film *When Saturday Comes*, Sharpe torments the Derby left flank again and again, and 20 minutes into the half his pass releases Lee Bowyer, whose cross is deflected by Derby defender Jacob Laursen into his own net and Leeds are in front. Completely forgetting I am sitting in a home supporters' section I leap to my feet. Halfway up I realise my mistake, alter my plans and peer goalwards as if to check that the ball has, in fact, ended up in the net, then sit down again in mock despair. 'Don't do that again,' whispers The Biggest Yorkshireman In London, gruffly.

The score remains 1–0 at half-time and the electronic scoreboard reveals Everton are beating Newcastle 2–0, with both goals by ex-Leeds man Gary Speed according to a rumour that spreads like wildfire, while Coventry trail 2–0 at home to Forest. The huge cheer that greets this news says everything about Leeds fans' frustrations at having lost their captain Gary McAllister to Ron Atkinson's side.

The second half brings nothing to suggest Leeds are going to win the league but somehow convinces many Leeds fans that (again to the tune of 'Football's Coming Home') 'Derby's going down'. Then, after about ten minutes, Deane tries to stare out a section of the Toyota Stand that is baiting him and only succeeds in winding them up still further. This antagonism seems to spread to the players with Bowyer fouled, Ian Rush booked for protesting, then Deane taking a boot in the groin that has most of the men in the crowd crossing their own legs in horror. Deane is stretchered off and replaced by 18-year-old Irish left wing-back Ian Harte, the nephew of Leeds' right-back Gary Kelly. With Sharpe fading badly after his promising start, he moves forward and Harte takes his place. After about ten minutes on the pitch Harte reverses the roles again and takes the ball on a forward run while the Derby defence impersonates the Red Sea. Harte unleashes a shot from what seems like miles out, then the net bulges and Leeds are 2–0 up. This time I stay seated and with 12 minutes to play I begin to feel smug.

Smugness lasts for six minutes until an excellent goal from Dean Sturridge drags Derby back to 2–1. Then, straight from the restart the hitherto infallible defender Richard Jobson makes one of the worst back passes imaginable and Derby equalise. The Baseball Ground erupts. With just five minutes to play Bowyer cements a fine debut with his first goal to lift the gloom, but, almost on full time, South African international defender Lucas Radebe decides that anything Jobson can do, he can do even worse, and so it ends 3–3. Leeds have thrown it away and only Derby fans leave the ground happy. Horrible.

Tuesday, 20 August: home to Sheffield Wednesday

Yesterday the Queen was reported to be on the verge of a major shake-up of the monarchy. Howard Wilkinson did his bit to drag an old establishment figure that has seen better days into a new lease of life by signing 34-year-old Mark Hateley on loan from Queen's Park Rangers. Ironic, considering the one player Wilkinson spent much of the summer trying to sign from QPR, Trevor Sinclair, is still there.

The Photographer and I ponder this irony (trying not to imagine how painful the kick in Deane's nethers must have been if, as reported, it is likely to put him out for a month) as we head up the M1 for the first home game of the season, against Yorkshire rivals Sheffield Wednesday. No one at Leeds apart from the manager, who seems to view them as something of a nursery club, likes Sheffield Wednesday very much. So a victory is important, especially as, at this stage of the season, Leeds only need to win by three clear goals to go top of the primordial Premiership. As we drive into South Yorkshire, the weather turns distinctly primordial and visibility is down to as far as the next thundercloud. By the time we park the monsoon eases, but we are still wet as we get to enjoy that unique thrill of approaching your team's home ground. Our approach is from the west. Our pace quickens as the crowds thicken, and there is unseemly excitement at the glimpse of the new car park and barely contained euphoria at the view of the West Stand's profile and, towering above it, the roof of the giant East Stand. We watch as a team of parachutists drop in and then hurry to Entrance Four to sit for the first time in our new seats, slightly to the left of our first choice – a rearrangement sorted out, just as Bob Baldwin suggested, by the girls in the East Stand ticket office. We now sit between the dugouts, right on the halfway line. We are in the second row but the steward assures us the front row here will always be empty. From where we sit, we get close-up encounters with Leeds' embarrassing elephantine mascot, Ellie of Elland Road, and exclusive insights into the machinations of the two benches. The subs are at the far right of the dugout but Howard 'Wilko' Wilkinson is only ten feet away and will surely hear anything we shout. This means he can probably also hear Helen The Ellie Fan behind me suggesting, in her best music-hall whisper, that he should seriously consider quitting his job. Despite what happened at Derby, it seems a little early for that kind of talk.

There is much happiness to be gained from the first home game of the season, although precious little for Leeds fans during the first quarter of an hour, with Hateley predictably struggling to fit into a side he met for the first time this morning. Then it gets worse. In a fundamental defensive error, Bowyer makes a weak pass that goes directly to Wednesday's Regi Blinker, who lets in Richie Humphreys to score. This mere seconds after I have told Ian The Moustache, who sits two seats to my right, that two of the goals at Derby were down to fundamental defensive errors that will probably not happen again all season. The already-muted atmosphere takes a turn for the funereal – except in the corner where the Wednesday fans are packed, beating the drum and chanting over and over about being top of the league.

From the restart Ian Rush finds himself one-on-one with goalkeeper Kevin Pressman but sees his shot come back off the post when it looked easier to score. I sit down in disbelief and wonder what Yeboah would have done in the same position. Bowyer hits a dipping shot that clips the bar soon after, but elsewhere there is next to nothing to be proud of. The Wednesday fans chant on and on. The Leeds players get worse and worse. And a Yorkshire voice is swearing profusely.

'Fucking hell! This is not good enough!'

It's Howard Wilkinson and it's good to know he's as pissed off as we are at the half-time whistle. I can't be bothered to stand up in the break and instead phone The Wolves Fan to tell him how depressed I am. Wolves are on the telly tonight and are, he says, rubbish as well. But at least he's suffering in the comfort of his own sofa.

Leeds begin the second half with more promise and Wednesday slip back a little, but the chances of us making it 4–1 and going top of the league are still remote. Wednesday manager David Pleat stands to shout instructions to one of his players and is rudely advised to 'piss off and sit down' by Ian The Moustache. Pleat, a man who has apparently spent the close season mutating into a bizarre cross between Brian Clough, Mr Punch and Russ Abbot's Teddy Boy character, appears the only person in the vicinity not to have heard the shout. Wilkinson is shouting again too and bringing on substitutes, but Leeds are making progress.

Harte is excelling as the left wing-back and Rush hits the woodwork again, then Lee Sharpe runs all around the penalty area and past one, two . . . four players, only to see his shot come back off the post, go along the line and be cleared for a corner. Young midfielder Mark Tinkler has a goal disallowed after referee Jeff Winter stops play for what looks like an innocuous Rush challenge, then, after soaking up all the pressure, Wednesday score with a breakaway goal at the death. Leeds have lost 2–0 at home and the bloody Wednesday fans are still singing.

Monday, 26 August: home to Wimbledon

I wake this morning forsaking the idea of a lazy bank holiday, concerned instead that the paper shows Leeds to be 16th in the Premiership. Once upon a time no paper published a table until after four games, but they have long since realised that everyone looks for the biggest win on the first day of the season and then immediately calculates the league table anyway. Leeds then need to win and to win they need to score. One man who might have helped is Tomas Brolin, but last week he joined FC Zurich on loan. When the squad numbers were announced in mid-August, Tomas Brolin's demotion to number 36 of 36 seemed to offer a pointer to how highly he figured in Wilkinson's plans. It seems likely that the club may never recoup the £4.25 million paid to Parma for his services.

Wimbledon fans have no reason to feel any better. Their team, too, have played only two games but haven't managed a point or a goal yet. This is a match Leeds must win. If they lose, they will sit one place off the relegation zone. And with matches against Blackburn and Manchester United (who fought out a lively 2–2 draw at Old Trafford yesterday) to follow, it could look very bleak by mid-September and I've already joked about placing a bet on First Division football for next season if Leeds don't get three points tonight.

If Howard Wilkinson is a betting man, I wonder if he wakes this morning contemplating the odds on his future. Last season he survived calls for his dismissal from a sizeable proportion of the following. This season he has been quoted as second favourite to be the first Premiership manager out of a job. Last Wednesday, when Kenny Dalglish announced he was leaving his post of director of football at Blackburn Rovers, his name was immediately linked with Wilkinson's job. Leeds moved swiftly to dismiss this idea but yesterday a report in the *Sunday Express* quoted 'a City source' as saying that elements within new owners Caspian were less than pleased with both the team's low-profile start and the manager's signings and personality.

I'm not sure. I *like* Wilko's dour post-match interviews, his frequently wacky programme notes. I also like the fact that he seems to have 'a plan' and isn't just taking each match – or season – as it comes. Sometimes I wonder what the plan *is*, but mostly I like the air of mystery.

The journey up is a blast as Penelope Pitstop, a Man City fan, is seemingly so desperate to watch a live match that she will drive me all the way in her Mazda MX3. It makes a change from the diesel-powered Ford Orion that I drive. But as the match is being shown on Sky TV for a live Monday broadcast, her decision seems a little eccentric. Sky's choice of match is a little eccentric too, but presumably showing two unfancied sides at once allows them to fulfil a quota by killing two birds with one stone. The cameras – or the two unfancied sides – appear to have had an effect on the gate as the ground is little more than half full at kick-off. Vinnie Jones, stalwart of the Leeds side that rose back into the old First Division as 1989–90 Second Division champions only to be dumped unceremoniously the season after, gets a warm welcome from both the home fans and a meagre Wimbledon

29

contingent that looks like it might all have come in the same coach. Or minibus.

'We can't afford another bad start like our first 45 minutes last Tuesday,' Wilko is quoted as saying in today's *Independent*. The Leeds team translate this as 'start badly and get worse', stroking the ball across the back three, knocking it back to Nigel Martyn, resting the midfielders and negating strikers Rush and Hateley altogether. Patience wears thin in the stands during a first half in which Leeds never look like scoring, and it's small consolation that Wimbledon don't either. Helen The Ellie Fan has less patience than most. 'Why don't I just stay at home and drill a hole in my head each week?' she moans.

That kind of gallows humour is already starting to spread around the ground, and murmurs of discontent grow to shouts of complaint and boos of disapproval at half-time as the teams leave the pitch. Wilko has made changes that haven't worked. Dropped from the side that lost here to Sheffield Wednesday are defender Lucas Radebe, replaced by David Wetherall, Mark Ford, whose midfield role has gone to Mark Tinkler ('as good a passer as there is anywhere' according to Wilko on Clubcall), and, shockingly, Gary Kelly. In three seasons Kelly has been virtually ever present, forgoing the number two shirt only because of injury, international duty for Eire and a one-game suspension. His replacement is young utility player Andy Couzens, who lacks Kelly's pace and looks less than comfortable at right-back.

In the second half, the bored Sky halfway-line cameraman and assistant, over whose shoulders we lean to watch every replay on their monitor, turn and offer us their box of chocolate misshapes. It takes our minds off both the cold rain that has started again and now blows into our faces and the chances squandered by Sharpe and Bowyer. Then, with half an hour to go, a spectacular long ball out of defence by Wetherall finds Couzens, who lays it off to Rush, who pushes it to Sharpe, 20 yards out in front of goal alongside Vinnie Jones. Sharpe switches the ball to his weaker right foot with a turn that embarrasses Jones and then shoots in a curler that embarrasses keeper Neil Sullivan – the same keeper embarrassed by David Beckham's opening-day shot from the halfway line. Sharpe's goal, his first for Leeds, isn't going to beat Beckham's for goal of the month but it's the best scored here for months and the place erupts. He sprints for the corner flag and everyone rises in the hope of one of his famous Elvis-style celebrations. Instead he dives full length and mimes a few swimming strokes – but this hardly matters: Leeds are in front and poised for their first win of the season.

The crowd are happier but unsympathetically continue to make Couzens's life miserable, and he looks tired, saddened and relieved when he is replaced – by Kelly – soon after the goal. Penelope Pitstop is shocked by the home crowd's treatment of one of its own and I can't help but agree. A 21-year-old so obviously playing out of position needs support, not criticism. But Elland Road needs results, not excuses.

The scoreline is not improved but the second-half performance offers many grounds for optimism. He's no Gary McAllister but Tinkler looks quite good. Rush works hard off the ball and distributes well, even forging a fledgling relationship with Hateley, who has a pretty good game too. Tonight's win is Leeds' first since 3 April when they beat a struggling Southampton by a similar score in front of a similar-sized crowd. As we file back to Penelope Pitstop's car we get colder and wetter, but I feel incredibly relieved: Leeds are up to 11th, and Sharpe's transfer fee seems a good investment.

On the way home, the phone rings and The Wolves Fan informs me that the first managerial casualty of the season is not Howard Wilkinson but Manchester City's Alan Ball. PP is relieved, too . . .

Saturday, 31 August: away with you

A polite but perfunctory letter arrives on Leeds United AFC stationery explaining that the club is unable to assist with this book because it will not be possible to grant the facilities The Photographer and I requested. Leeds obviously don't want us nosing around in what is starting to look like the season of their greatest need. As it happens, we can manage on our own. And besides, we certainly wouldn't want to make it any worse . . .

Chapter Three

September

Sunday, 1 September: away to Moldova and Liechtenstein

There are no Premiership games this weekend because of World Cup qualifiers and Under-21 internationals. Even with Speed and McAllister gone, Leeds, encouragingly, have a number of players in the frame. Mark Ford and Lee Bowyer are both in the England Under-21 squad for Moldova. Ian Harte and Gary Kelly are named in Mick McCarthy's squad for the match against Liechtenstein and Andy Gray is chosen for Scotland Under-21s versus Austria. The last two named withdraw with injury but it's good that at a time like this, when the team itself is struggling to match potential and expectations, individuals at least are winning plaudits. Both Ford and Bowyer play and England Under-21s win 2–0 on the Saturday. Better yet, the 19-year-old Harte – who picked up three caps and a goal during the summer – scored again in Eire's 5–0 Sunday-afternoon romp over Liechtenstein.

At home, Wilkinson's battle to sign quality players produces tabloid rumours linking Leeds with bids for Spanish sweeper Miguel Angel Nadal from Barcelona and Liverpool's Neil Ruddock, but I'm already ignoring everything I read in the papers except the league tables.

Wednesday, 4 September: away to Blackburn Rovers

About 20 miles away on the M6 another Leeds fan signals to The Photographer and me from the fast lane, and he follows us into the next services. He's a complete stranger who doesn't know the way and wants to follow. As we have a cup of tea, he turns out to be the man who will buy The Man From Birmingham's unwanted ticket. He also tells us he hasn't missed a single match for five seasons. We don't know whether to congratulate or pity him.

Resisting the temptation to approach from the south on the Devil's Highway, the A666, The Photographer and I lead him into Blackburn from the east. I had been unreliably informed that Blackburn was full of dark satanic mills and was a pig of a drive from London, but it only takes four hours and we arrive at Ewood Park a full hour before kick-off.

We park in a street where three urchins, one wearing a Scotland shirt, stop kicking a ball around long enough to threaten to let our tyres down. I think they're kidding because they also take the piss out of the mid-'70s Admiral replica kit (complete with Allan Clarke's number eight on the back) that I wear.

'What's that?' asks Scotland. 'Is it a baseball team? What's that badge?'

I point out how the 'L' and the 'U' stand for Leeds United and combine to make a smiley.

'How is that a smiley? It's only got one slitty eye . . .'

Ewood Park resembles a massive out-of-town shopping mall but is cheered up no end by a huge black police horse that is having a fit. We stand well clear while its rider takes it to a car park to calm down and wander off in the opposite direction to buy a tray of chips from Mother Riley's Café, passing a similar establishment that still advertises a Shearerburger, currently far more popular on Tyneside.

We take our seats in the same block where, just five months ago, Newcastle fans dreaming of the title were reduced to tears by a Geordie, Graham Fenton, wearing a Blackburn shirt. Looking far happier is Kay From Blackpool, whose Elland Road season ticket is just behind mine and who has driven here alone tonight. She says she saw the Leeds team bus parked outside a Blackpool hotel this morning. I like Kay From Blackpool because in her household she's the Leeds nut, trying to indoctrinate her son, while her husband stays at home, a football widower.

The first half is remarkable chiefly for a number of fruitless sideways passes by most of the Leeds team and a whole series of mind-bogglingly unproductive forward runs by Carlton Palmer. Then, with half-time about six minutes away, Blackburn caretaker manager Ray Harford makes an inspired substitution when Garry Flitcroft replaces the injured Paul Warhurst. The former Manchester City hero's first involvement is to upend Mark Ford just outside the Blackburn penalty area. Sharpe curls in a free-kick and Ian Harte rises to head it past Tim Flowers. Hot on the heels of his blaster at Derby, as full-backs go, Harte is starting to look like one hell of a centre-forward.

At half-time the mood is almost ecstatic because Coventry are losing too, and in the second half Leeds withstand some intensive Blackburn pressure, with their Greek winger Yorgos Donis looking very troublesome, as the makings of a new Leeds pass-and-move system become almost visible. Far more fun, though, is watching Blackburn struggle. To the tune of 'Football's Coming Home' – fast becoming the most durable soccer anthem ever – Leeds' travelling support torments the Ewood faithful with 'He's fucked off home, he's fucked off home, Shearer's fucked off home' and 'You're going down, you're going down, Blackburn's going down', apparently convinced that anyone bad enough to be beaten by Leeds must be prime relegation fodder. When the whistle goes, Leeds suddenly look anything but, and back in the car Radio 5 confirms that Leeds have seven points from 12 and that, unbelievably, after all the pessimism of recent days, Leeds are sixth. One point ahead of Manchester United, who come to Elland Road on Saturday. For the first time this season I enjoy the luxury of phoning mates to gloat because their teams have done worse . . .

Saturday, 7 September: home to Manchester United

Yesterday it was a static Eurofighter 2000 at the Farnborough International Air Show, today I'm back in the cockpit of a Ford Orion on the M1. It may be technically inferior but its instrument panel is considerably less migraine-inducing. Today, if I want a headache, I only have to think about the dire consequences of losing to the old enemy, Manchester United.

I meet The Photographer, as I always do, outside the Luton Gateway hotel by junction 11 of the M1. Here he leaves his car and we travel in mine. This hotel is a haven for weary travellers and small businesses seeking conference facilities as well as an ideal meeting-point for footie fans, as it offers parking spaces and access to both carriageways of the motorway. Coaches for the Chiltern branch of the Leeds United Supporters Club regularly rendezvous here, as does a contingent of Man U fans. Sadly, the Gateway doesn't like people in football shirts dropping in to use the toilets or the telephones, but we still like to think of it affectionately. And sometimes sneak in anyway.

As we leave it behind, The Photographer tells me he too saw a tent pitched in the middle of the big sloping meadow overlooking the M1 about one mile to the south. He too saw a girl sitting cross-legged in front of it. And he too agrees that as no one in their right mind would camp in such an unpicturesque spot, beneath an electricity pylon, and we both saw it, this is clearly an omen. Because the girl was dressed all in white.

The Photographer has with him various newspapers including the *Sun*, in which Lee Sharpe is featured. He reveals that he has briefed his new team-mates on some previously unknown shortcomings of his old team-mates. Fired by this news and the suggestion from Ceefax that United's woefully underachieving £7 million centre-forward Andy Cole may play today, I remain encouraged that the improvements witnessed at Blackburn will be enough to overcome our opponents for the third season running. And when United's manager Alex Ferguson suggests to Radio 5 that Leeds only beat his side the last two seasons because they had weakened line-ups and we scored from set pieces, we are incensed enough to be confident.

Fixtures between Leeds and Man United are as important as they come in the eyes of the fans. The antipathy between the two sets of fans borders on pure hatred, uncomplicated and far from pretty. Such rivalries exist between other clubs all over Britain but surely none can compare with the depth of feeling that will bubble in the ground this afternoon, turning Elland Road into a cauldron of hate. As long as this doesn't spill over into actual violence, it should be good for a laugh.

Having read the papers, The Photographer turns to *FHM* magazine's '100 Sexiest Women of the '90s' supplement. Driving up the fast lane while glancing sideways at that many photos of scantily clad women is hardly recommended by the Department of Transport, but he draws my attention constantly by discussing their relative merits and complaining that the photographers are poorly credited. He waves a pin-up of *Goldeneye* Bond girl Famke Janssen in my direction as proof, clearly trying to disguise this quality time as 'professional research'. As we get close to Leeds, he finally reaches the top ten. When we should be discussing team selection, we instead find ourselves ridiculing the choice of red-head Gillian Anderson as number one. At least it has distracted us from the tension ahead.

Elland Road's once-feared atmosphere has all but evaporated over the last three seasons, but today it's intimidating indeed with angry noise and chanting coming from all four sides of the ground. The 3,000 or more Man United fans behind the goal to our right are being drowned out by the sheer passion of fans who normally only shout when Leeds run on to the pitch or score. When the Leeds team is announced over the PA, every name is saluted with a roar, including those of the substitutes. Every name in the opposition line-up is lost under a tidal wave of jeers, boos and whistles.

A similar welcome greets the first man on to the pitch, Eric Cantona, former Leeds hero now savoured with the kind of affection originally invented for Judas Iscariot. Terribly unsporting but strangely satisfying. Yet seeing the faces of the Man United substitutes as they step into the dugout to our immediate left, I feel uncomfortable to watch them stoically ignore the torrent of abuse raining from all around me. It's ugly and unwarranted and does Leeds fans no credit. At least we could wait until they've come on and kicked someone in a white shirt.

As the balls used in the warm-up are booted off the pitch, the figure of Karel Poborsky is the Manchester United player closest to us. Looking around I see

Ryan Giggs, Jordi Cruyff, David Beckham and any number of footballers who suddenly look as menacing as they are famous. When the whistle blows they look something much worse – confident. It's suddenly blindingly obvious that they are so much more confident than Leeds and within three minutes first Lee Bowyer, then Ian Harte both kick the ball off our own line only for the latter to see it rebound into the net off Nigel Martyn for an own goal.

The crowd gets behind Leeds immediately and the team respond but as Leeds attack, Manchester United merely retreat a few yards and soak up the attempts. Then a minute before half-time Cruyff is held by David Wetherall and referee Martin Bodenham points to the spot. Up steps Cantona to take it. Didn't Bill Shankly once suggest that the collective will of Liverpool's Kop could suck a ball in that might otherwise be going wide? Nonsense, of course, but somehow the collective will of Elland Road persuades Cantona to send Nigel Martyn the wrong way but hit such an ineffectual shot that the ball merely trickles over the line the wrong side of the right post. It was without doubt the worst penalty I have ever seen, and worth every penny of my season ticket to witness.

At half-time the post-miss euphoria is still at fever pitch and the ground stands to applaud Leeds off the pitch. The tannoy DJ supports the mood by playing Freddie Mercury and Montserrat Caballe's 'Barcelona' to remind the Man United fans of a 4–0 defeat. It certainly doesn't feel like we're a goal behind and somehow we convince ourselves that we are still in this match. Then the half-time statistics come up on the electronic scoreboard and the reality is grim: Leeds have not yet had a shot on goal . . .

The second half starts just like the first with another early goal (this time from Nicky Butt), after which Leeds' grip on the opposition coat-tails gets looser and looser. When Bowyer gets a ball in the face, Wilkinson goes for broke and makes a triple substitution, replacing him, Ford and the useless Rod Wallace with Lucas Radebe, Andy Gray and Mark Hateley. Fired by the change, Leeds chase the ball and the red shirts for just ten minutes but then concede a third, fittingly going to Poborsky, who has played magnificently. The away fans are ecstatic, making more noise than the rest of the ground because they know what I dare not say: Leeds are being humiliated. The difference between the sides is immense. We could be leagues apart. Leeds are a Ford Orion to the Eurofighter 2000 of Manchester United. Hundreds of Leeds fans start voting with their feet, leaving patches of empty blue seats all around.

There were times at Blackburn when I thought I could see what Wilko was trying to get the players to do, but today they look incapable. Soon, a chant familiar from the tail end of last season begins: 'Wilkinson out! Wilkinson out! Wilkinson out!' Angry individual voices shout at the manager just yards to my right, screaming for him to resign. The away fans join in with a cry of 'Wilko for City!' and a Leeds fan comes down the aisle to our right to shout at Wilkinson through the back of the Perspex dugout. And Wilko just sits there, a forlorn figure in his grey sweatshirt and white football shorts, powerless to do anything, pretending not to hear the chorus of disapproval.

How can a man withstand such pressure? Should he even try? It surely doesn't get any worse than this – and then it does. In the last minute Cantona gets a fourth and the rout is complete. The Frenchman salutes the Kop that once idolised him in a provocative gesture, but most are too drained to care and Giggs pulls him away before any harm is done. The final whistle comes mercifully quickly after that and I feel grateful that Leeds have lost only 4–0. Goodness knows what might have happened if Lee Sharpe hadn't told his new team-mates all about his old team-mates' weaknesses . . .

Monday, September 9: Wilkinson out!

Today's papers are no kinder to Leeds than yesterday's, and the greatest testament to the team's abject failure comes from Narciso Pezzotti, the Juventus assistant manager at Elland Road spying on his team's Wednesday-night Champions League opponents: 'This was not a real test . . . because the opposition were so poor.'

The *Independent* lists four Leeds players in their Premiership 'Team of the Weak'. McAllister is in there too. Alongside that hall of shame was another classic Howard Wilkinson quote: 'To the untutored eye it can sometimes look as though you are not fit, you're not trying, you can't trap, you can't tackle, you're scared. To be fair, hardly any of that is true – but it looked like it at times.'

He wasn't the only one to notice. I'm at my desk at ten to eleven when the phone rings and The Photographer's voice says just two words: 'He's gone.'

Hardly a defining moment in a lifetime, I guess – not compared to where you were when Kennedy was shot, England won the World Cup or the O.J. Simpson verdict was announced – but it's something I'll never forget. First and foremost, I recall Wilko sitting in the dugout ignoring the fan yelling at him and feel a sense of sadness.

Clubcall still starts with Howard Wilkinson's voice but the next voice explains it will be for the last time. I hang up. The phone rings again: it's my mum. Yes, I've heard, thanks for ringing. Unbelievable. The phone rings all day; nearly everyone tells me George Graham is the man and Leeds will be fine. This is odd.

After Alan Ball and Man City parted company, a number of potential candidates queued up to say they didn't want the job. But the line of most likely candidates was headed by the recently disgraced Graham, who seemed to be summoned to interview at Maine Road by a combination of Radio 5 pundits and Ceefax appeals. Graham's replacement at Arsenal, Bruce Rioch, did not apply because, rumour had it, he was biding his time in case there was a vacancy at Leeds.

Then I call Clubcall again and hear Howard explain with immense dignity his regrets. He is a proud man and I again feel great sympathy for him as he prepares to walk out on the club he has given his all to for almost eight years, never reaching the culmination of his glorious ten-year plan. Leeds were sixth before the United game and had been steadily improving. The squad is plagued with injuries and stymied by the summer's court case holding up funds. Ironically, Wilkinson reveals that one of the Euro 96 stars he had bid for but was unable to secure amid all the uncertainty was Leeds' chief tormentor on Saturday, Poborsky.

But that was then, and right now Leeds have to move on . . .

Tuesday, 10 September: Graham in!

At work when the phone rings it's like *Groundhog Day*. Except this time it's around ten to two and The Photographer's two words are 'George Graham!'

It had been on the cards for so long, even back in the summer, that it comes as no surprise. Only an anticlimax. One door opens, another one closes. One day your team is managed by a Yorkshireman, the next there's a Scot whom everyone thinks of as Arsenal. Clubcall is still introduced by Wilko's voice, but an hour later there's this Scotsman, apparently surprised to be doing this on his first day, saying, 'Hello, this is George Graham, er, speaking to Clubcall, the new manager of Leeds United . . .'

The phone at work rings constantly; working in London, I know many Arsenal fans.

'Congratulations! He'll be brilliant for you. He'll sort your defence out,' says The Gooner.

'There's only one . . . Georgie Graham,' sings Duncan Donut.

'So, Leeds United . . . new manager who's a crook, then?' offers The Big Boss – a man who claims to have forgotten all about his '70s Leeds allegiance and now follows Arsenal.

Me, I don't like change. If we win the next six games on the trot, I'll shout his name. Leeds have brought in big-name managers in the past to no avail. Brian Clough and Jock Stein each held the job for just 44 days. So ask me again on October 23 . . .

Saturday, 14 September: away to Coventry City

A new grudge match. Coventry are the club who took Wilko's much-vaunted successor and former club captain Gordon Strachan as their player/assistant manager, then bought our most promising home-grown striker Noel Whelan and the jewel in the Leeds crown, Gary McAllister, by reportedly offering him a salary of £800,000 a year, double what Leeds were prepared to pay. That they now languish at the bottom of the table with only one point and a single, solitary goal at least gives me much satisfaction and George Graham the easiest of starts.

According to the frenzied atmosphere of excitement pervading the Radio 5 build-up, including an interview with 'celebrity' Leeds fan and *Loaded* editor James Brown, Graham's arrival has 'fired up' the players and some have even asked for extra training sessions. This, then, is a game Leeds can't lose. The fairy tale rebirth starts at Highfield Road at 3 p.m.

Actually, it starts at 52 seconds after 3 p.m. when good work by Andy Gray gets the ball to Rush, who lays it into the path of Couzens to belt in our fastest goal for aeons. Leeds fans, who fill more than half the M&B Stand along the north side of the ground, go bananas, and the news photographers search out our new manager who has just seen his charges make the kind of opening that fairy tales normally leave out for being too unlikely.

But as the euphoria subsides, an earlier ugliness resurfaces. Vast sections in the stand are chanting 'He's going down, he's going down, Macca's going down'. I know this, because I am too. I do this because I think it's funny, but steadily I realise it isn't. Leeds fans are jeering at a man who gave their club impeccable service for six years then finally did something for himself. He is booed whenever he touches the ball, cheered when he loses it. Short memories.

The game continues, interrupted by chants of 'Judas, Judas!' and 'There's only one greedy bastard!', while I consider instead the changes from Wilko's last team. Palmer has pushed forward into midfield from where it takes me some time to notice that Lee Sharpe is missing, presumably injured. Our front line is Hateley and Rush, both of whom continue to improve – but the revelation of the team is Rod Wallace. Recently he has run around like a red setter, completely barmy and with no sense of direction. Today he is transformed into a terrier, attacking Coventry and the ball like he believes this to be his last chance of first-team football. Which it may well be. But Graham has said he wants effort and this kind of effort I'll applaud all day. Sadly, though, effort gets Leeds nowhere and at half-time it's still only 1–0.

Fifteen minutes into the second half, John Salako makes a completely unchallenged diagonal run towards goal before scoring with a shot into the one spot that Nigel Martyn couldn't reach. Coventry, fired up by the lifeline, redouble their efforts, and no one should have been surprised when seven minutes later they score again, through who else but Whelan. Leeds fans fall as silent as they've been all season. This wasn't meant to happen. The script wasn't supposed to be like this. Behind me a family outing is going horribly wrong and junior, dressed in a kiddie's replica strip, has seen enough. He squirms with boredom and mum and dad are kind enough to excuse him from watching the football.

The yellow shirts of Leeds throw caution to the wind but the closest they come to an equaliser is a penalty appeal when Carlton Palmer is bundled over. In fairness to the otherwise annoying referee, a Mr G. Willard of Reading, this was one decision anyone could get wrong. Palmer has a gait which could best be described as gangly-cum-about-to-fall-over. And so Leeds get nothing except egg on their faces and a marvellous Wallace volley crashing against the bar in the dying seconds.

Rising to salute the gallant but toothless attempts to equalise, Leeds fans applaud the team off. Then something wonderful happens. Whelan walks back towards the away contingent, his arms above his head, applauding the Leeds fans for supporting him. Just like Vinnie Jones . . .

Wednesday, September 18: Ceefax at home to Darlington, Coca-Cola Cup second round first leg

I'm lucky. I've got a job that allows me to get plenty of time off. But not tonight. I have to work late and by the time I get home the match has kicked off. Ceefax shows it's 0–0 as I switch on both the kettle and Radio 5.

I wanted to be there tonight for a number of reasons. Not least to witness Elland Road almost empty. But mainly to see George Graham and his new number two, former Arsenal and Eire centre-half David O'Leary, sit in the dugout for the very first time. O'Leary was a Leeds player for two seasons but played only ten times due to the injury that ended his career.

Prior to the miserable appearance in the final last season, Leeds' record in this competition has been abysmal, so when Radio 5 announces there has been a goal at Elland Road, I'm cheerfully surprised to learn it has been scored by Rod Wallace, in the right end.

With West Ham and Chelsea both a goal down at Barnet and Blackpool respectively, I feel confident enough to turn down Radio 5, tune into BBC1's *Big Cat Diary* and mix the Ceefax page with images of lions, leopards and cheetahs on Kenya's Masai Mara. Purely with the interests of this book in mind, it seems appropriate to photograph the page of Ceefax. Then, when the *Big Cat Diary* shifts to infra-red footage of lions with eyes like headlamps, it seems appropriate to photograph these with the scores overlain – purely in the interests of art. Or something. As half-time approaches with no sign of a second Leeds goal, Darlington then spoil the picture completely with an equaliser and the phone rings. It has to be The Wolves Fan, so I insult him rather than saying hello as soon as I answer it. It *is* The Wolves Fan. I let him have his gloat, then promise to phone him back later when normal service is resumed.

Five minutes into the second half he gets a phone call and a brief chorus of 'There's only one Rodney Wallace' after the little diamond has bagged a second. What is George Graham feeding him on? Ten minutes later it's heart-in-the-mouth time as Brian Butler namechecks Elland Road then cuts to the sound of nothing more than a microphone falling over. When it's picked up again I hear that Rush, needing just one goal to equal Geoff Hurst's all-time record of 48 goals in this competition, has had one disallowed for offside. Then, with a little over a quarter of an hour left, Darlington equalise again. I watch the phone and wait for The Wolves fan to call. But he knows not to kick a man when he's down . . .

Saturday, 21 September: home to Newcastle United

It's getting painful now. After failing to beat Darlington, what chance do we have against Newcastle United, Alan Shearer, Faustino Asprilla et al.? The realisation that I will drive backwards and forwards along the M1 to endure this kind of pain right through until next May stretches before me in a way far more daunting than the 190 miles of motorway. George Graham has said that the depth of the problem was greater than he anticipated and has spoken about the need for time and patience. All I can muster right now is dread.

As The Photographer and I take our seats, the injury crisis has got to the stage where I don't even recognise two of the Leeds subs. On Newcastle's bench sit Les Ferdinand and four others who could probably give the 11 in white a run for their money. With the game ready to begin, Shearer runs to the dugout to speak to Newcastle manager Kevin Keegan. Ian The Moustache yells at Keegan, who thinks he wants his autograph. No, we explain, just keep Shearer exactly there for the next 90 minutes. Keegan grins but Shearer runs back and the whistle goes. It's almost the last thing the referee gets right all afternoon.

Referees are an easy target. But just like luck, questionable decisions normally even themselves out over the course of 90 minutes, or at least a season. Refs are human and, just like players, they make mistakes. But today, Paul Alcock of Redhill is abusing the privilege. David Wetherall probably wouldn't complain about his first-minute booking for a horrible challenge on Peter Beardsley, but Rodney Wallace, whose only crime is backing away slowly from a Newcastle free-kick, is surely hard done by. A series of stoppages for petty offences baffles fans and players alike. Worse is to come. David Ginola is awarded a free-kick after theatrically exaggerating the attentions of Gary Kelly. The Leeds crowd is then incensed when the Frenchman throws himself into another outrageous dive, which Alcock completely fails to notice. Justice is perversely served when Ginola is booked after a push by ex-Leeds man David Batty. If Alcock is unable to tell the difference between the two, you have to ask yourself if his optician is able to sleep at night.

Shortly after, Keegan substitutes Ginola as an apparent safety precaution while the Kop reminds the winger that he is 'just a shit French bastard'. So much for European unity. But this is funny. Sending off Carlton Palmer is anything but. Likewise Alan Shearer's protestations to Alcock that seem so instrumental in Palmer's second booking and mandatory red card. As O'Leary says, escorting a nonplussed Palmer to the dugout, 'He's ruined the game . . .'

And he has. Up to this point, Leeds have been giving Kevin Keegan's quality-soaked side a real run for their money. Despite the constant interruptions for cards and whistles, the match is a thriller and Leeds' performance is far exceeding the very best The Photographer and I dared hope for when heading up here. But at half-time Alcock has to be escorted from the pitch as the boos rain down and the mildest man in football, Mr David O'Leary, has to be restrained from registering his complaints. Immediately, O'Leary achieves hero status and I forgive him for blocking my view as he paces the touchline.

As just ten men trot out for the second half, we get our first close-up glimpse of new manager George Graham, who habitually watches the first 45 from the directors' box. I feel a small glow of pride as he and O'Leary go deep into impassioned conference and reflect that all I really heard from Wilko in recent weeks was 'Fucking hell! This is not good enough!'.

The former manager sounded cheerful on Radio 5 this afternoon, where he was working as an expert summariser. All signs of pressure had gone from his voice and he sounded like a man reborn. 'Now I know why thousands of people go to watch football on a Saturday afternoon,' he said. 'It's actually really good fun, isn't it?'

It can be, Howard, it can be, but as the game recommences Leeds are unable to maintain their momentum and chief tormentor Shearer, booed every time he touches the ball for his apparent role in Palmer's dismissal, gets the one goal that separates the teams with half an hour to go.

But Leeds fight bravely and hope springs eternal. The two unknown youngsters on the bench make their debuts and turn out to be Mark Jackson and Wesley Boyle. Boyle's name and number aren't even on the squad list and checking the programme shows he plays regularly for the youth team. An equaliser never comes but there is a spirit shown that prompts something akin to an ovation as the beaten Leeds team leave the pitch.

The drive back is therefore not a depressing one but does provide The Photographer and me with a surreal near-death experience. As we hurtle along the fast lane somewhere near Sheffield, the car ahead switches to the middle lane and half a mile or so ahead I see a white swan. The bird stands perfectly still making no attempt to move. I take my foot off the accelerator but cannot change lanes due to traffic on my left. I resign myself to picking white feathers out of the radiator and going home on the back of a Green Flag recovery vehicle, but at the very last minute a gap appears to my left and I swerve into it. In the mirror, the swan remains absolutely motionless, frozen in either terror or madness. Yet it looked so serene and beautiful, I prefer to believe it was a guardian angel that only The Photographer and I could see. Yes, that must have been what it was. A hallucination. And the very next thing I find myself believing is that Leeds will start to be worth watching again . . .

Wednesday, 25 September: not away to Darlington, Coca-Cola Cup second round second leg

Work tonight means I also cannot be there as Leeds play Darlington away in the return leg. The swan seems to bring good fortune, however, as Ceefax on the office TV shows us to be 2–0 up after 30 minutes. According to the screen, Wallace has got both of them. The display later changes to credit the second to Harte and the mind boggles as to how anyone could have confused Wallace, short and black, with Harte, stocky and white. Unless Paul Alcock works for Ceefax . . .

Saturday, 28 September: away to Leicester City

The Man From Birmingham gives up. It's doing his head in already, and so he sells his tickets to The Biggest Yorkshireman In London who has been using the excuse of just having moved house for missing so many games of late. He drives Radio Rhys, The Photographer and me, to the last parking space in Leicester, near a canal flanked by an eye-watering mural stretching as far as the eye can see. Walking to the ground we agree on a prediction of 2–1 to Leeds. Leicester are one of those teams we must beat to get our season going again. So 2–1 it is.

Looking down into the canal to our right, a swan swims out from under the bridge. Then another. And another. In all, 11 of them. In white. My mind leaps back to the close encounter on the M1. This is an omen of the highest order – although a nagging doubt is raised when someone remembers that Leeds will wear the change strip of yellow today.

We reach the Filbert Street ground in time to watch David O'Leary leading the squad through a new regime of co-ordinated limbering-up exercises. The team's spirits look down. Looking to the left, the Leicester players are warming up in a far more lively fashion. And laughing among themselves as they do so.

This thought is still in my mind as the match begins and Leicester immediately look the more sprightly. The Leeds team has an odd look to it, plagued by an injury list that I cite to anyone who laughs at the results. Left-back Tony Dorigo is missing presumed lost. Central defender John Pemberton is on the long-term list, too. Tomas Brolin, although currently on loan to FC Zurich, has suggested he might return now Wilko has gone – but he has a knee injury. The Leeds fans chant his name a couple of times just to remind George Graham of how popular he was at Elland Road – with everyone except Howard Wilkinson. Lee Bowyer is also out, with a detached retina suffered in the defeat by Manchester United. And young Andy Gray – a 'player most likely to' according to a young Premiership dream team published in *Total Sport* magazine – is another one whose backside is keeping the treatment table rather than the subs' bench warm. And then there's the depletion of the forward line: Yeboah, Rush, Hateley and Deane all out.

This sad total of nine players injured is why George Graham has today fielded three midfielders and two wing-backs whose average age is just 20. He has no choice. And he has no choice but to play Rod Wallace, nominally a midfielder and a short one at that, as the target man in a forward line that consists of him and Lee Sharpe, who runs around bravely but gets almost nowhere.

And so, as the half-time whistle goes, Leeds have looked worse than hopeless. Nobody boos, which makes a change, until half-time's lap of honour by members of Leicestershire's county cricket championship side, waving their trophy at the Yorkshire faithful.

After the restart, a shower of rain that falls only in the south half of the ground and not at the Filbert Street end is instantly the most exciting event of the second half. Leicester fans, presumably, get more joy out of another awful piece of Leeds defending that lets in Emile Heskey to put the home side 1–0 up on the hour. Leeds have had a few chances, but the whole truth is told by Leicester fans chanting, 'We're shit, and we're beating you'.

At this, Leeds fans in the corner next to their tormentors rise to the bait and, after hearing the one about Leeds slums and dead rats, stoop to a level far worse than the team's performance and chant 'Just a town full of Pakis'. Within minutes a small fight ensues and, as if the football wasn't bad enough, it's 1973 again with stewards piling in to restore order.

On the pitch, Leeds rally slightly when Radebe replaces the injured Couzens and Wetherall leaves defence to do a passable impersonation of a centre-forward, but Leicester almost score again and a Wallace header against the bar notwithstanding, we never look like saving it.

Trudging away, no one is quite sure why Leeds resorted to playing the long-ball game to Rod Wallace, who is virtually the smallest player on the pitch. On the way home in the car, Radio 5 covers the news live as another chap who couldn't win a ball in the air against a Leicester defender, Frankie Dettori, wins his seventh race of the afternoon at Ascot. The odds for this are 25,092.5–1. The other news is that Leeds United are now fourth from bottom of the league. Ladbrokes' price for Leeds winning the Premiership has gone out to 250–1 . . .

Chapter Four

October

Saturday, 5 October: Barnet vs. Torquay United, Division Three

The Premiership is on hold again because England play Poland at Wembley next Wednesday. Leeds' international contingent has dwindled this month with only Ian Harte likely to win a cap when Ireland play Macedonia. The Irish manager Mick McCarthy has dropped Harte's uncle, Gary Kelly, presumably because he has noticed what Leeds fans have known all season: Kelly is a 22-year-old exhausted by three consecutive seasons in the first team missing only five games.

In the papers, the Tomas Brolin fiasco rumbles on but Lee Bowyer makes far juicier copy. Yesterday's *Daily Star* reported that Bowyer was one of four young men arrested in a drive-through McDonald's in London at 6 a.m. last Sunday. The paper suggests he was involved in a fracas when trying to order breakfast. It's barely credible that while nursing an eye injury and earning X grand a week, all he wants is a Big Mac or a fight. Brian Deane is another Leeds player finding unusual ways to occupy his time while recovering from injury. Thursday's *Sun* has a preview of a feature in the new *Company* magazine with Deano modelling only a smile and a pair of shorts, proclaiming, 'Football always comes first with me.' And on my doormat this morning is a letter from Leeds explaining that the club's position regarding this book hasn't changed as a result of the recent managerial changes. It has, actually; they've moved from ninth in the table to seventeenth.

Away from the pain and heartache of a Leeds fixture, I find myself wondering what football can be like if there's no love involved, only curiosity. And so Lord Percy, an Arsenal supporter, and I find ourselves paying just £5 to watch Barnet, the local Nationwide Football League Third Division side, entertaining Torquay United at the quaintly named Underhill.

The ground is impoverished but cute, with a couple of meagre stands, uncovered behind-the-goal terracing and a pitch that ripples like a duvet with someone under it. At kick-off, less than 2,500 people are there and of those only Percy and I are genuinely relaxed. It doesn't hurt us at all when chance after chance is missed and the only time I get remotely passionate is when Torquay's Jon Gittens hoofs the ball out of the ground three times in succession when gently into touch would have sufficed. Barnet don't look like they can afford to lose so many match balls. The match ends 0–0 and still I don't care. Which confirms what I knew all along: love of a football team should be an affair of the heart, not one of local convenience . . .

Saturday, 12 October: home to Nottingham Forest

If, as the theory goes, a week is a long time in politics, then a fortnight is a bloody eternity in football. Maybe the visit to Barnet served as a distraction, but the defeat at Leicester could have been two seasons rather than two weeks ago and a renewed feeling of optimism fills me as I point the car northward once again. The Photographer is unable to attend today because his wife gave birth to their first child just three days ago. It was clearly with a heavy heart that last night he offered me his season ticket, wishing that I lend it on his behalf to someone who would appreciate it.

The Wolves Fan, who has a number of unhappy memories of watching Leeds United in my company, draws the short straw. Had the performance of the team in recent seasons not been so uniformly poor, I might suggest he was some kind of Jonah figure – but sadly this is not the case. As the teams take the field, he points out optimistically that at least David Wetherall plays well whenever he watches.

Today Nottingham Forest are the team one place below Leeds in the Premiership and face a home side 'welcoming back' Ian Rush and Mark Hateley. Then again, Nottingham Forest have Jason Lee up front. Carlton Palmer is suspended but Leeds reintroduce Lucas Radebe alongside Wetherall and Richard Jobson across the back. Nottingham Forest have what sounds like a firm of solicitors: Blatherwick, Cooper and Pearce. Okay, so Stuart Pearce may be the best player on the field, but surely Leeds can win today.

With most of the first half gone, I remember there is a partial eclipse of the sun this afternoon but it doesn't get noticeably darker and nothing could be as dull as what's happening on the pitch. Pearce is by far the most entertaining player on the pitch, if only for his shorts, which he clearly has tailored three sizes smaller than everyone else's to emphasise the size of his leg muscles. The atmosphere around Elland Road has dwindled from something that could once be cut with a knife to a mire that needs stirring with a wooden spoon. The Forest fans sense a chance but their team are weak too, and at half-time the score remains 0–0. Behind me a youngster called Jack has the situation in a nutshell.

'Leeds used to be brilliant,' he pleads, wise beyond his years. 'In Division One they were really good.'

'They might be there again next season,' suggests Ian The Moustache.

Interval hopes are firmly pinned on an appearance by left-back Tony Dorigo, who might have made the England number three shirt his own were it not for a cruel run of injuries and the form of one Stuart Pearce. I live in hope of his first run-out since being carried off in last season's second leg of the Coca-Cola Cup semi-final against Birmingham City.

But when the second half begins it's the old codger Hateley whom Leeds have to salute, as his fine jump and header lets in Rodney Wallace to score within seconds of the restart. To be a goal up is a wonderful feeling but one which has so often been short-lived this season. And as Ian Woan bears down on Martyn's goal just minutes later I can't help but wince. Woan lets loose a fine shot and the ball skids towards the line and crosses it – the wrong side of Martyn's left post. The relief is incredible. To my right, the emotions felt by Forest manger Frank Clark are slightly less enjoyable. He turns and grips a steward's arm in disbelief and I suddenly like Frank Clark very much. An amusing man with a face like Deputy Dawg, he is in fact blessed with a similar ability to make people laugh. Shouting at the referee, swearing at his own assistants when they fail to produce number boards when he opts to make a substitution and – best of all – instructing Des Lyttle: 'Tell Jason [Lee] to calm down. He's springing around like a fucking idiot.'

Chesterfield Ken, a long-suffering veteran sitting just behind, chuckles at Clark. 'These seats are priceless . . .'

Well, almost, but when the football is as indifferent as that being played by these teams, being close enough to hear the likes of Clark being driven as mad as I am at least offers some compensation. So too does the miss by Woan. Leeds gather strength from it and Forest have theirs sapped. Soon there are only ten minutes to go and O'Leary is waving number boards 23 and 3. Couzens is coming off and Dorigo is going on.

All around the ground, a buzz of anticipation rises into a massive roar and standing ovation as Dorigo trots on. Small hairs stand to attention as memories of blistering overlaps, deft crosses and crunching tackles are replayed in thousands of minds. If Dorigo is remembering too, he must also be acutely aware that he is still off the pace. For minutes all he can do is shadow opponents and watch the ball be passed away from him. In apparent frustration he lunges into a tackle and is booked before he has had a meaningful touch. This hurts, but hope springs eternal. Sure enough, with less than a minute to go, it is a Dorigo tackle that is crucial in setting up a run by a second substitute, youngster Mark Jackson, that lets in Wallace to cleverly sidestep Forest keeper Mark Crossley for his and Leeds' second goal. The Forest fans in the corner and The Wolves Fan are the only people in the ground not on their feet. Looking down I notice that the cover of today's programme bears Wallace's picture and the coverline 'On target for United'. Spooky.

The Photographer telephones to ask if it is all over yet even as Ford and Sharpe are exercising a frankly ludicrous goal celebration. He is unaware because Radio 5 hasn't broadcast the news yet and so instantly hails his three-day-old son Mackenzie as a good-luck mascot. Then the whistle blows and George Graham has his first league win as Leeds manager to look back upon, even if he won't look back upon it with any great relish.

Back home I discover the last time Leeds won a Premiership match by two goals was on 13 January against West Ham United. For the first time all season I watch *Match of the Day* live rather than on video, and while Graham's post-match interview proclaims that the team's performance is 'not fooling anyone', my elation will not be diluted.

All the fear of relegation has gone. Suddenly I recognise what I have known all along: that it matters not how badly the team play as long as they win. I go to bed happy in the knowledge that I have not been fooled but I have been cheered up and even the thought of getting up at 4.30 a.m. to watch Damon Hill's final attempt at the Formula One championship in Japan seems like fun. If Leeds can win by two clear goals, then surely nothing can stop Damon . . .

Saturday, 19 October: away to Aston Villa

Nothing did stop Damon, but come this morning all I'm concerned about is Leeds stopping their recent miserable run of form against Villa. Last season there was the shambolic 3–0 Premiership defeat at Villa Park (when Wilkinson preferred to give a debut to youth-team player Alan Maybury than pick Swedish international Tomas Brolin, who travelled with the team but was told to carry the kit on and off the bus) and the Coca-Cola Cup final at Wembley in March when Leeds put on a display so poor that the same scoreline flattered.

All of which isn't exactly conducive to a cheerful drive up. Having missed last week's game, The Photographer has today taken the life-affirming step of leaving the week-and-a-half-old Mackenzie in the arms of his wife. Life goes on but I sense he feels guilty about it.

We arrive in Aston almost an hour and a half before kick-off, a unique experience, and pay £3 to a very jolly man marshalling a car park opposite the Aston Villa Leisure Centre. From here on in things start to slide. The Man From Birmingham calls to say he's on his way and to ask me to buy another ticket for one of his mates. This done, The Photographer and I approach a pub called The Witton Arms where, with another phone call, The Man From Birmingham is told to meet us.

Getting into The Witton Arms costs £1 per head and, once inside, it jumps right to the head of the list of Worst-Spent Pounds of All Time. Moving out of a bar that more closely resembles a cattle truck, we stand in the corridor by the toilets and get talking to a young lad who spots The Photographer's Puma top and decides we are safe to talk to. 'I wouldn't dare go in there,' he says, jerking a thumb in the direction of the bar we have just left.

I realise this is because he is wearing an old Leeds training top and is in fear of his life while his father has gone to the bar. Not wishing to frighten him, I tell him he'd be fine and that there are several Leeds fans in there. But he persists in the idea that there will be 'trouble'. He announces he is afraid to go to Arsenal on Saturday and then asks us if we get to many away games. Today's is only his second. 'My first was at Leicester and I was very close to the trouble . . .'

A sickening thought occurs to me: here's a youngster whose first experience of football at another team's ground has been soured by idiots who taunted and finally punched each other at Filbert Street. Now this polite and talkative lad will go to every game expecting to see a fight. Very sad.

Giving up on The Witton Arms and The Man From Birmingham, The Photographer and I attempt to salvage the afternoon with a plate of fried plantain and egg (with bread and butter) for just £1.45 in the Caribbean café across the road. Then my phone rings and outside the window is The Man From Birmingham, pointing at me. It's a quarter to three and we're not even in the ground yet. True to his recent form, he has been unable to get any tickets for the Arsenal game. I shrug and explain that it's okay as I have made a contingency plan. His eyes light up. 'Could you get me one, if there's a spare? I'd really like to go . . .' I can't. There isn't. He's mad.

The team this afternoon looks halfway decent. Although Carlton Palmer is back from suspension. Tony Dorigo has disappeared again but Hateley and Rush are fit and with Wallace just behind them and Sharpe as left wing-back, I fancy our chances. Our chances, as it happens, have slimmed considerably within minutes of the kick-off as Villa take the upper hand and use it to shake their visitors by the throat. The only light relief is a new chant, 'Stand up if you hate Man U', which prompts every man, woman and child in the Leeds support to surge to their feet, before sitting down laughing and feeling far happier than anything on the pitch had given them cause to.

Nigel Martyn is Leeds' best player by a mile but even he is beaten by a fantastic Dwight Yorke shot that cannons into the bar so hard that the goal is still shaking seconds after the ball has ballooned into the crowd. Unbelievably, the score remains 0–0 at half-time, during which I agree to settle for it remaining so for another 45 minutes.

When the teams return, Villa keeper Mark Bosnich makes his way towards the goal in front of the Leeds fans and a few taunt him with stick-on moustaches and Basil-Fawlty-as-Hitler salutes in reference to his 'joke' that misfired at Tottenham last week. It should be funny but it isn't. Bosnich ignores it.

After the restart, the inevitable happens. Villa's Serbian midfielder Sasa Curcic, superb all afternoon, tears Leeds apart in the 58th minute with a sprint and a pass that Dwight Yorke converts into a magnificent goal. I want to applaud but figure the guy to my left will punch me so sit in silent awe instead. Even as Villa celebrate, Hateley has only just got up off his arse after lousing up a half-chance at the other end. He'd had a better chance in the first half but messed that up too, and his performance today is so awful many in the crowd are giving him a hard time. Villa score again seven minutes later through Tommy Johnson and I sense a rout, but somehow it doesn't come. It does get worse, though. Graham makes a substitution that baffles everyone, taking off David Wetherall and replacing him with Paul Beesley. Beesley is another of Wilkinson's bargain-basement forays into the footballing hot-pot that is Sheffield and is regarded by the Leeds faithful with about the same degree of affection as a herpes scab. Which last year was slightly more popular than the Northern Ireland left-back Nigel Worthington, free-transferred to Stoke City in the summer. Beesley's introduction prompts The Photographer to suggest that the next thing that will happen is that someone will shout 'Come back Wilko, all is forgiven', and as the last syllable leaves his lips, someone does.

I keep trying to look for positives. We have caught Villa offside many times so presumably the Graham/O'Leary/Arsenal ethic is getting through to the defence. Unfortunately the ball is not getting through to the attack and to all intents and purposes we don't have one. Rush is almost a forgotten man, and a shadow of the goal machine he used to be when wearing a Liverpool shirt. Leeds have bought him at least two seasons too late. Palmer, Kelly and Wallace keep getting in each other's way on the right flank, while Sharpe is having his worst game yet.

Just when it appears things can't get any worse, and with many Leeds fans already leaving, it begins to rain, a cold wind blowing it right into our faces. Villa are well on top but seem to be toying with us. But for Martyn they could be 6–0 up. It's too depressing, and instead of the rallying cry of 'We're Leeds, and we're proud of it', the miserable section in the corner chant 'We're shit, and we're getting wet'. The whistle goes and in the last three matches against this team we have conceded eight goals and never looked like scoring once. This is bad; the idea that we have to play them again on Wednesday in the Coca-Cola Cup is far worse.

During the drive home, a Leeds fan phones David Mellor's 606 show to complain that the team are just as bad as they were under Wilkinson . . .

Sunday, 20 October: Newcastle United vs. Manchester United

It's cold. It's wet. I'm miserable. And I'm convinced Newcastle's defence will collapse again, Manchester United will beat them 2–0 and they will go top of the league. But against my gut instinct I pick up The Wolves Fan, drive round to The Gooner's and sit down in front of Sky TV. The goals rain in: from Peacock, Ginola, Ferdinand, Shearer and finally a peach of a chip from Philippe Albert. The three of us are beside ourselves with delirium. I realise that I have completely forgotten how football can actually make you happy, ecstatic even, just by delighting in other people's suffering. It's cruel. But it's wonderful. Because Man United have lost 5–0. Football really doesn't get any better than this . . .

Wednesday, 23 October: not home to Aston Villa, Coca-Cola Cup third round

I awake to news on Capital Radio that a helicopter containing football fans has crashed, killing its five occupants on the way home from Chelsea's 2–1 defeat at Burnden Park, Bolton. Ceefax tells me first that one of the occupants is Matthew Harding. Although I would normally have delighted in Chelsea's exit, this morning there is a sense that at a time when football is being spoiled by businessmen with money, today it has lost a true rarity: a fan with money who stood up for the hopes and dreams of others like – only far poorer than – him. On arrival at work the news takes a sadder twist when I learn that among the other passengers was John Bauldie, a Bolton fan who did the same job as me in the office next door, for Q magazine.

I have to work tonight so when the game kicks off a ticket goes unused and I am still at my desk, but I leave in time to find a pub to watch most of the game on Sky 3. The local is showing golf, the next pub's TV is tuned to boxing. The telly in the third is blank and the Alanis Morissette album is the predictable soundtrack, but a girl behind the bar promises to switch the TV on for me. She has to disturb a table of drinkers to reach the set and it feels like everyone in the pub is watching me. I tell her to leave the sound down and await the numbers in the top left-hand corner. Amazingly, although 20 minutes have gone, it is still 0–0.

I then sip my beer and watch in agony as the match unfolds silently above my head to the accompaniment of Alanis. Leeds survive what in slow motion looks a justified penalty appeal. At regular speed, Leeds seem to be quicker than they were under Wilkinson but look just as unlikely to score. Hateley has gone, his loan period having elapsed, but still Leeds play the long ball. Rush seems to have given up on being a forward and is now only any good at gathering the ball near the halfway line and giving it to someone else who will lose possession within a second or two. At half-time I can only watch expert summariser Gary McAllister's lips move and wonder what might have been if he still played for us.

For the second half I replace my empty glass with a full one, while one of the bar staff replaces Morissette with Garbage, an irony I can't help but smile at. Elland Road looks pitifully empty, and who can blame the faithful after the performance last Saturday at Villa Park? After it, George Graham was widely quoted as saying that, with the exception of Nigel Martyn, the performance had been his team's poorest since he took over. When asked which areas he was dissatisfied with he replied succinctly: 'The back, the midfield and up front.'

With the clock on the screen showing 68 minutes, Wallace on the byline by the virtually empty South Stand lays the ball back into the path of Sharpe who hoofs it into the roof of the net. I throw caution to the wind and order a third pint. Sadly, before I get anywhere near the bar, Jobson louses up and Ian Taylor makes it 1–1.

The Photographer, whose ticket is also going unused tonight, phones to express customary discontent – tinged, ironically, by the news that the 20 minutes I missed featured Leeds playing quite well – and before the call is ended Beesley trips Dwight Yorke and the referee points to the penalty spot. Yorke takes it himself, a soft one into the hole vacated by Martyn diving to his left post. The Photographer rings off and minutes later Tommy Johnson hits Martyn's left post from a distance, and despite a late rally, Leeds never really deserve to equalise. When the game ends I thank the barmaid for tuning the telly in and head off to the tube station.

The pain of watching Leeds lose has become a familiar feeling, a dull ache, like the remnants of a hangover. I had expected Leeds to lose tonight, but for the 60 seconds or so after Sharpe's goal celebration I was happy. Perhaps things will improve when Yeboah returns, when Deane and Dorigo and Bowyer are fit. And when Graham makes his first decisive swoop into the transfer market. Then again, perhaps not. It has already become easier to expect the worst and avoid disappointment. But as *Sportsnight* begins, it directs my thoughts towards the family and friends of those on board Harding's helicopter. The hurt I feel seems altogether trivial . . .

Saturday, 26 October: away to Arsenal

'He's comin' home, he's comin' home, Georgie's comin' home!' sings The Gooner down the phone, on the pretext of arranging to meet up before the game. He, like Arsenal fans everywhere, is frothing at the mouth at the thought of not one but two erstwhile heroes – George Graham and David 'Spider' O'Leary – returning to Highbury. The red half of north London surely effortlessly musters more enthusiasm than Leeds fans at the prospect.

The back pages are full of Graham wanting to bury the past – but suggesting a bust in the marble halls of Highbury wouldn't go amiss. He speaks of wanting to meet old friends – but get a win for Leeds United. The man is clearly deluded. Only one thing is certain: he and Spider can expect a far greater reception here than they are currently getting at Elland Road.

I walk past the car for a change and instead take the tube to meet not one but four Arsenal-supporting friends – The Gooner, Lord Percy, Fucking Phil and Video Steve – in what they assure me is the finest greasy spoon in north London: Holloway Road's Paradise Restaurant. The owner is convinced Arsenal will lose, and that they should sell Paul Merson and buy Donis from Blackburn. But like Donis, the owner is Greek. He's also clearly mad and should stick to bacon, egg, beans and chips, which goes down very nicely while I try to explain that there is no way Arsenal are going to do anything but win today and the only way Leeds are going to score is if Arsenal put one through their own net. The Photographer rings to say he's running about an hour late, so while the others take their seats in the North Stand I get to stand outside Arsenal tube station for half an hour with nothing to do but reflect upon how many good-looking girls support Arsenal.

The Man From Birmingham's ticket-fixing reputation now firmly a thing of the past, The Photographer and I have had to resort to a rather embarrassing Plan B. He has borrowed a pair of Arsenal season tickets off Duncan Donut and his friend, the latter having chosen today to get married with DD as his best man. The Photographer shows up 15 minutes before the kick-off and surreptitiously hands me one of the tickets. It's red, says 'Arsenal' on the front and I don't like it. (Although it did cost £54 less than mine for Elland Road and at just £303 permits entry to seven home cup ties – Leeds grant none – with refunds available if less than seven such ties are played.) Actually, that I like. But I don't like trying to find the seat while pretending I am a regular. When I do find it, the Leeds fans I would rather be with are just 50 yards to my right in the Clock End.

Shortly before three, the crowd roars its approval as the Diamondvision screens show George Graham and David O'Leary emerging from the tunnel to take their unaccustomed place in Arsenal's visitors' dugout. The reception is incredible and both disappear behind a scrum of press photographers that orange-coated security men try vainly to disperse.

When the commotion and the Arsenal fans' chants of 'One George Graham' subside, the officials and 22 players stand in the centre circle for a minute's silence in respect of Matthew Harding and the 81 people who were crushed to death at the Guatemala vs. Costa Rica World Cup qualifier two weeks ago. Leeds fans have no love for Chelsea and some unpleasant disruption seems inevitable, but when some Neanderthal bellows 'Chelsea scum' it comes not from the away supporters but somewhere to my left in the Lower West Stand. There are a few angry shouts of disapproval as an otherwise eerie and moving moment is spoiled. When the referee's whistle brings the period to an end, however, the full fury of the Lower West Stand is unleashed. The Neanderthal is removed by police and runs a gamut of angry abuse from almost everyone around him.

But the bitterness turns to joy all around me as Lee Dixon rockets a shot past Martyn to score inside the first minute. The Photographer's and my meagre efforts to fit in are exposed the instant we hang our heads instead of leaping out of our seats to celebrate. But I am past caring. All I feel is indignant at the ease with which French midfielder Patrick Vieira sprinted through the right of our midfield and at the gaping hole through which Dixon ran unchallenged. Just four minutes later a long clearance by David Seaman bounces over Lucas Radebe and Dennis Bergkamp – starting his first game for Arsenal this season – shows just how off the pace he is by rounding the defender to rifle the ball past Martyn for 2–0. The West Stand is ecstatic, the Leeds fans in the Clock End rally valiantly but the Arsenal fans capture their real mood with chants of 'You're going down, you're going down'.

The anticipated landslide does not materialise. Arsenal, seemingly sensing that their work is already done, take their foot off the gas and even let Leeds have the ball. This makes matters worse, because it only gives Leeds the opportunity to show how little they can do with it, except give it back to Arsenal. The team playing in yellow are so lacking in fire power that an overhit back pass from Lee Dixon is the closest Leeds come to redressing the balance with Ian Harte up front partnering Ian Rush. There is no Rod Wallace today as he got off the bus when his pregnant wife phoned to say she had gone into labour. And so he gets to spend the afternoon beside her rather than Rush.

For the Leeds number nine, time and patience among the fans is running out. When Wilko signed him he was clearly duped by an identical twin brother whose parents could think of only one name. His brother used to play for Liverpool and was one of the most prolific goalscorers of all time. But Leeds ended up with a bloke that couldn't hit a cow's arse with a banjo if he was standing next to one and holding the other. Further evidence is provided when Rush gets the ball and runs towards the Arsenal goal from 25 yards out. As he reaches the edge of the area he swings his right leg and the ball flies away in the direction of the corner flag. The Arsenal fans laugh. Leeds fans wince.

With Richard Jobson injured, Carlton Palmer has moved back into defence, allowing 19-year-old Paul Shepherd to make his first-team debut in midfield. Shepherd holds his own but the only real moment of promise in the whole of the first half is a flash shot on the turn from Harte that whistles into the side-netting. To the tune of 'Those Were the Days', the Leeds travelling contingent celebrates: 'We've had a shot on goal, we've had a shot on goal . . .'

Although Leeds are desperately short on firepower, sitting on the bench behind Graham, kicking his heels like a petulant schoolboy waiting outside the headmaster's study, is Brian Deane, back in the reckoning for the first time since being carried off in the opening game of the season. His return is the next glimmer of hope after the promise of Tony Dorigo's reappearance was put on hold once more with his hamstring injury apparently needing further recovery time.

The half-time interval comes and goes and, sure enough, first out of the tunnel for the second half is Deane, replacing Couzens. The tall, muscular figure makes an instant impact and an anxious Arsenal voice behind me urges his team's defence to stay close to him because 'he's dangerous'. Ironic, considering Deane must be some way off peak fitness but is instantly Leeds' best player. He looks like a Premiership footballer stepping down to play for a First Division side. And next season he might be if Lee Sharpe doesn't take opportunities like the one Deane presents him with just minutes after the restart. Sharpe, with virtually an open goal and standing about four yards out, heads the ball high, wide and not very handsome.

At the other end, Ian Wright is predictably far less profligate and picks up Arsenal's third with Leeds struggling to pick up anything other than yellow cards. It begins to look as if just when Yeboah and Bowyer and Dorigo et al. make it back to full fitness, the other half of the squad will be out on suspension.

At the end of the game, Leeds escape with a 3–0 drubbing and my only consolation is another statistic flashed on to the screens: Southampton are beating Manchester United 5–2. Filing out of the ground, someone with a radio says the final score was 6–3 and for a minute it almost doesn't matter that Leeds are back down to 17th, one above the relegation zone.

I make my way to The World's End pub to meet the Arsenal fans I had lunch with. Walking slowly, I try and prepare myself for their gloating, consoled by the thought that at least they will buy the drinks. Annoyingly, I get there first and have to buy my own. I take it outside and await their arrival while all around people use mobile phones to call friends and family and yell 'We are top of the league' – because that's precisely where Arsenal sit after Newcastle lost 2–0 at Leicester and Wimbledon (who had previously won seven games on the bounce since Leeds beat them at Elland Road) have only drawn. My phone rings and it's The Wolves Fan.

'Have you heard the shock news?'

I presume he means that Man United have been thrashed again.

'No, no. It's Graham and O'Leary. They've just resigned!'

'You're kidding!' I exclaim, as a dozen thoughts swim around my head. Today's the 26th . . . he lasted 47 days, three more than Cloughie. Who can blame them? Just when I thought things couldn't get any worse. What are we going to do? Across the road a TV set in a shop window is showing the classified results and The Wolves Fan is talking but I'm hardly hearing what he's saying.

'You're right,' he says.

'Sorry?'

'You were right,' he repeats. 'Earlier – when you said I was kidding. I am kidding and they haven't resigned . . .'

I don't know whether to laugh or insult him so I do both, and when the friends (who I will insist buy me a beer) arrive, I try the same wind-up on them. They all fall for it too. So that's all right . . .

Thursday, 31 October: he's coming home

Not far beneath Teletext's lead news story about Manchester United's first European home defeat at the hands of Fenerbahce is a headline that reads like every Leeds fan's dream come true: 'Yeboah on way back.'

'It's good news,' says George Graham on Clubcall, with a measure of understatement akin to suggesting that a National Lottery jackpot might improve a punter's financial situation, 'and it's a bit earlier than we expected. Tony has been doing a lot of running, but we'll just have to see how he progresses when he starts twisting and turning.'

The manager's note of caution is wholly appropriate, but it's not one I feel like sharing. On Monday night Leeds' season could have gone from bad to worse, but Everton managed to beat Nottingham Forest 1-0. Had that result been reversed, Frank Clark's team would have leapfrogged over Leeds in the table, pushing them into a relegation slot . . .

Chapter Five

November

Saturday, 2 November: home to Sunderland

Predictions *en route* to matches are rarely worth the hot air they're made of, but today I tell The Photographer I am absolutely certain Leeds will win and suggest 5–1. He guffaws, but when I explain that this confidence is almost wholly based on having seen Allan Clarke on TV last night on *There's Only One Brian Moore*, arrogantly making mincemeat of his erstwhile Chelsea rival Alan Hudson, he begins to understand. Then, seizing on the memory of the all-conquering Clarke, his hero also, he too predicts a win – but settles for 3–1.

My car is currently heading north rather faster than is strictly legal due to The Photographer's baby-delayed arrival at Luton. In the back today is Big Andy, who looks down on us during matches from the nosebleed seats of the East Stand. For reasons known only to himself, Big Andy would be happiest if he were at the ground already. Perhaps it takes him a long while to muster the energy to climb the steps to his season-ticket seat.

But our delayed departure apart, the mood in the car is good. The Photographer is flaunting his lucky Swatch – a hideous black and white patterned affair capable of inducing migraines – but it worries me deeply that he even thinks we might need a lucky Swatch to beat Sunderland. If the fourth passenger in the car, Big Andy's brother-in-law and another bloody Arsenal fan, agrees, he remains tight-lipped. Given the performance he witnessed when his own team destroyed Leeds last week, this is best explained as discretion.

Peeling off the M1 at junction 41 through Ardsley East, I wonder aloud what everyone thinks might be wrong with Leeds and whether Graham has made a difference. The Arsenal fan is quick to speak in the manager's defence.

'It's very early days for him yet and it's not his team he's having to play,' he says, in a practised manner that suggests he has been working secretly as a publicist for Leeds United. But his opinion, of course, is true and echoes what George Graham has said himself.

'He'll sort out your defence first, get that right, then work forwards.'

But I want to see him work forwards a little more quickly. I want to see him drop Ian Rush. No one objects to the idea in principle, but The Photographer and Big Andy remind me that according to Ceefax, Brian Deane is unlikely to play because he has tonsillitis so Leeds will need Rush up front. It's a depressing thought, but at least on arrival at the ground a blonde-haired girl with perfect teeth and a baseball cap gives me a free Slim Jim 'spiced and smoky meat snack' strip.

Once in our seats we watch both teams completing their warm-ups and wearing Leeds training tops are Lee Bowyer, showing no sign of either his eye injury or the rumble in the burger bar, and Brian Deane, showing no sign of tonsillitis. The story must have been yet another put about by the Leeds United Bureau of Misinformation, either to lull the opposition into a sense of false security or to worry us fans for a bit of a laugh. Ian Rush is, as usual, absent, but only because he is in the unique position of moving so slowly that he does not need to warm up.

At the kick-off, Rush, confusingly, stands on the right wing in front of us. As the game gets under way Deane and Wallace lead the line and, sure enough, Rush is playing wide in a new midfield role – Graham's apparent reward for his recent services to goalscoring.

Goalscoring, despite my earlier prediction, is soon the furthest thing from my mind as Leeds conjure yet another horrible display and Sunderland, with matching generosity, conspire to spurn chance after chance. But the army of Sunderland fans behind the South Stand goal are undaunted. Their noise is awesome, making them easily the loudest visitors to date, but in the occasional lull a confusing sound can be heard: that of a drummer and what may or may not be brass instruments. People stand to look then sit down again, their faces bearing a mixture of amusement and concern. Leeds United have, from somewhere, acquired the services of a band.

They've also acquired a telephone in the home dugout. This is glued to David O'Leary's ear almost all the half and it's certain that Graham isn't whispering sweet nothings to him from his vantage point in the directors' box. The word is that Graham is sitting today with Newcastle manager Kevin Keegan and Everton manager Joe Royle, whose teams both have the day off. I wonder if they enjoy seeing Graham squirm.

Then, after 27 minutes of teeth-grinding, Gary Kelly pumps a long ball out of defence that is cleared only as far as Wallace. Wallace moves forward and hits over a cross that flies straight to the head of Mark Ford. The young midfielder can hardly believe it when the ball hits the net. Neither can I. For one, his was virtually Leeds' first shot, and, secondly, today's programme has yet again compared him to David Batty, not least because of his notable lack of goalscoring. While I wonder whether to feel embarrassed about Leeds being in front, Ford is wondering how to celebrate. At first he untucks his shirt and considers a Ravanelli-style run. Then his fists pump and his arms wave awkwardly in a manner suggesting goal celebrations are something he has never felt the need to rehearse. As if to spare him further ridicule, Ford is quickly mobbed by Deane, Wallace and Bowyer, while nearer the centre circle captain Rush is unamused and waves urgently at the posse to stop clowning and get back for the restart.

Leeds carry this scarcely deserved 1–0 advantage into the half-time interval, when I set about biting my way through the wrapper and into the Slim Jim. I'm still spitting out bits of silver foil and wondering what a 'spiced and smoky meat snack' strip might taste like when the second half begins.

Leeds play better after the restart, with Rush making impressive headway in his new position, Deane looking dangerous and Radebe masterful at the back. Best and most surprising of all, though, is Paul Beesley. His performance in the centre of a three-man defence that has clearly been working hard on the training ground is a revelation.

O'Leary, though, is not satisfied and continues yelling 'tighter' at Beesley and Radebe's partner, David Wetherall. Eventually, poor 'Wethers' loses patience and yells back in helpless protest. Formerly Wilkinson's blue-eyed boy, he looks unhappy but is trying hard and deserves the distraction of Deane bulldozing down the left, into the penalty area, and chipping the impressive Sunderland goalkeeper Lionel Perez. Deane sees his chip bounce back off Perez but swiftly steps aside as the rebound falls to the on-rushing Sharpe, who blasts the ball into the net. As Sharpe begins his first ever Elvis-style corner-flag celebration since coming to Elland Road, the crowd mostly ignore him and chant 'Deano! Deano! Deano!' instead. Deane gets a thoroughly deserved goal of his own seven minutes later, and with Sunderland looking deflated Leeds push for a fourth, which Rush, ironically, almost snatches with a shot from a distance saved spectacularly by Perez.

The Leeds team leave the pitch looking ecstatic at their win, presumably unaware that it is the biggest league victory seen at Elland Road for two seasons. It's tough luck on Sunderland, but that's quickly forgotten when the scoreboard shows that Man United have lost 2–1 at home to Chelsea, their fourth consecutive defeat. A fine day indeed.

The drive home offers distant glimpses of countless fireworks parties but it's not until I get there that I learn from Ceefax that Leeds are still fourth from bottom. No matter, because for all George Graham's protestations on *Match of the Day* that he is still looking for 'some of that northern grit', his grin tells it all: injured players are coming back and the corner – if not yet turned – may at last be in sight . . .

Saturday, 16 November: home to Liverpool

England won 2–0 in Georgia last Saturday. In the car today are myself, The Photographer and Kentish Scouser, a Liverpool fan who has promised to behave herself on the way back if Leeds lose. For some reason (Liverpool's 3–0 drubbing by Blackburn Rovers two weeks ago, perhaps) I admit to feeling optimistic.

'You say that every week,' moans The Photographer.

Ah, but I mean it a little more since seeing the George Graham article in the new December issue of *Goal.* I read it whenever England's World Cup qualifier win in Georgia got dull (and consequently finished it well before half-time) and felt myself newly attracted to the man my Arsenal-supporting friends have been singing the praises of all these years. The story, written by Graham Wray, portrays Graham as a strict disciplinarian with a dry sense of humour, a true love of the north and the ability to coax goal-shy defenders into practising curling free-kicks past Nigel Martyn in training. Wray paints an aura around Graham that makes me believe in him and doubt only his players.

Suitably encouraged, I predict a 1–1 draw. Such scorelines are triumphant when your team is fourth from bottom and about to play the side fourth from top. When your team has Ian Rush and the opposition has Robbie Fowler, Steve McManaman, Jamie Redknapp et al. . . . .

Rush was in the headlines nine days ago when a *Daily Mirror* back page read 'Graham, Rushie in Pitch Bust-Up'. The story alleged a slanging match had occurred between the manager and his '£14,000-a-week' captain over Rush's Wilkinson-era agreement that it was okay for him to miss Monday training whenever he had played a weekend game. The *Mirror* suggested the row signalled the end of Rush's time at Elland Road. I was excited. But on Clubcall, Graham was quick to denounce the story as 'absolute rubbish'. I was disappointed. The manager went on to explain: 'Rushie told me when I first came here that he had an agreement with Howard Wilkinson that he could have Mondays off after a game. I am quite happy with the arrangement. If making an exception and allowing him to spend an extra day at home extends his career I have no argument.'

As we speed towards Sheffield, talk turns to a rumour, first told to me last

Wednesday by Kentish Scouser but repeated within hours by everyone I know, about Arsenal manager Arsène Wenger, and the dignity he displayed refuting it. It was actually a very good week for mad rumours. Even less credible was the one about Michael Jackson becoming a father and marrying his nurse, the mother. Or Tomas Brolin being on the verge of a loan deal with Sampdoria until medical advice suggested the metal plate holding Brolin's ankle together should be removed.

Passing the cooling towers beside Sheffield's Tinsley Viaduct, The Photographer remembers 17-year-old schoolboy midfielder Andrew Quinn, signed without publicity by Howard Wilkinson from Sheffield Wednesday at the start of the season. The signing has become news this week because an FA tribunal has ordered Leeds to pay record compensation to Wednesday, beginning with an immediate £75,000 credit plus extra payments in the event of first-team appearances and international honours. The total bill has a fixed ceiling of £490,000 but also necessitates Leeds paying Wednesday 20 per cent of any future sell-on fee. He'd better be good. And soon.

As we park the car and walk past stalls displaying but not selling any Ian Rush T-shirts, of more immediate import is whether the old geezer will finally score this afternoon. Against his old club, the stage could not be better set for him to break his career's longest run of games without scoring a goal. But it's still hard to feel upset for anyone other than Leeds United. The Photographer says Skytext ran a poll this week inviting readers to vote on whether he should be dropped, with 52 per cent of respondents saying 'yes'. As we take our seats and the PA announces the Leeds line-up, Rush's name gets a huge cheer and warm applause – but from the 2,000 or so Liverpool fans seated behind the South Stand goal. Perhaps many of them were among the 48 per cent who voted for him to stay.

This afternoon, Elland Road is buzzing with an uncharacteristic expectancy. The normally empty seats to our left and right behind the two dugouts are all full and there are no gaps to be seen even in the furthest corners of the ground. The teams trot out to an enormous roar that represents easily the best atmosphere of the season. At kick-off the collective passion sends chills up my spine but Liverpool's fluent passing quickly gets me sweating nervously. Fowler has soon tested Martyn and McManaman is rampant. Within ten minutes Leeds are barely hanging on. In the directors' box, George Graham has already seen enough to know Leeds won't survive and the phone in the dugout, unheard by everyone except David O'Leary amid the roars and complaints, tells the assistant manager to get 19-year-old defender Mark Jackson ready to replace Rod Wallace, playing again as a striker alongside Deane. Everyone is mystified and while Jackson is still stretching, Liverpool win a corner on the right.

Wallace trudges off with a face like thunder and on trots Jackson, while everyone in the stands tries to fathom Graham's plan. Kelly and Palmer both fail to clear the near-post corner and the ball bounces to Neil Ruddock, who lashes it towards the post Mark Ford is guarding. On the way it clips Palmer's leg and Leeds are 1–0 down with 13 minutes on the clock. Some time after the restart mere mortals like myself spot the thinking behind Graham's substitution: Jackson plugs the gaps in front of a back three comprising Radebe, Beesley and Palmer. It doesn't help Leeds going forward (where Deane and Rush now wait . . . and wait) but, together with tighter marking on McManaman and Fowler, it does stifle the team in red. Liverpool, to be fair, are under par today and making Leeds look better than they really are, but Graham's snap decision leaves me in awe because it works so well and allows the half to end at just 1–0.

The second half brings much improvement from Leeds but still no clear-cut chances. Nigel Martyn brilliantly denies John Barnes, while Radebe and a once-again impressive Beesley keep McManaman and Fowler much quieter. Lee Sharpe, however, continues to give the ball away every time he makes a pass, but at least Rush is giving it his all despite some appalling service. He goes close trying to turn in a ball at the near post and then narrowly fails to get his head to a Kelly cross between Ruddock and Mark Wright, when Wright appears to turn the ball out with his hand. Rush immediately protests to the referee and things turn ugly. Players rush in and push each other around. At one point McAteer has Rush by the throat. It's odd to see former team-mates at loggerheads, and Kentish Scouser isn't sure who to side with.

But it all helps Elland Road become the cauldron of noise that once made visiting teams so nervous. The Tannoy announces today's crowd is 39,981 – the biggest for two seasons – and there is an almost tangible conviction that Leeds deserve an equaliser. Working to far lesser effect is the band, periodically making a noise in the south-west corner under the scoreboard. Not far enough away to be an amusing novelty, close enough to be a pain in the arse.

Sadly, Leeds are woefully short of creativity to match their passion. No one typifies this more than Carlton Palmer, pumping long balls hopefully forward every chance he gets. When Graham has seen enough he runs out of the dugout to yell at Palmer, even though he is on the other side of the pitch and out of earshot. Sure enough, Palmer's long ball goes high, wide and distinctly unhandsome. Graham looks to the heavens in frustration and returns to the dugout swearing.

Liverpool are defending as desperately as Leeds are attacking. When McManaman belts a clearance into the East Stand, it's obvious they are rattled. Then Ruddock belts a corner clearance into the Leeds half and the hitherto faultless Martyn, almost at the halfway line, fails to control it, McManaman is able to run 50 yards for a second goal his team always threatened to score but one which I cannot admit they deserve.

Walking back to the car The Photographer and I discuss what went wrong. In front a disgruntled Leeds fan turns round and puts it in a nutshell: 'We're shit.'

Saturday, 23 November: away at Southampton

You know you've got it bad not because you go to a game on your own – thousands of people do that. Or because you arrive almost two hours before the kick-off and choose to hang around in the car park awaiting the team bus – there are almost a hundred people doing that. No, I realise how bad I've got it when that bus arrives.

Until it does, I stand around in the car park surrounded by kids clutching autograph books. While I reflect that at the age of 36 there ought to be better ways to kill time, one of these kids, a Southampton supporter, gives me the evil eye.

'Oi, mister, you a Leeds fan then? Brian Deane? He's a load of rubbish!'

I smile and explain he's Leeds' secret weapon, then ask him whatever happened to Frankie Bennett.

'Who on earth is Frankie Bennett?'

I point his picture out in the programme: squad number 21. 'Frankie Bennett,' I repeat. 'He's a right winger, came on as sub against us last season and instantly looked like the best player on the pitch?'

'Never heard of him . . . 'Ere, I got Simon Charlton's autograph. That's his car over there.'

Now it's my turn to be unimpressed and I turn my attention to the family who travelled down from Leeds and stayed at a hotel in Eastleigh. Like me, they are shivering with the cold, stamping their feet and suggesting a walk to the nearest refreshment van for a warming cup of tea. This idea is nixed by mum who points out that if they do, the bus will arrive and her sons will miss their chance of a Tony Yeboah autograph. I pretend to be with them, stand around and shiver some more, then start a conversation about the great man's first-team comeback, presumably against Chelsea next Sunday. Perhaps after a run-out for the reserves against Oldham on Wednesday.

'I can't wait,' says mum. 'Then we can drop Ian Rush. He's hopeless . . .'

On Wednesday, Tony Yeboah played and scored in his first match of any description since last March in a private practice game against a Carlisle United XI at Leeds' allegedly state-of-the-art training ground at Thorp Arch, near Wetherby racecourse. If Yeboah, named in *Goal* by no lesser a man than the great George Weah as one of his favourite five players, can now return to full fitness then the waiting will have been worth all the pain Leeds fans have been through lately. Until then at least we can take comfort from Manchester United's midweek 1–0 home defeat by Juventus in the Champions League . . .

Leeds United's Wallace Arnold bus pulls up alongside the car park, slows, then keeps on going. The Dell, as surely every Southampton fan would admit, is a less-than-imposing stadium from whichever direction it is viewed and it doesn't take a great leap of the imagination to believe the driver simply didn't notice it. But then the bus reappears, reversing in so that it can park with its door as close as possible to the players' entrance. As the bus trundles backwards I move to stand alongside it and give myself a view of the door. Looking up I see Andy Couzens and Gary Kelly looking down at me. I look away feeling embarrassed, looking for a small autograph hunter who might pass as my son (if I had one). The door opens and the passengers alight. Mr Graham and Mr O'Leary get off first, followed by the players, in no obvious pecking order, behind. Everyone looks very smart in the matching blue suits Graham has recently let them choose, as they didn't like the designs given to them back in August. As these familiar faces in unfamiliar garb step into the throng one-by-one I check them off and am aware of a rising feeling of excitement. I'm looking for Rod Wallace and Andy Gray (who are both rumoured to be injured) but see neither. Suddenly, though, there is a cheer from those closer to the bus door as off steps Tony Yeboah. I invent a new word and yell it instinctively. It's a mixture of 'Tony' and 'Hooray!' and as it escapes I recognise myself as a shameless romantic. But this season has been miserable enough without denying myself this tiny crumb of excitement. A small but heartfelt chant breaks out: 'Ye-bo-ah! Ye-bo-ah! Ye-bo-ah!' I grin like an idiot and realise the hairs on the back of my neck are standing up, not with the cold but with excitement. I have got it bad and I don't care.

I phone The Photographer, who is *en route* from Portsmouth. When he answers I blurt instantly, 'Yeboah's on the bus! I've just seen him.' He is excited too, I can tell, but a little anxious because he is lost. I tell him not to worry and to meet me in the pub behind the goal in Archers Road, a familiar rendezvous.

When I get there I consider sharing with the Leeds fans around me the news about Yeboah, but chicken out and instead take my pint outside and read the programme. I don't normally buy away programmes due to the hugely romantic misconception that the home team will rue the loss of my £1.50, but Southampton are such a small club that I decide to make a contribution to their meagre coffers. Today, this shamefully patronising gesture is also strongly influenced by the fact that I am alone and kick-off is still an hour away. The programme is deadly dull. But I do learn that Frankie Bennett is currently on loan to Shrewsbury.

First goal of the season, away to Derby County

First monsoon of the season, home to Sheffield Wednesday

Posing at Blackburn

Stand up if you hate Man U

Bored at Coventry

Eddie Gray studies youth-team form through December fog at Thorp Arch

Gary Kelly breaks his duck, Southampton

Leeds fans can't believe their luck

Nigel Martyn

Early arrivals brave the freezing cold at Goodison Park

Leeds and proud of it

Gary Kelly

Leeds and worried about it

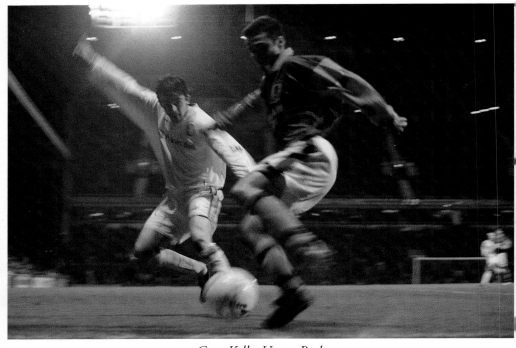

Gary Kelly, Upton Park

David Wetherall

Irony ahoy: 'We are the champions! Champions of Europe!'

Referee escorted off the pitch, home to Arsenal

Police and stewards brew a storm in a teacup at Roker Park

Lucas Radebe

*A traditional greeting to match the
Old Trafford welcome*

Rod Wallace vs. Crystal Palace, FA Cup. (Ever-attendant referee Dilkes, yards away, far left)

Nigel Martyn's last-minute penalty save, same match, sends the away fans barmy

George Graham's first signing, Gunnar Halle

Howard Wilkinson's last signing, Lee Sharpe

Saluting the FA Cup triumph at Highbury

Another Martyn penalty save, FA Cup vs. Portsmouth

Lee Bowyer

Some joy at last, away to Forest

Downpour at Anfield

Robert Molenaar

Save for the future, Elland Road car park

Across the road, members of the Hampshire constabulary are videoing those of us outside the pub, presumably to aid in the identification of any troublemakers. But they waste their time as Leeds and Southampton fans mix happily. Eventually the icy wind forces me to go into the ground so I phone The Photographer to tell him to meet me in the East Stand.

If The Dell is less than imposing from the outside, inside it beggars geometry. Every single stand looks like it was designed by some small child with no concept of perspective, or some architect with a Picasso-like obsession with cubism. On the pitch (which gives the impression of being rectangular, but you never know . . .) Matthew le Tissier and a few of the other Southampton players are warming up, but in front of my seat I find the sight of Ian Harte, Andy Couzens and coach David Williams firing balls at keepers Nigel Martyn and Mark Beeney far more interesting. The handful of Southampton fans behind the goal appear in near-mortal danger, as more than half the shots Harte and Couzens fire off crash wide of the goal and ricochet around the upturned red and white seats. The programme quotes both players at 20–1 to score the first goal but I sense if anyone from Ladbrokes is watching, they might well lengthen those odds considerably. Predictably, when the rest of the team trot out, Yeboah is not among them. The most enthusiastically greeted players, therefore, are the Lees, Bowyer and Sharpe.

The Photographer arrives and takes a few pictures, encouraged by the bright winter sunshine that can do nothing to lift the temperature. The stand opposite is too small to offer any shade and as the match begins all Leeds fans can do is squint and shade their eyes if they want to see what's going on.

Through the haze we see Rush miss a certain chance to break his duck then Egil Ostenstadt find the Leeds net for a goal that is disallowed for offside. The celebrating Southampton players are the last in the ground to realise.

When the sun finally sinks below the stand opposite about 15 minutes into the first half, a terrifyingly clear view of the atrocities being committed on the pitch emerges. The ball is pumped skyward time and again. The Photographer begins to count aloud consecutive passes by either team and never once gets further than four. Even before le Tissier limps off, I cannot believe that just a month ago Southampton beat Manchester United 6–3. It is, however, easy to see how they lost 7–1 to Everton last week. Leeds are no better and very possibly this is football at its worst.

I'm just pondering that immortal line in the film *Young Frankenstein* where Gene Wilder, standing over Marty Feldman as he re-excavates a recently filled grave the pair intend to rob, tries to cheer his shovel-wielding servant with some kind words: 'Could be worse . . . could be raining!' At which point the heavens open and Feldman is wet and cold as well as dirty and tired. God has seen this film and recreates that scene for the Leeds fans at The Dell this afternoon as, with a minute or so to half-time, the heavens open and spill some of the coldest rain ever known to man. As the whistle goes and the players run off, God delivers a double-whammy and turns the rain to snow. This is so ridiculous that it prompts a number of Leeds fans into equally ridiculous behaviour. It begins with the mindbogglingly inappropriate and tediously repetitive chant of 'We are the champions! Champions of Europe!' (normally saved for situations which have no conceivably worse variations) and ripens with the hare-brained idea that as it is snowing and we are all thoroughly cold and uncomfortable, then we should also be naked from the waist up. In truth, only about a dozen hardy souls are this committed, but the rest of us are fired up by the stupidity of the idea and take up the chant. The snow turns back to rain and the rain doesn't last long, but the chant and the shirts-off singalong continues for the whole of the half-time break. The Photographer wanders off to take pictures and returns with the news that there is at least one individual who has taken his jeans off too. When the teams re-emerge they bring an end to the best entertainment of the afternoon.

On Clubcall yesterday George Graham said he would settle for a point. With ten minutes to go I'd settle for anything that would make the referee blow the final whistle ten minutes early. Two more minutes grind by until Deane receives a throw-in near the left corner flag. His cross drops right in front of the Southampton goalkeeper Chris Woods, who makes no attempt to catch it then can only watch as it bounces over two defenders and into the path of Gary Kelly. In 163 games for Leeds United Kelly has never scored and his odds today of 66–1 seemed generous in the extreme. But lo, he cocks his left leg (he is right-footed) and volleys the ball into the net. Kelly is beside himself with delirium and shock and sprints directly towards us. I make plans to give up my seat, sit him down and kiss him, but this proves unnecessary as he swan-dives to the touchline in front of me and is mobbed by Leeds players and fans sitting rather closer.

With just eight minutes to go the game has finally come alive, as have Southampton, who get a series of corners and threaten to score.

'They're going to equalise in the last minute,' predicts some harbinger of doom to my left.

Not so, I tell The Photographer. Teams managed by George Graham don't concede last-minute goals – they score them. Just minutes later, with injury time in progress, this wishful thinking is enacted before our eyes when Deane is released by Rush ten yards inside the Leeds half, then runs almost to the Southampton penalty area, where his pass finds Sharpe unmarked to his left, perfectly positioned to wellie first time past Woods for 2–0. Leeds players enact a bizarre bow-legged walkabout celebration. The Photographer laughs and explains that it's the Vic Reeves and Bob Mortimer-styled 'Cockney walkabout' as featured on last night's *Shooting Stars*.

When less than a minute later the whistle goes for the end of the match, the Leeds players come over to the stand to give and take applause. Most of those around me have come a lot further than I have and deserve nothing less. But all of us deserve moments like these. Leeds United were awful today. The game was just as bad. But two goals and three points in eight crazy minutes have wiped all those memories away.

Driving home listening to Radio 5, David Mellor on 6.06 gives an FA representative a hard time over the new England kit, launched now when most parents have already bought their youngsters the old one for Christmas. Because I have *Match of the Day* to look forward to, I even feel sorry for the FA representative. On it, Gary Kelly is wheeled out for an interview in which he too looks forward to some of our 'great players' returning from injury and declares: 'We're not just saying "let's stay in the league for next year", we want to do as best as we can and, fingers crossed, we can be up there and fighting for a place in Europe.'

The goal has clearly gone to his head . . .

Wednesday, 27 November: away to Oldham Athletic Reserves, Pontin's Central League Division One

I'd be lying if I said Leeds United Reserves are my second-favourite team. My second-favourite team varies enormously, depending on who Manchester United are playing. But this afternoon, as The Photographer and I head north once again, we are prepared to switch our allegiances to the team about to brave the freezing conditions at Bowerfold in Stalybridge, normally home to Stalybridge Celtic FC. The reason is simple: Tony Yeboah is playing centre-forward.

Finding the ground is our only problem. I opt to stick to what I know and leave the M1 north of Sheffield at junction 35. This allows us to spend as long as possible in Yorkshire and gives me what looks on the map to be a reasonably straight 30-mile run across the Pennines into Stalybridge. When we get there, that run climbs on to a fog-shrouded Howden Moor blanketed in snow which looks altogether nothing like the kind of place that would be a good one to break down in. And so we cling to a convoy until the lights of the fabulously named Tintwistle indicate we have rejoined civilisation and have only six miles to go. Bowerfold appears unexpectedly on our left and we pull over to park, making our way to the adjacent Hare and Hounds to await the anticipated invasion of Leeds fans. Strangely, save for eight hardy souls, it never materialises. Walking the 50 yards from the pub to the turnstile, a reason suggests itself. The temperature is below freezing point and falling. But the thought of seeing Yeboah play in such an unlikely arena is insulation enough and when just £2 gets me through the turnstile, I feel a little warmer inside. The ground is like Barnet's, mainly uncovered terracing, with spectators free to wander around all four sides. The players are out on the pitch warming up – although the frost taking hold of the crisp green grass and the plumes of breath that float up towards the less-than-impressive floodlights suggest that warming up may be a relative concept. For a second, my heart sinks as Yeboah is nowhere to be seen. On the far side, I spot a knot of schoolboys pestering a man in a yellow shirt for autographs. The shirt bears the number nine and the man is Yeboah, so The Photographer and I lengthen our stride and walk around towards him. Just before we reach him, he peels away and returns to his warm-up.

The Tannoy man announces the two teams, Oldham first, then Leeds. 'Number five, David Wetherall; number six, Paul Shepherd; number seven, Wesley Boyle; number eight, Lawrence Davies; number nine, Fred Smith . . . just kidding, Tony Yeboah . . .'

Despite the cold, this is beginning to seem like fun. The players return to the dressing-room and we take up a place behind the goal. The teams re-emerge and when it becomes apparent that Leeds will kick towards this goal, two TV cameramen – from Sky and the BBC – take a position in front of our vantage point and a dozen or so Leeds fans drift round from the other end of the ground. The turnout is less than impressive, with perhaps only 200 people scattered around the ground.

For the first 15 minutes Yeboah doesn't get a touch and Leeds barely have an attack. The BBC cameraman in front of us is as bored as we are and says he will only switch his camera on when Yeboah gets the ball. But steadily Leeds get better, and their improvement coincides with Yeboah's apparent decision to stop waiting imperiously in the centre for the ball and instead to drift left or right to seek it. Soon he mesmerises a young Oldham defender, plays some neat flicks, then just fails to connect with a good cross from the right. When Leeds win a corner he pushes and shoves a centre-back he knows he can leave for dead while an Oldham defender yells: 'Someone pick up the number seven!'

'It's not him you need to worry about,' scoffs The Photographer in a voice obviously loud enough for the number seven to hear, as he looks over and scowls.

The corner comes to nothing but minutes later a powerful Wetherall header is cleared off the line by former Leeds right-back Ian Snodin. Someone congratulates him and, while a Leeds player receives treatment, Snodin strikes up a conversation.

'I was such a great player when I was younger.'

'Aye, I know, I've got your autograph. You looked much better with a moustache, though . . .'

Some heroics by Leeds keeper Mark Beeney at the other end aside, this exchange proves the highlight of the first half until a last-minute header from Ian Harte grazes the bar. When the half-time whistle goes The Photographer and I consider our verdicts. One, the match has been pretty awful, but much better than watching the first team at The Dell last Saturday. Two, Yeboah's performance improved as the match progressed and he'll probably play 30 minutes on Sunday. Three, tonight is the coldest we've ever been.

An old gentleman in a flat cap asks the name of our goalkeeper. He nods sagely but is unimpressed with my potted biography, waiting only for me to finish.

'And the coloured lad up front?'

'That's Tony Yeboah,' I reply, and he nods and wanders off. His judgement is clearly faultless. Perhaps Leeds should employ him as a talent scout.

As we make our way around to the Joe Jackson Stand at the other end, we pass a man in an Oldham scarf going in the opposite direction. He smiles and greets us: 'Real supporters, eh? Coming all this way on a night like this?' Then we tell him we've come from London and he scuttles away with a glance that suggests he thinks we're insane. All the proof he might have needed arrives a minute before the second half is due when the whole world suddenly goes dark. Floodlights, streetlights and houselights have all gone out and only a handful of generator-powered bulbs in the main stand shine on, making scant impression in the all-encompassing gloom. Half an hour later, with the blood near frozen in our veins, a whistle blows and unseen in the darkness the ref's voice announces the match is abandoned. Someone boos and yells 'Why?' but the answer is obvious – because two idiots have made a 400-mile round trip from London.

The Photographer is flabbergasted but I can only laugh and suggest it could be worse: we might be a goal down, or leading by a goal that Yeboah hadn't scored. Where would the romance be in that?

Driving back over the moors, where the fog has lifted and a brilliant moon reflects off the snow and Longdendale Reservoir, things get no worse and a whole lot better with the news from Radio 5 that in the Coca-Cola Cup, Manchester United are a goal down at Leicester. Then Alan Green's voice suddenly spoils the atmosphere.

'There's a penalty at Filbert Street . . . Up steps Butt . . . he's hit it over the bar!'

And immediately 400 miles for 45 minutes and no goals doesn't seem so far after all . . .

Chapter Six

December

Sunday, 1 December: home to Chelsea

I've been a laughing stock at work all week but have gained a perverse pleasure in telling the story of the fruitless trip to Stalybridge anyway. And so the question of whether Yeboah is fit enough to return remains unanswered, and a bigger question emerges: how on earth are Leeds going to deal with Gianfranco Zola, Gianluca Vialli . . . maybe even Ruud Gullit?

Football matches weren't meant to be played on a Sunday. The Photographer, who assumed 1 December was a Saturday and arranged to entertain friends, strongly agrees. When he tells me this is a date he cannot cancel, he is confident his wife will understand when he introduces Sky TV coverage into the mix to stimulate the afternoon's conversation.

At this stage of the season Sky coverage could be very embarrassing. If Leeds play like they did at Southampton they might be humiliated by the currently high-flying Chelsea and everyone will know why, as David O'Leary told Clubcall during the week: 'This season's all about consolidating and getting the club up into mid-table.'

So was he worried about relegation, asked the interviewer?

'We've got to be worried . . .'

Not just me, then.

And so The Wolves Fan gets to visit Elland Road yet again. When we get there, I see someone selling issue ten of *We Are Leeds*, a fanzine I've never seen before. It has, he apologises, been a long wait since issue nine but I forgive him and buy its successor. A quick scan reveals *WAL* to be a little less bitter than its ubiquitous rival *The Square Ball*, but is nevertheless a fanzine troubled by its *raison d'être*, as the editorial admits: 'When you have been campaigning vociferously for the manager's head for nine issues, what do you write about when they finally sack him?'

Closer to the ground, thoughts of the more gutsy performances against Newcastle and Liverpool lead me to believe George Graham might be inspiring the team to raise their game against superior visitors. A picture of Paul Beesley looking like Monty Python's D.P. Gumby on the programme's cover momentarily dampens this new burst of confidence. Then I spy more girls handing out impenetrably foil-wrapped Slim Jim sausages and The Wolves Fan, who views such things as haute cuisine, snatches a handful and follows me in through turnstile four, muttering how he hopes David Wetherall will play well again today.

Once in our seats, a glance at a monitor beside the Sky cameraman in front of us reveals that 'Wethers' plays in defence alongside Palmer and Beesley, with Radebe pushed into midfield. Equally unexpectedly, Yeboah is one of the subs alongside Wallace. Ah well. The Ghanaian is out there warming up. For the time being, however, it is not Yeboah but a small child who is the centre of the crowd's attention. For playing 'keepy-uppy' with Gary Kelly and Mark Ford is a boy half their size who appears just as good. He is nine-year-old Richard Hanley of Oldham, today's mascot, with ball-juggling skills so accomplished that the West Stand cheers his every touch. He leaves the pitch with the full-timers, still juggling, but his innocent modesty is exposed as an act when he pauses, waves and milks the applause. I just hope he's under the wing of the club's Centre of Excellence and that he is very definitely not a girl – as was the ten-year-old Del Morton which last Tuesday's *Daily Mirror* said Leeds scout Ces Pod tried to sign recently . . .

Hanley leads the teams out just before 4 p.m. but is quickly forgotten once the referee Gerald Ashby's whistle blows. From the start three things are apparent: Radebe is man-marking Gianfranco Zola, Deane is chasing every ball like a thing possessed; and the atmosphere in the stands is as good as it's been all season. The collective will to beat Chelsea stems from their victory over Leeds in the 1970 FA Cup final replay and not because this season Chelsea have been getting so much attention for having a star-studded skilful team playing attractive football. But that helps, too.

Those stars are, however, having trouble staying on their feet on a surface that appears to have been only recently greased with chicken fat. George Graham has complained about the quality of the pitch recently, and it's easy to see why, but the only reason Gianluca Vialli goes down after an innocuous challenge from Bowyer is that the expensive Italian striker is a big girl's blouse. Vialli's dive is so theatrical, Leeds fans all around the ground leap to their feet to offer something less than sympathetic condolences.

Seconds later Beesley plays a long ball out of the Leeds half which curls seductively around the Chelsea right-back and into the path of Deane. Chelsea keeper Frode Grodas is off his line quickly, forcing Deane wide but the big forward evades the challenge then, off-balance and from the narrowest of angles, tucks the ball into the unguarded net with his left foot. Leeds 1, Expensive Italians 0. Elland Road is ecstatic.

In today's programme Graham has written: 'I want my teams to be committed, to win the ball back as early as possible, and to be a forward-looking team.' It looks like he read that passage aloud to them before they left the dressing-room as Chelsea are being run ragged – and there is more to come very soon after. Sharpe races into the penalty area and half connects with a cross from Kelly. The rebound evades Chelsea defenders Dan Petrescu and Michael Duberry and Rush is in like a shot to stab the ball home. As I leap out of my seat I mentally replay the incident as the player rushes away to celebrate. R-u-s-h. Yes, it was. Nine minutes into his 16th game for Leeds, the old-timer has finally found his touch. All his previous transgressions are instantly forgiven and even The Wolves Fan is at least as excited as any Leeds supporter in the ground. The Kop is momentarily lost for anything other than roars but then a golden oldie rings out, 'Ian Rush, Ian Rush, Ian Ian Rush, he gets the ball, he scores a goal, Ian Ian Rush.' The way Leeds have started suggests we might hear that one again this afternoon. This is obviously going to be a rout.

Except Chelsea come back with a string of hyperspeed near-post corners taken by Zola, but Leeds defend them well and even produce a couple of scrambles at the other end. When despite these the score remains at 2–0, questions about Rush's finishing hang in the air once again, but chiefly I'm distracted by a genuinely new experience: an exciting game and quality football, with Leeds outplaying a team beaten only once this season. It's going so well, that even the sight of Yeboah getting off the bench for a warm-up seems almost irrelevant, because as Chelsea get their game together, the Leeds defence is a wall they cannot breach. Tackles go flying in and Chelsea don't appear, as Corporal Jones would have been quick to recognise, to like it up 'em. Bookings for Kelly, Deane and Ford raise the temperature on and off the pitch, while the Kop slams Frank Leboeuf for some crime I didn't see with a heartfelt appeal for European unity: 'You're just a shit French bastard.'

In this hostile atmosphere, Zola plays peacemaker, gathering a ball that Wetherall has just shielded out of play and politely handing it to the defender. It's about the only time this half the Italian has got away from Radebe. Just before half-time it begins to rain and the turf gets a little slippier. Chelsea substitute Eddie Newton begins warming up just in front of me, but stretches one high-kick too far and falls flat on his backside. Seen and laughed at by the whole West Stand, Newton recovers what's left of his dignity, stretches some more, then returns sheepishly to the dugout.

He comes on without falling over at the start of the second half, along with his player/manager Gullit. Graham sticks with the Leeds starting eleven that have forced Gullit into this rethink. Within five minutes Deane has headed just over, Rush has had the sweetest of 30-yard chips cleverly saved and Sharpe sees a pair of close-range efforts saved. Perhaps mindful of how impressive this must look on Sky, Elland Road effuses a collective smugness. But I'm desperate for Leeds to score again. The weather has cleared but it's raining chances and against Chelsea, second best all over the park, this is too rare to waste. When Gullit is booked for uncharacteristically scything down Sharpe it's obvious the visitor's sense of helplessness is upsetting them. Mark Hughes tries to look helpless when he is booked after fouling Beesley from behind, his protestations that Beesley dived only increasing the special level of antipathy Elland Road reserves for the former Man United star. I always feel Hughes should be congratulated for weakening his former employers by moving on before his sell-by date, but I'm clearly in a minority here this afternoon. When Hughes is stretchered off after a horrendous-looking challenge by Deane, the Chelsea striker is cheered off the pitch. Sometimes this beautiful game is not pretty.

Gullit misses a chance and the Kop fine-tunes its appeal for European unity: 'Shit Dutch bastard, you're just a shit Dutch bastard.' The unbelievably cocky Chelsea fans, who have only recently sung 'We'll win, and you know we will', can only sit and suffer the ignominy. It gets worse for them, too, when Leeds start to tire in the last ten minutes and substitute Frank Sinclair crashes a header into the bar as final proof that this is Leeds' afternoon.

After the whistle goes and we file out I am disappointed that it was only 2–0 but still pleasantly stunned. The result puts Leeds up to 12th and the wag in charge of the PA plays Lighthouse Family's 'Lifted'. On the way home, the day is complete when The Wolves Fan – ecstatic also because his own team have beaten Manchester City 3–0 today – finally stops spitting out little pieces of foil and discovers how to open a Slim Jim . . .

Saturday, 7 December: home to Rotherham United, Northern Intermediate League, and away to Middlesbrough

Much fuss has been made about Leeds United's new training facility at Thorp Arch this season, but it's closed to the public and so few people except journalists have been able to see it. On every other Saturday, however, its main pitch is home to the club's youth team, and for no fee at all anyone can lean on the wooden fence that separates the car park from one touchline. And watch the club's nursery team beat seven bells out of all-comers.

The Photographer and I have followed the side's progress in the Reserves and Youth pages of the programme and have regularly pointed out to anyone that laughs at the first team that although our 'kids' did get knocked out of the Northern Intermediate Cup at the end of August (by a team they subsequently beat 5–0 in the league), that hiccup has long since been forgotten. Leeds United's Northern Intermediate League record to date reads: played 13, won 12, drawn one, lost none; goals for 48, goals against three. They are also through the first two rounds of the FA Youth Cup.

Unfortunately, for those of us who live in London and might like a beer of a Friday night, their matches kick off at eleven o'clock. But at least today Thorp Arch (just a Carlton Palmer clearance away from Wetherby racecourse, north of Leeds) is virtually *en route* to Middlesbrough and so a six o'clock alarm call seems as good a way to start the day as any.

The forecast frost hasn't materialised but the M1 threads its way through clouds of icy fog as The Photographer attempts to keep us both awake by reading aloud football pitch dimension records from a book he has inexplicably brought along for the ride. It's 7.30 in the morning and he is quoting an endless stream of statistics alongside ground names that threatens to drive us both insane. He somehow keeps reading like this for fully 15 minutes, after which he slumps into awed silence and I breathe a sigh of relief.

The weather doesn't improve at all and if anything gets a whole lot worse as we move on to the M18 and then the dreaded A1. The lady on Leeds United's switchboard gave impeccable directions but as visibility and temperature both plummet with the ground just two miles away, I begin to wonder if (a) I have a cat in hell's chance of finding Thorp Arch and (b) if the game will be played at all.

But through the mist I see Wealstun Prison and so know we are close. In fact, I've driven right past the entrance so turn, double back and approach more slowly, this time noticing a very discreet sign announcing 'Thorp Arch Grange', where the trainee professionals of the youth team apparently live, with no club badge to suggest anyone from Leeds United ever even visits. Further up the drive marked 'Private' is a car park, containing a few people in training anoraks and a mud-splattered minibus marked 'Rotherham United'. On the left are a couple of dozen young footballers warming up and so I park behind the fence, three yards from the pitch.

I get out, but the air I let into the Orion is so cold that The Photographer sulks and insists he will watch from the passenger seat. But after the Leeds squad warms up (methodically, in identical fashion to the first team) spectators lean against the fence in front of him, and he is forced to brave the elements.

At kick-off the entire touchline is occupied, presumably with proud parents or relations, together with the odd local and occasional out-of-towners like The Photographer and me. Unlike being in the big crowd at a first-team match, here I feel a bit like a gatecrasher at a party populated by a few familiar faces but no one who would actually speak to me. Easily recognisable is Eddie Gray, now coaching the youth team but formerly left-wing wizard between 1965 and 1983. Also familiar, but considerably less so, is Paul Hart, formerly a central defender with Leeds from 1977 to 1983. Now director of youth coaching, he has managed the youth team for the last four seasons and led Leeds United to victory over Man United in the 1993 Youth Cup final. The majority of the beaten eleven now form the backbone of Alex Ferguson's current side. The victorious Leeds players have either moved on or are still struggling to break through. Which wasn't the plan at all . . .

Looking through the icy fog at the players in white, I can name only four and have to listen to shouts of encouragement then match shirt numbers and faces to the alphabetically listed squad list handed out by the club photographer. The tall number nine is Lee Matthews, who played in the pre-season friendly at Grimsby. Number two is Alan Maybury, who made his sole first-team appearance away at Aston Villa last season. Number three is Australian youth international Harry Kewell, who played twice last season, once as sub. But the only other face familiar to first-team watchers is that of the number eight, Wesley Boyle, seen recently at Stalybridge and who came on as sub for Ian Rush against Newcastle nearly three months back.

Kewell, especially, looks superb even before he rifles in a long-distance shot to open the scoring. Later, picking up the ball on the halfway line, he feints round three challenges and lashes in a second that is the best goal I've seen anyone in a Leeds shirt score this season. The half-time score of 2–0 does not reflect the home side's dominance and says nothing about the accomplished style in which they have played, passing the ball around elegantly in a way the first team would love to emulate. Rotherham's number nine is, as the gentleman to my left observes, 'a bit of a lad'. This means he likes to kick people almost as much as the ball, but generally the match has been played in a uniquely refreshing spirit, with no diving or whingeing or abusing of the referee. It's a long way to come for free entertainment, but I've paid £20 or more and travelled much less to watch games that have paled in comparison.

For the second half, with Leeds playing from right to left, Eddie Gray leaves the benches on the far side and walks the line in front of us, yelling encouragement. He calls names of players off the ball and they respond by moving into positions only his wise old eyes have spotted.

Centre-half Jonathon Woodgate scrambles a third goal and Leeds appear to be cruising until a Rotherham forward chases on to keeper Simon Briggs's clearance and the rebound makes it 3–1. Matthews gets a fourth and Kewell completes a well-deserved hat-trick with a brilliant 20-yard chip near the end to make the final score 5–1.

Back in the warmth of the car The Photographer and I are stunned. We've just seen a truly impressive performance and a genuinely exciting game. I think of Howard Wilkinson and how in his long tenure at the club he had always put great store in building a youth policy. Judging by the performance just witnessed his efforts were wholly justified, but it's a shame he won't be around to reap the rewards . . .

*　　　*　　　*

Middlesbrough is only 60 miles away from Thorp Arch. More importantly, by The Photographer's reckoning, Thorp Arch is five hours away from breakfast. I pull in at a roadside greasy spoon on the A1 and park in front of a sheep. It just happened to be standing there. The café is deserted when we enter but as if by magic, just like the shopkeeper in *Mr Benn*, someone who looks like he used to be in Thin Lizzy appears at the counter. The breakfast is good but as we eat The Photographer and I are both having trouble adjusting to the fact that it's lunchtime and we've already seen a football match. The sheep runs off when we return to the car but I thank him for minding it anyway.

The rest of the journey to Middlesbrough is uneventful, if foggy. It's clearer in the city itself, which means we get to see the ground from a distance but can't seem to find a sign or a road that doesn't take us in an elegant 180 degree sweep away from it. Finally, we seem to be close enough to walk and park in a muddy scrap-yard next to the Tees, paying the man £3. He looks like he'll break bits off my car and sell them while I'm away, but then he nullifies the impression by politely apologising for charging so much. Along the road is a stall selling Brazilian replica shirts bearing the names of Middlesbrough's celebrated samba contingent for just £3, so maybe we have been ripped off in the car park. On the other hand, Emerson is AWOL and rumours persist that the injured Juninho won't stay here either, so who wants a shirt at any price?

The Riverside Stadium is odd. I didn't go last season, its first in use, but it still looks too new to be true. It looks impressive from a distance but then I walk another hundred yards and almost bump into it, and realise it is nowhere near as big, impressive or far away as I first believed. The ship moored beside it is actually bigger and more impressive, although The Photographer is far more excited about a burger caravan called Sophie's Choice whose proprietor looks nothing at all like Meryl Streep.

Inside the ground, I have a fantastic view of both the ugly holes left by the two empty corners of the ground and the Leeds team warming up. In fact, because our tickets are in the front row behind the goal and the security is so casual, The Photographer and I lean against the barrier and watch goalkeepers Martyn and Beeney take pot-shots at each other. They wisecrack constantly and it's strange to reflect that they seem such good mates when in effect the former is keeping the latter out of a job. As the Leeds supporters file in most watch him – and Ian Harte – as they bombard Martyn. One shot on the run from Beeney flies into the top left-hand corner in magnificent fashion. Maybe he should push for an outfield position. 'Beeney! Beeney! Beeney!' chant the Leeds fans while Martyn points at him and laughs. The weather is cold but the mood is light, with last week's win over Chelsea and Middlesbrough's struggling and much-weakened team pointing to an easy win. Everywhere people speak of Yeboah not starting but coming on as a substitute for the last half-hour. To grab the headlines and goal of the month.

Kick-off brings another story and a new kind of pain. That of the crushing disappointment felt by watching Leeds underachieve and appear content to do so. In the 12 weeks of the season to date, 'Boro have picked up just four points and haven't won any of their last ten matches. Surely here are three away points for the taking? But Leeds appear not to think so, throwing men in numbers behind the ball whenever they lose possession and making no urgent efforts to go forward with it when they don't. Within the first five minutes Bowyer and Ravanelli tangle in the penalty area and, while lying on his back, Bowyer kicks Ravanelli in the shins. The players are pulled apart and booked, prompting a rash of five yellow cards in the first 35 minutes. But these and the rest of the first half pass in a horrible stalemate with only the continued excellence of Nigel Martyn and the tireless efforts of Ravanelli to admire. The Italian belts a free-kick just above Martyn's fingertips and over the bar, gestures at how close it was by holding his finger and thumb together while Martyn smiles back at him, exaggerating relief. In the first 45 minutes, it is the only thing worth paying to see. Just when last week suggested it had all come good, everything's gone wrong again.

The half-time whistle brings groans tempered with the relief that at least there are only 45 minutes to go. During half-time, the 'We are the champions! Champions of Europe!' chant starts up again and about half a dozen remove their shirts. But the vast majority are too miserable to even think about joining in.

The second half is no better, with Leeds playing towards (but very definitely not attacking) the goal at the end holding their supporters. It's a bad-tempered game and many of the Leeds fans are in a mood to match. All around us seem to be idiots who think everyone in a red shirt is a bastard and chant 'Eng-er-land! Eng-er-land!' every time Ravanelli tries something but fails. It's presumably supposed to be patriotic but seems only xenophobic.

Ridiculous, too, considering that Leeds' best player, Tony Yeboah, is Ghanaian.

Thoughts turn to Yeboah again and again. He was indeed named as a substitute and has run down the touchline towards us several times this afternoon, but George Graham has shown no signs of bringing him on. Sitting cold and bored, this becomes a matter of increasing annoyance. When with 13 minutes to go a Leeds substitute stands and takes his tracksuit top off, it is Mark Jackson, nominally a defender, in place of midfielder Mark Ford. I am appalled. In a game here for the winning Graham has settled for the draw and for the first time ever I am tempted to leave early . . .

Saturday, 14 December: home to Tottenham

Scraping the ice off the car windscreen to reveal more ice underneath on the inside confirms two things. One: it's going to be another cold, miserable day, and two: this car is not what it used to be. A bit like my enthusiasm for watching Leeds.

Thursday's *Sun* and *Daily Mirror* gave over most of their back pages to rumours that Yeboah is about to leave Elland Road, officially the most depressing thing to have happened since Man United beat Leeds 4–0. 'I Quit' screamed the *Mirror* headline, with 'Yeboah wants out after Graham bust-up!' followed by 'I need to play, not be a sub!'.

Yeboah told the papers he was unhappy at his having been asked to sit, and remain, on the bench for two consecutive matches. So am I. He also issued a threat to move elsewhere. I cannot. I'm stuck with Leeds. No man is bigger than any club, but in Yeboah's case he comes a damn close second. He is the most gifted player at the club and, when fit, easily its best asset. On Clubcall, again Graham stressed his belief that Yeboah is not yet fit and needs a game in the reserves before he will be. 'I think Tony's come out with these comments through frustration,' continued George, sounding just like Margaret Thatcher addressing an old Tory wet. 'The most important thing is that Tony gets back to full fitness. And gets in the frame of mind to commit himself to getting back into the team to help Leeds climb up the table . . .'

Earlier in the week, on Monday, Liverpool's John Scales, Harrogate-born and a Leeds United fan, was to be unveiled at Elland Road as George Graham's first signing. Instead, Scales went against the advice of his agent Eric 'Monster' Hall and opted to join Tottenham. Leeds chairman Bill Fotherby was confident when Scales left to sleep on the offer. But Scales spoke to Spurs and changed his mind due to 'football reasons'.

And so with much less fuss and, indeed, much less interest, Graham's first signing for the club became 31-year-old Norwegian international Gunnar Halle from Oldham Athletic for £400,000. Ironically, he had been due to sign for Leeds on the day Wilkinson was dismissed. News of his arrival quite underwhelmed me and was completely overshadowed by the FA Cup third round draw in which Leeds United were drawn away to Crystal Palace. For a London-based Leeds fan like myself or, say, John Scales, this is a local tie and therefore good news . . .

When The Photographer gets into the car at Luton with Little Andy (not because Big Andy set off hours ago, but because he cannot make today's match), the papers they bring say Yeboah is listed as injured and won't even sit on the substitute's bench. Halle is expected to make his debut in place of the 'tired and jaded' Gary Kelly. John Scales appears to have a 50:50 chance of playing for Spurs . . .

The Photographer, Little Andy (showing no obvious signs of tension at leaving later than he's used to) and I can think of nothing encouraging about the forthcoming match. Or the future. We discuss instead what other people do on a Saturday. Watch all of Sky's *Soccer AM* football show in comfort, suffer the computer graphics behind Gary Lineker on *Football Focus*, go to a supermarket, wash the car. All of these seem more enticing than the match ahead of us.

The mood is still glum when I park in our preferred spot in the garage forecourt at the western end of Elland Road. The man taking £2 off me for the privilege is cheerful enough, but then he doesn't watch the matches. As we approach the ground our pessimism mingles with that of everyone around, creating a huge fog of misery. I explain that a friend who supports Coventry, an ex-pat who will be back home from Berlin, wants to come to watch them play at Elland Road on Boxing Day so I intend to queue up and buy a ticket for him. The Photographer looks at me incredulously.

'You expect there to be a queue?'

He's right. I walk straight up to the window and am told by the helpful chap in the office that my seat, and the one next to it that I want to buy, are listed as 'obstructed view' and cannot be sold. Strange, I've bought it before.

'Sorry . . . I'll tell you what I'll do, and I know this'll sound daft, but I'll sell you a "restricted view" seat nearby and then your friend can sit where he likes . . .'

Daft it is. Inside the ground, daftness is the order of the day. The news is that Halle will play, but so will Kelly. Instead, Graham has dropped Lee Sharpe. Kay From Blackpool spreads a rumour that Sharpe has been disciplined for being at a Manchester nightclub earlier in the week when Everton's Terry Phelan was attacked. It's certainly a more exciting idea than the team's line-up, although Wallace is back from injury and the youth team's hat-trick hero Harry Kewell is on the bench. Spurs were daft enough to bring Scales with them and he apparently met with a very hostile reception as he got off the bus. More wisely, Tottenham manager Gerry Francis has not named him even as a sub. Strangely, though, at five to three he emerges to sit on the bench, running the gauntlet of abuse from the West Stand as he approaches us. It's a cold day and he looks very uncomfortable so as he approaches the away dugout to my left I take off my scarf and offer it to him. John Scales, Leeds fan and Tottenham player, ignores me completely.

Within minutes of the kick-off Scales is forgotten because the impossible has happened. Leeds United are playing with even less flair and invention than they did at Middlesbrough. Tottenham pass and move and threaten, Leeds scramble, run nowhere and drive supporters to distraction. Before the last home game, against Chelsea, the empty row of seats in front of us had been removed but the extra leg room had gone unnoticed as everyone spent the whole 90 minutes either on the edge of their seats or on their feet with excitement. Today the on-pitch proceedings afford much time to contemplate the gap in front of row BB. With the match spiralling to ever-deeper levels of frustration, this gap now offers us the luxury of putting our feet up and reclining. Hell, we even have room to stretch and yawn. The only thing to disturb our peace is the dugout telephone and David O'Leary yelling at Gary Kelly. The phone rings about 45 times in the first half. It feels good to know Graham is as unhappy as I am.

Gunnar Halle is doing his best to impress, but does so in a kind of two-steps-forward, one-step-back kind of way. Gradually, though, he becomes more assured and at least gives us something to think about in the absence of anything resembling forward play. Ironically, it is he who puts in the cross – after over 30 minutes of play – that marks Leeds' first assault on Tottenham keeper Ian Walker. Equally ironically, the head it connects with belongs not to our centre-forward but right wing-back Gary Kelly who merely deflects it into Walker's comfortable grasp. Meanwhile, only the close attentions of Lucas Radebe on Teddy Sheringham is making the Spurs attack as blunt as Leeds' own. A Ruel Fox header hits a Leeds post but the game is as dull as the swiftly darkening sky.

Spirits are briefly raised when a thunderous shot from Wallace cannons out to Kelly who, inspired by opening his account at The Dell three weeks ago, rifles it back. But, sadly, he miscues and the ball skitters across the face of the goal towards Rush inside the six-yard box. To this point Rush has shown some clever touches, but now takes a leaf out of his early-season form book, as the ball hits his shin and skews wide. By half-time I am numb not with cold but with frustration. Spurs have had many chances, notably falling to Norwegian striker Steffen Iversen, but all of them have been gathered by the magnificent Nigel Martyn, inspiring chants of 'England's, England's Number One!' which grew louder as the half progressed. With England and Arsenal's David Seaman currently injured, the idea doesn't seem too far-fetched. Presumably England manager Glenn Hoddle has better things to do than watch Leeds, so Martyn can only hope that the word has reached him.

During the interval Elland Road is miserably quiet and quietly miserable. Once under way, the second half at first seems a little better because wing-backs Kelly and Halle push forward. But up front, Deane and Rush wait so long for crosses that never come that they stop running altogether. At the back, Radebe is doing such a sterling job of closing down Sheringham that the England striker isn't getting a look-in. In apparent frustration he flattens Lee Bowyer and is lucky to remain on the pitch after an earlier yellow card. This at least gives the crowd something to be passionate about. Radebe, meanwhile, is fast becoming Leeds' most solid defender, having man-marked a string of top-flight players in recent weeks. Sheringham's is the most recent name on a list that has included McManaman, le Tissier, Vialli and Ravanelli. But looking around for flair and entertainment, surely even George Graham would admit that the empty crisp bags spinning around in the wind are far more enthralling than anyone wearing a white shirt.

Leeds escape again about ten minutes after the restart when a David Howells header smashes into the bar. Leeds have come nothing like as close all afternoon and finally Graham loses all patience, leaves the dugout for the line and begins cursing and waving his arms around. His actions restore my faith in him if not the team. He makes two substitutions – Mark Jackson for Ford and Kewell for Wallace – soon after, but neither makes any real impact. It's disappointing to see Kewell caught out by the pace of the game, but illustrates well how far a stunning youth-team player can be from an experienced first-teamer.

Five minutes from time Spurs have a decent penalty appeal turned down and Gerry Francis becomes animated for the first time in the afternoon, swearing at the referee. At full-time Graham steps forward to shake Francis's hand. The Leeds manager rolls his eyes heavenward and shakes his head. Francis shrugs and both seem to understand that this must have been just one of those days. But driving 900 miles to watch two consecutive goalless draws isn't filling me with much charity. I can't even be bothered to stand up, let alone applaud the teams off. On the journey back the three of us are all sullen. There is a crumb of comfort in that Leeds have now kept four consecutive clean sheets and are unbeaten since the Liverpool game – the team's best run for 13 months – but the M1 south looks very long tonight.

Radio 5 reports that the fourth of Robbie Fowler's four goals in Liverpool's 5–1 home win means he has scored 100 goals for Liverpool one game sooner than Ian Rush. Rush's 100th goal for Leeds will presumably establish another record, making Leeds the only club in the Premiership to employ an octogenarian. The fact that the team Liverpool took apart today was Middlesbrough, including Emerson, makes Leeds' failure to score there last week even more annoying. Halfway back to Luton, The Photographer suggests I am driving very aggressively and I realise that yes, I am. A little ashamed, I ease off and stop tailgating the Peugeot in front. Leeds might be boring us to death at the moment, but there's no sense in driving towards it too . . .

Saturday, 21 December: away to Everton

For most of the week I've convinced myself that I'm suffering from football fatigue. Admittedly, Ceefax, Teletext and Clubcall have proved as irresistible as ever and I still wish I had access to Skytext page 218 so I could check out three whole pages on Leeds . . . but I worry that I have lost enthusiasm for this travelling lark. Actually, it's not so much the travelling as the arriving and the 90 minutes in the middle. I blame George Graham. Yet at the same time I am nursing a growing faith that, like Baron Frankenstein, he is doing something almost too terrible to watch yet so miraculous that everyone will be in awe.

Even top Spice Girl Mel B announced in Monday's *Sun* that she was a Leeds United fan. Actually, her dad is, but she once went out with 'a Leeds trainee' and has met David Batty. In fact, she used to see Batty 'quite a lot' and reckons he is 'a bit of a lad'. He certainly was on the pitch, but we had to sell him to help pay for a grandstand. Such is football. Ask your dad . . .

My dad doesn't like football but he does like getting up early. So I think of him as I pour milk on my cornflakes in the dark, lit by the eerie glow of Ceefax. Once again, I'm actually up earlier at the weekend than I would be to go to work. Which is never ideal in late December, this being the Christmas party season and all. Ceefax rubbishes last week's rumour about Lee Sharpe, saying the reason he did not play against Tottenham was that he was injured. He's fit again today along with Wallace – and Yeboah. I finish the cornflakes, switch off the TV and head out shivering to the car. Today The Photographer, Andys Big and Little and I will meet in the UCI Multiplex car park, just off the M40 at Wycombe. But I have left far too early, or driven far too fast, and arrive with 40 minutes to spare. With the dawn not yet fully broken I close my eyes and doze off. I awake to find the car surrounded by Wycombe Wanderers fans awaiting the coach to Bristol Rovers. Some are smirking at me. With all the dignity I can muster I ignore them, stifle a yawn and finally remember to switch the headlights off. Daylight has finally arrived.

It is closely followed by The Photographer, one minute early, as he stresses with immense pride, followed in a two-car flourish by both Andys, today leaving as late as they dare. Little Andy volunteers to drive, so I put my warm clothing in his boot and take the chance to doze most of the way to Birmingham. We arrive and park in Liverpool's Stanley Park, in the shadow of Anfield's main stand, around 2.15 p.m.

Everton's Goodison Park ground half a mile away is not the most impressive in the Premiership. Close up, its Bullens Road Stand, into whose corner away fans are billeted, looks plain 'old-fashioned' rather than 'classic' and no amount of steel-cladding can disguise the fact. The whole ground seems to shrink in embarrassment at the more imposing sight of Anfield. Rather than go in, The Photographer and I wander around looking for something photographically more interesting than a roadside stall selling Duncan Ferguson T-shirts, but can find only caricatures purporting to be Nick Barmby but looking not even related to the forward Everton signed from Middlesbrough. And so the thought of watching Beeney belting 20-yarders at Nigel Martyn becomes the best option and we go in.

Leeds fans are not tolerant of shortcomings of any description and were, I'm sure, the first to bait opposing fans with the chant, to the tune of 'Oranges and Lemons', 'Shit ground, no fans!' Elland Road is no San Siro and is not often full, but Goodison can offer little defence on either count. Repeated at regular intervals, 'Shit ground, no fans!' manages to fill much of the time until kick-off. Next to me, also struggling to get warm, are a father and son who have travelled from Ipswich and explain that to get to the top of the main stand opposite, you have to take a lift. This, and a tiny clock in the far corner with its Mothercare logo, is the final proof that Goodison is rubbish.

Yeboah scored for the reserves in a 3–3 draw against Man United this week but no one expects Graham to pick him today. Friday's *Sun* reckoned Yeboah had made his peace with the manager. In the short piece, the striker admitted that it was the manager's job to pick the team. But it read like the statement of a man who had been force-fed humble pie, and when the teams trot out (and are finally announced over the PA) Yeboah sits once again on the bench – alongside Wallace, Jackson, Ford and Beeney. Which means Graham has finally gone for a bit of flair, playing Sharpe in midfield instead of Ford.

The Leeds contingent is in a lively mood and within seconds they have something to stand up for other than the chant of 'Stand up if you hate Man U!' when a Deane through ball into the Everton goalmouth is chased by Rush and Sharpe. Rush's first touch puts the ball at Sharpe's feet but keeper Neville Southall races out to make a quite brilliant save.

Everton's attack of Ferguson and Barmby is backed by Andrei Kanchelskis and ex-Leeds man Gary Speed. It's a scary proposition not made any less terrifying by the oceans of space Everton's right wing-back Earl Barrett is getting on Leeds' left flank. The pace is fast and the football is end to end, bordering on entertaining. A Gunnar Halle cross finds Gary Kelly who shoots just wide, Wetherall forces Southall to concede a corner with a shot from 35 yards, Rush heads narrowly wide. No one came prepared for anything like this. When the ball from Rush's header rolls harmlessly to a stop halfway to the corner flag, the lack of ball boys in front of the Park Stand prompts an Everton fan to sprint from his seat ten rows back to retrieve the ball. A steward spots his run but cannot intercept and the spectator makes it to the touchline and throws the ball to Southall amidst much cheering, tempered by good-natured chants of 'You fat bastard!' from the Leeds fans. Suddenly the memories of last week's match against Tottenham seem as distant as they are painful and the truth is inescapable: this is actually fun.

Minutes later Rush hits a shot on the turn but Southall saves, easily. Rush has a good record of scoring against Everton but not, as yet, in a Leeds shirt. We live in hope but chant Yeboah's name every ten minutes anyway.

The pace of the game shows no sign of abating and Everton's Ferguson twice goes close at the far end. Kanchelskis runs across the Leeds defence and, with two white shirts colliding in confusion, looks certain to score . . . but Martyn blocks his shot superbly. Because he opted to sign for Leeds at the eleventh hour after talks with Everton, the home fans boo him whenever he gets the ball; Leeds fans, increasingly aware of the difference he makes, smile and chant 'England's number one!' in response. Leeds fans, meanwhile, jeer Speed every time he gets the ball and cheer when he loses it. It's all very silly but it keeps spirits high because despite Speed being Everton's top scorer to date with seven goals, all the evidence suggests that Leeds got the better of the two players.

At half-time, neither the PA nor the electronic scoreboard above the Park Stand brings any news of scores from other matches so Leeds fans make their own entertainment with the 'We are the champions!' chant while the madder ones take their shirts off. Police, stewards and Everton fans look on in bemusement.

As the teams emerge from the dressing-rooms for the second half, Leeds have made a substitution – but Yeboah remains on the bench and instead Jackson has replaced Radebe, hurt early on in a clash with Ferguson. After good work in defence, Jackson releases the ball to Sharpe, who gives it to Rush, who puts Deane clean through with a superb pass through Everton's defence. Deane bears down on Southall, chips – and fluffs. The agony grows. Leeds have not scored for 21 days, so the chant of 'Yeboah! Yeboah! Yeboah!' is redoubled, mixed with 'Georgie . . . Get Yeboah on!'. Graham is apparently exasperated by Deane also and is on his feet yelling at the big number ten, but still Yeboah remains on his backside in the rear of the dugout. 'Deano' gets another chance minutes later but is body-checked 25 yards out. A couple of seasons ago, as I suggest to The Photographer, Leeds would have scored from a free-kick in this position but without McAllister this is going to be a waste of time. Then Kelly's free-kick lands on the bar and, with Christmas just five days away, today's game seems just the present I needed. The minutes tick away, Ferguson, Barmby and Kanchelskis all go close for Everton. But while Bowyer comes close at the other end, Yeboah goes nowhere except for another warm-up run.

With barely ten minutes to go, Jackson chips a pass that sees Rush onside and goalside of the last Everton defender, 20 yards out. Horribly, his first touch leaves him 19 yards out with the ball five in front of him. Rush's subsequent shot is blocked but rebounds to Kelly, whose return ricochets to Rush once more, this time nine yards out. His first touch leaves him seven and the ball six and so his shot is screwed wide, too – but no matter, because Deane is rushing in and only has to connect to score. With everyone on their feet in anticipation, time stands still . . . Then from no more than one yard out, with Southall on his backside at Rush's feet and an open goal ahead of him, Deane hits the post. He will, as someone once said, look back in horror. I can only look across the pitch at the dugout at a Ghanaian striker who, match fit or not, would have scored from any one of the four chances just offered to the Leeds attack. When the final whistle goes seconds later, this is all anyone filing out can talk about. Surely, now, Graham must drop Rush.

The walk back across Stanley Park is the kind of trip that would make Scott of the Antarctic wish he'd packed an extra pair of thermals, and as The Photographer calls his wife, the news is even more chilling. Graham has just been interviewed on *Final Score* and explained that Rush is in the team because he is playing well. I wonder aloud if it's too late to get George Graham a copy of last season's review video so he can see what Yeboah is like when he's playing well . . .

In Little Andy's car, Radio 5 says Leeds have now gone five games undefeated and without conceding a goal. For that much we are grateful. We agree that Graham has sorted the defence. But we cannot agree that Yeboah would have missed as often as Rush or Deane. David Mellor's 6.06 show boasts its new freephone number, and countless fans use it to witter on about how Middlesbrough should be punished for declining to play at Blackburn today because they cannot raise a team. I let it drift into the background and, making the most of the luxury of not having to drive, fall asleep dreaming . . . dreaming . . . well, of nothing at all actually. It's obviously going to be one of those seasons.

Match of the Day condenses the game into 11 minutes, after which Graham looks pleased (with everything except Deane's miss which he could only smile ruefully about) while Des Lynam and Trevor Brooking are both impressed that Leeds had 'worked so hard', dropping expressions like 'excellent performance' and 'fully committed'. I look up when Leeds last put together a run of five clean sheets and discover it was begun in December 1988 when they were in the old Second Division. This, then, must be progress . . .

Thursday, 26 December: home to Coventry City

I feel slightly silly eating breakfast at my parents' house in Lowestoft wearing my '70s Leeds replica shirt. They politely say nothing but I can tell what they're thinking, even as they offer helpful remarks about the snow having held off and suggesting the best route across East Anglia to the M1. I feel even sillier stretching a scarf across the parcel shelf of the car as neighbours' curtains twitch. I effect a wry smile that is meant to suggest I realise how daft the ritual is and, anyway, round these parts most of you are stuck with supporting either Norwich City or Ipswich Town.

All except Berlin Mark, who for reasons best known to his psychiatrist is a fan of Coventry City and will therefore be accompanying me like a lamb to the slaughter. Coventry are the only team in the Premiership to have scored fewer goals than Leeds this season, and given Leeds' recent run of defensive intransigence, the Sky Blues are clearly without a prayer. I know this. Berlin Mark knows this. He knows I know this and we let the knowledge hover there in silence.

His presence alongside me follows no small amount of familial trauma. Working in Berlin means he rarely comes home to see his relatives. This being Boxing Day, his Canadian wife, two children, mother, sister and various in-laws are all expecting him as the guest of honour at a big family get-together. But if Berlin Mark is feeling guilty he's saying nothing. He's far more concerned that of the last five times he has watched Coventry City in the flesh, they have never won. On the last three occasions they have failed even to score. He is a jinx and I am happy to have him in the car today.

Reaching the M1 takes almost three hours, but immediately it puts me in full football mode. Christmas is quickly forgotten and I look forward instead to arriving in time to see Noel Whelan getting a warm welcome, Gary McAllister getting a hostile one, and new manager Gordon Strachan taking his place in the dugout. The *Daily Mail* this morning quoted Graham as being unconcerned about matching 1981's run of six consecutive clean sheets, saying he wants the points and would rather win 3–2. This is fighting talk and surely means Deane's or Rush's backside will be planted on the bench while Yeboah knocks in a hat-trick.

At the ground, in the queue for West Ham tickets, my confidence is dented by The Photographer, who meets me there and announces that according to this morning's *Sun*, Yeboah is threatening to quit Leeds unless Graham plays him. Which immediately suggests Graham has told him he won't. Berlin Mark beams like a Cheshire Cat.

Inside the ground, Yeboah warms up wearing a tracksuit suggesting he is once more only a substitute. There too is a stocky, slightly round-shouldered man with dark, curly hair. It is Tony Dorigo, happily back from injury once more. There is not much in the way of Christmas cheer around the ground, however, save for one woman to my left who has tied her blonde hair up with tinsel and decorated a small child (probably a girl) like a blue, white and yellow Christmas tree complete with frightwig. The only other Christmas cheer is in the hip flask that Ian The Moustache passes around. The team news is less titillating. Yeboah remains on the bench, Deane and Rush remain up front. Graham has once again named five centre-backs – although two of them will operate in midfield.

Within minutes of the kick-off Radebe, dragged into shooting range because his marking target McAllister is being forced to defend, unleashes a shot from 25 yards. He has never scored for Leeds and doesn't now, but the attempt is promising. Another follows soon after and Leeds are soon well on top. Gunnar Halle is looking very sharp and good work by him leads to half a chance for Rush, bobbling into the path of Deane, who belts the ball into the roof of Coventry keeper Steve Ogrizovic's net. Nine minutes gone, 1–0. Deane runs all the way along the touchline past our seats waving his fist in triumph. Idiotically I wave mine back then turn round and sit down. Berlin Mark is sitting too, his arms folded, a look of here-we-go-again resignation spreading across his face. The idea of sympathy flits across my mind but I ignore it and gloat instead. I am certain this is going to be a whitewash.

With Bowyer playing well and Radebe keeping McAllister subdued the chances begin to mount up. And evaporate. With about 30 minutes gone Howard The Student, son of Chesterfield Ken, sagely announces to the world in general and no one in particular that these are the hardest kind of games to win. How right he is. Leeds are oozing confidence but relaxing and Coventry are sensing they have more room to manoeuvre.

Almost on the half-hour Darren Huckerby, their lively new signing from Newcastle, switches from right to left wing and latches on to the ball just inside the Leeds half. From there he sets out on an arcing run that earns him admiring glances but no tackles from a collection of white shirts, and takes him to a point somewhere near the right-hand corner of the Leeds penalty area. Seemingly bored with making the Leeds defence look non-existent, he shoots and rubs out Nigel Martyn's sheen of invincibility to make it 1–1. Beside me, Berlin Mark doesn't expect the joy he can barely hide to last. And neither do I. But just eight minutes later Coventry take a left-sided corner to Martyn's near post that no Leeds player attempts to clear. The ball drops to Dion Dublin, who without needing to jump heads it into the net. Palmer, Radebe and Wetherall all stand looking at each other while Dublin first shrugs then celebrates. Two minutes later, Huckerby is given the ball by Carlton Palmer, who attempts to make amends with a desperate tackle that sends Huckerby flying and prompts referee Martin Bodenham to point to the penalty spot. Up steps McAllister, boos ringing in his ears, to plant it confidently to Martyn's left. After going 480 minutes without conceding a single goal, Leeds have let in three in ten. The phone in the dugout rings again but Graham is clearly not telling O'Leary to follow the crowd's suggestion to put Yeboah on.

At the interval everyone is shell-shocked, including Berlin Mark. But when the teams emerge for the second half no one is really surprised to see that the substitute coming on is not Yeboah but a defender, Dorigo replacing Beesley.

Within minutes, Graham's master plan becomes clear. Anticipating Coventry will sit on their lead, he has switched Kelly to a kind of sweeping role, moved Halle to the right wing and told Dorigo to take over from him on the left, giving Leeds the option to attack down both flanks. This they do but they create no real chances other than a Kelly free-kick that beats the Coventry wall but not Ogrizovic. Then Leeds lose possession and Coventry break quickly towards the Kop. The stage is set for Leeds-born Whelan to score in front of the fans he used to stand among, but he misses badly and is furious with himself. Attempting to make amends, he makes one excellent challenge, closely followed by a reckless one, on Bowyer. Without waiting for the referee to reach for his pocket, Whelan turns and begins the long walk off the field. He remembers what most around me have forgotten, that he was booked in the first half also. The young striker is already halfway to the touchline when Bodenham holds the red card aloft. As he approaches the Coventry dugout he is close to tears, seemingly unable to face the shame of being sent off at his 'home' ground as he heads for the tunnel, boos ringing in his ears. Given that Whelan has been dismissed for showing the very spirit that Elland Road applauds in one of their own, I am appalled and can only sympathise with him. Short memories, again.

For me, Whelan's dismissal casts a shadow over the rest of the match, but just two minutes later Deane goes to ground after rounding a defender and Bodenham awards Leeds a penalty, their first of the season. Deane looked to have made a meal of the challenge and the sight of Paul Telfer leaning over and shouting sweet nothings into the top of the 'stricken' forward's head suggests Coventry may have thought so too. But up steps Gary Kelly to take it. Before I can express my surprise that a right-back and not a striker is taking it, Kelly has stroked the ball to Ogrizovic's left where the keeper has dived to save it.

Yeboah's name is chanted again and again and Elland Road is getting very impatient. Four minutes later Graham appears to have relented, as two yellow number boards are selected and Yeboah takes off his tracksuit. As he performs stretches directly in front of us, Berlin Mark, in something approaching panic at the thought of the assault Coventry might now endure, is moved to remark on the size of the great man's thighs.

'Yes, they are quite magnificent, aren't they?' replies a voice which I recognise as my own. Just the sight of that number 21 on his back is doing strange things to me.

When the game finally pauses and Yeboah trots on to the pitch, Elland Road rises to its feet, a truly awesome moment on a truly horrendous afternoon. The player coming off is number six, David Wetherall, although I had assumed that the board was upside down and Ian Rush would be replaced. Once again, George Graham knows best, going for broke with a new formation that has 18 minutes to salvage something against a team of ten men.

It seems like an age before Yeboah even gets a touch, while his shirt gleams all the whiter for him not having been on long enough to get it dirty. One muddy splodge appears after he dives in a futile attempt to win a penalty and then a few more appear as he gradually works himself into the game. A little of the old magic reappears when he controls the ball with his chest, turning a defender by feinting one way and moving the other, and again a few minutes later when he dribbles at a retreating blue shirt. He sets himself to shoot but instead delivers a superb pass to Deane. Who plants it in the South Stand.

Coventry manager Strachan raises a laugh when he yells at their last-minute substitute Eoin Jess, who is warming up casually on the touchline: 'Run, Jessy! You know you'll have to do it when you get on the pitch!' On he comes, and he runs a bit, but then the match ends. Coventry have three goals and three points. Leeds have nothing despite a one-man advantage, a three-man attack and a striker called Yeboah. All of this is unable to make amends for ten minutes of madness in the first half. The Leeds players trudge off to almost total apathy from what is left of the crowd, the hordes of blue seats suggesting that dozens of those who have waited eight months to see Yeboah return watched him for less than the 18 minutes he played. The electronic scoreboard makes it worse: Man United, whom Leeds must play in two days' time, appear to have returned to form and have today won 4–0 . . .

Saturday, 28 December: away to Manchester United

'Manchester United Football Club have requested that we advise Leeds United supporters to remain seated at all times, to avoid the possibility of supporters being ejected from the stadium, in accordance with ground regulations.'

This joyous message of goodwill is typed on to a white piece of paper and attached with a paperclip to every ticket sold by the Leeds United ticket office. It's about as welcoming as this fixture ever gets for a visiting supporter. With every mile up the M1 and the M6 an ever-heavier sense of dread sinks upon the car, as if we were four little hobbits approaching the Dark Tower of Mordor. Of all the games in a season this is the one Leeds United fans most want to win and least expect to.

I have broken a solemn vow by coming here today, having sworn I would never return after a visit for a cup match in 1995 that Leeds lost 3–1 and which was about as enjoyable as root canal work without anaesthetic. The result itself was almost irrelevant; far worse was the home crowd's air of smug satisfaction mixed with liberal amounts of undiluted hatred. Perhaps they feel the same visiting Elland Road, which means that this antipathy is a sad fact of life that may never go away. On Christmas Day, my four-year-old nephew told me his favourite football teams were Leeds and Man United and I heard myself chastising him even as he completed his innocent triumvirate with the word 'England'. I had no right to pass on my prejudice and I'm not proud that I did. He and others should be allowed to grow up and go to matches where opposing fans taunt and tease, not threaten and intimidate, each other. Off the field the two clubs work hard to bridge the divide, but the problem in the stands and around the grounds just won't seem to go away.

The thought occurs again as the Orion I'm driving grinds to a halt in the traffic-jam capital of England, otherwise known as the M6 through Birmingham. The Photographer and Andys Big and Little are all joking about us turning around and going home because it's not too late. But we have stuttered along in first or second gear for half an hour when The Photographer, scanning the TV listings, gives our dilemma a new sense of proportion, exclaiming, 'Shit, we could be at home watching *Bedknobs and Broomsticks* . . .'

The approaches to Manchester are fast but uninspiring and eventually lead us into Chester Road, where all the £3 forecourt parking spaces seem to have been taken. We head a little further east and manage to squeeze on to a kerb between two driveways in the poetically named Byron Road. It's a name far too pretty for its locale, but walking to the ground we have other worries. Old Trafford is one of the few Premiership grounds I don't wear colours to. Walking towards it, gradually surrounded by an ever-growing sea of red and black, I feel more and more conspicuous. We all do. Voices all around loudly utter sentences containing the words 'Leeds' and 'bastards' and I imagine hostile eyes boring into our backs. Anyone not wearing colours is almost certainly a Leeds fan around here, and along Sir Matt Busby Way that makes you about as welcome as a herpes scab on an archbishop's lip. Mounted police in fluorescent yellow vests patrol the area but I see no Leeds fans, even though it is just 20 minutes to kick-off. A friend calls my phone and I am careful not to say anything which gives away my allegiance. As we speak, The Photographer begins patting his pockets looking for his ticket. Foolishly, he has stuffed it into his Leeds season-ticket wallet and is waving the latter around as he attempts to extricate the former. I stand close to him so that no one around us can see what he is doing. This is 1996 and there are police all around us, but still we feel we have to take such precautions because of the football team we support and where we are standing.

As we move to entrance E231 the press of bodies gets stronger as the open space at this corner of the ground gets narrower, and suddenly a couple of hundred Leeds fans are visible. These are being funnelled to the right of a line of mounted police, home fans instructed to keep moving just to the left. Behind us suddenly comes the sound of running and shouting as one bunch of morons charges towards us. No one has any idea who started it but some turn to voice their anger anyway. The police react quickly, keeping the two groups at bay and mobile, but the atmosphere has changed from cautious to tense. One mounted officer barks orders and when another skirmish develops I am grateful for the half a tonne of horseflesh alongside my left ear, separating me from someone I may well have much in common with but who would probably just punch me for standing the wrong side of a horse. I head briskly to the turnstile, cursing Old Trafford and the idea that we have to come here at all. Inside, some faces look relieved, some frightened, some seemingly angry that they were unable to meet threat with force. For me the match cannot start – or end – soon enough. This is no atmosphere in which to watch football.

Which is a shame because the ground is clearly one of England's best. This is the second conclusion any visitor would come to. The first is that the public-address system is England's loudest, although that may just be above the visiting supporters in an effort to subdue them. The same technique was employed by the CIA at Waco with slightly less successful results. Five minutes before kick-off the cursed speakers are cranked up way past eleven to deliver 'Ooh Ah Eric Cantona', or something, to remind us that (a) the teams are about to emerge and (b) that Leeds United sold the Frenchman to their greatest rivals for just £1 million. Point (a) we can handle, point (b) we ignore. Which is far from easy when around 53,000 people are singing along with relish and gesturing in your general direction. And yet, arms folded and standing tall, I study various areas of the pitch below with casual enthusiasm.

The roar as the teams emerge is almost as loud as the PA, but not quite, until latecomers and all-comers spot a number 21 shirt filled by Tony Yeboah, who is starting a game at last. He is Leeds' main hope today, surely, assuming our defence can refrain from committing suicide as it did against Coventry 48 hours ago. Within minutes of the kick-off the ball reaches him, back to goal, on the penalty spot. Yeboah turns quickly and although his shot drifts harmlessly to goalkeeper Peter Schmeichel, it is an encouraging start. Yeboah has the ball again a few minutes later and starts to bear down on the penalty area, only to drag it to a red shirt at the last minute. Then the home team break at a frightening speed and Ryan Giggs races forward into oceans of room. He escapes one challenge but is forced wide, to where Gary Kelly opts to fall on to his heels in the kind of challenge only ever likely to concede a penalty, and so it does. Old Trafford erupts and as Cantona steps forward 2,000 Leeds fans in the eastern corner shout or pray for him to miss – but he doesn't and Leeds are a goal down with just nine minutes played.

But after that terrible beginning, nothing really happens. Giggs and David Beckham look menacing but Radebe matches Cantona more or less step for step and Carlton Palmer is having a near-faultless half. Yeboah gets very poor service, however, and doesn't appear to be as quick as he used to be. Rush, asked to play wide right to make room for Yeboah, is slower still, much like a Robin Reliant going uphill, an old man against the boys of Manchester United. Meanwhile, Lee Bowyer is a boy playing like the man he was supposed to learn from but has been forced to replace – Gary McAllister. I try to work out where he's supposed to be playing but as he crops up all over the pitch, the answer seems to be 'everywhere'. Bowyer has matured hugely and has doubtless learned a life lesson after being found guilty and fined £4,500 earlier this month for his part in the affray in McDonald's. This is good, Leeds are growing to depend on him.

He takes a corner while the notorious K block, at the far end of the goalline we look down on, roars discouragement. The ball sails over the Man United defence and as it does so Radebe peels off the near post to meet it at the rear. Unchallenged, he heads it just wide with only Schmeichel to beat. The Leeds contingent groans, knowing that such a chance was too good to waste. Amazingly, the referee empathises and gives Leeds another, because Bowyer had taken the kick with the ball positioned just outside the 'D'. The home crowd are incensed by the second chance but Bowyer merely places the ball correctly and attempts the same set piece once again. This time, Schmeichel comes out to meet it but misses. This time the ball drops to Radebe's feet. And this time Radebe's control fails him and he stabs it agonisingly wide. When the half-time whistle goes that double effort remains Leeds' only chance, with the home side having gone much closer on occasions too mentionable to numerate.

Half-time brings a sense of relief, more deafening PA broadcasts and some otherwise inaudible bare-chested bravado from a Leeds contingent preferring to ignore their sorrows. The second half brings deepening confidence in the Man United side, content to let Leeds do the running. Leeds are happy to oblige but their running is either too late, too soon, too slow or in the wrong direction. When Yeboah finally manages what only a statistician might count as a shot on target, George Graham has seen enough and substitutes him with Andy Gray. It's musical chairs at the front as Gray plays wide right moving Rush to wide left and Deane from left to centre. In front of me a man slaps his forehead in despair. 'Making a substitution without taking off Rush is like opting to play with ten men,' he groans to the similarly exasperated man alongside him.

Manchester United replace the almost-invisible Ole Gunnar Solskjaer with Andy Cole, supposedly rubbish, but who looks ten times more likely to score than Rush. In the end, neither of them does and the match ends with a whimper, not a bang.

During the second half a politely spoken lady had almost deafened us with the announcement: 'Visiting supporters are invited to remain in the ground at the final whistle so that the ground can be cleared before they are escorted back to their transport.' The 'invitation' sounded kind, but as I am certain the lady doesn't know where I parked the car – and I don't want to be part of a body of Leeds fans, then peel off and walk the streets alone – I suggest to The Photographer that we try to leave immediately. Strangely, we are not locked in at all and we can leave straightaway, under the watchful gaze of a phalanx of smartly dressed security men pointing us in the direction of the exit gate and the cold evening air. Outside, we are immediately exposed to the scrutiny of the departing home fans and so move quickly towards the back of K block before doubling back to walk among them. It's impossible to look as happy as those around us so I fix my face in what I hope is a grimace of chilly discomfort. When my phone rings I smother it quickly, certain in the belief that the call will involve a question about the match I have just left but am in no position to discuss. In the event, no one threatens us and the walk to the car is mostly silent and uneventful. We meet Andys Big and Little quite by accident at a Chinese chippy, stuff our faces and return to the car.

Radio 5 says Leeds are down to 14th, sixth from bottom. Alex Ferguson, when interviewed, says it was a close game with some scary moments for him, but he's only being kind. No matter how much Graham has improved the Leeds defence, the attack is ending 1996 as the most toothless in the Premiership. As of today, Leeds have scored just 16 goals in 20 games and look to be in relegation trouble once again.

On the M6 through Birmingham an hour or so later the car grinds to a halt in traffic, and so does its occupants' enthusiasm for the season. We have all independently opted to miss the New Year's Day game away at Newcastle, and as the Toon have today stuck seven past Tottenham, it might be just as well. This year's string of fixtures has produced little but depression. There has been scant reward for the weekly toil of slogging up and down the country. Following the team has become merely a habit, not a leisure activity, and I am tired of it. Sick and tired of it. I'm going home, I'm going to sulk, and I'm going to have a New Year's break in Cornwall. Leeds will just have to get through the Newcastle game without me, without us . . .

Chapter Seven

January

Wednesday, 1 January: (not) away to Newcastle United

At about the time I would have been looking for a parking place near St James' Park, my car is parked in one outside a farmhouse in Cornwall about 450 road miles away. Football is very far from my mind and I need to be reminded to collect the 'terrace trannie' which will be my mobile link with Leeds United. Today, mine is the second of two cars bound for ye olde unspoilt Cornish fishing village of Polperro, but as kick-off time approaches two problems arise. First, the car radio reception is worse than unlistenable, and second, the car's temperature gauge is rising alarmingly quickly. This is surprising considering the fact that the wind-chill factor means the outside (stationary) temperature is down to around -14. Our short convoy makes an unscheduled stop in Liskeard and while I am now concerned about events due to unfold all those miles and hours to the north, the possibility of being stranded this far from home (never mind Elland Road) seems very real. With the bonnet up, The Tottenham Fan who has been sitting in the passenger seat turns smart-arse mechanic, and with the icy wind doing its best to do to our ears what it has done to the water in the car's cooling system, he cheerfully massages the frozen hoses until the ice in them starts to break down. Something called antifreeze, he explains, would have helped.

By the time we reach Polperro my Leeds woolly hat has revived my ears and serves to hold an earphone in place too. The game at St James' is already 20 minutes old and the first round-up of scores reveals that Leeds are 1–0 down and – surprise, surprise – Alan Shearer has scored the goal. Polperro is a beautiful village but is not improved any by listening to commentary of

Chelsea versus Liverpool while hoping against hope for news of an equaliser scored by Tony Yeboah. I am in a pub sipping a pint of Cornish mild when the news of the only goal scored anywhere in the Premiership since the second halves got under way interrupts proceedings at Stamford Bridge. It has gone in at St James', Leeds are 2–0 down and – surprise, surprise – Alan Shearer has scored again. The Tottenham Fan, still smarting from his team's 7–1 hammering at the feet of Keegan's team two days ago, reckons Leeds are getting off lightly. A pint of mild has never lasted so long but I manage to stretch it out to something like 4.30 when there is news of another goal at St James's. Leeds are 3–0 down and – surprise, surprise – it's not Shearer but Les Ferdinand who scored it. The full-time report ten minutes later says nice things about Leeds having chances but naturally tells of Rush missing them and makes no mention of Yeboah, who I presume was dropped. There was a point before the car froze up when I thought Leeds might cause a surprise and win. I was clearly mad but I'm not proud and so I will admit it. Right now all I can think is how mad I might have felt if I'd forgone the New Year's Eve celebrations and driven all the way from Cornwall to Newcastle to watch the game.

In the end I watch it in highlighted form on *Match of the Day*, surrounded by people getting far more enjoyment out of throwing felt balls at others while wearing Velcro-covered helmets. It is a far from ideal environment to watch Shearer claim a second goal that was an own-goal deflection by Carlton Palmer and then see Rush spurn three excellent chances. The first has me hurling insults at the telly in a manner which I know is normal for a man in the stands but rather extreme for a man in my present situation. The room goes momentarily quiet until Tony West Ham offers sympathy and agreement. Then the noise level soars again and I am unable to hear the after-match interview with George Graham even with my ear against the TV's speaker. Right here, right now it makes no difference anyway, so I give up on the telly and pick up a felt ball . . .

Wednesday, 4 January: frozen off

Spared the trip to Selhurst Park, because the Crystal Palace versus Leeds tie was postponed due to a frozen pitch, I extended my stay in the south-west to ensure I'm fully recharged for the rest of the season. Or something. And so the sight of the grounds of Bristol Rovers and Brentford at either end of the M4 are as close as I get to the football until watching Ceefax at home at half-time. It's not the 12 surviving FA Cup scores that catch my eye, however, but page 323 which says Yeboah disagrees with George Graham, who says he is unfit, and has gone to Africa to play for Ghana. He will be away next weekend so won't play against Leicester and won't be back in time for the rescheduled

Wilko looks a beaten man, last game in charge, home to Man United

George Graham looks a worried man, third game in charge, home to Newcastle United

Youth team overcome Manchester City at a near-deserted Maine Road

Pensive, away to Leicester City

Mark Jackson

Martyn and Beeney warm up

Fans in the stand chill out

Anything dad can do

Tony Yeboah, back in the dugout but still out of favour

Catering at Riverside. The book, the film, the burger?

Brian Deane in the clutches of the West Ham defence

Letting it all hang out

Assistant manager David O'Leary

Letting it all hang out. A few bellies more

Club captain and ex-goalscoring legend Ian Rush

Irish international and new goalscoring prodigy Ian Harte

Disbelief when Carlton Palmer is named as sub, away to Forest

Sharpe, Molenaar and Harte await the call-up in the dugout, home to Aston Villa

The next generation

Physio Alan Sutton with David Wetherall

Loud and proud

Leeds' travelling support watch Tony Yeboah's last game, vs. Tottenham Hotspur, 15 March 1997

Real Madrid wearing Leeds United shirts, Hillsborough

George Graham holds court, press conference after Blackburn

Watch the game

Tony Dorigo keeps watch on Forest's Chris Allen

Youth team parade Northern Intermediate League trophy in front of the Kop

Can we go home now?

Wilko era youngster Mark Ford ponders his future under new manager Graham

Deane scores Leeds' 28th and last Premiership goal of the season. And thereby relegates Middlesbrough, Juninho et al.

FA Cup tie with Palace on the following Tuesday. Surely Yeboah will now leave Leeds and the club will need more than a fortune to replace him.

I'm still chewing this over when the classified football results, filled out by the pools panel, are broadcast. The panel have clearly got wind of the Ian Rush phenomenon and the George Graham revolution and put today's game that never was down as a goalless draw . . .

Tuesday, 7 January: away to Manchester City, FA Youth Cup third round

The latest available youth-team statistics now read, played 15; won 14, drawn one, lost none, goals for 56, goals against five. This record so far is even better than the 1973–74 Championship-winning Leeds United side that enjoyed a record run of 29 games undefeated at the start of the season. Twist my arm and I'll admit that the quality of opposition is rather more variable in the Northern Intermediate League (the only other Premiership clubs among its 18-strong line-up are last season's winners Newcastle United, Sunderland, Middlesbrough and Sheffield Wednesday), but this is nevertheless just the kind of thought needed to inspire taking an afternoon off work, putting on an extra layer of clothing, and then driving north into a snow flurry to make a 4.30 p.m. rendezvous outside the Luton Gateway Hotel.

Before I set off, The Photographer phones to say he'll be half an hour late, so I call Maine Road to check the game is still on. The ticket office says it is, and seems surprised that anyone should ask. Perhaps the weather is better up north. This seems unlikely as matches everywhere else tonight have been postponed due to freezing conditions, and yes, Stockport County's Coca-Cola Cup tie against Southampton is also off – and this at a ground just three miles east of Maine Road. But isn't undersoil heating a wonderful thing? Arsenal are reportedly keeping seven miles of it on around the clock, at a cost of £1,000 per day, so that goalkeeper David Seaman can train and return to match fitness. Anyone who watched their stand-in keeper, John Lukic, play for Leeds last season will consider this a good investment.

The motorways are free of ice and snow and, miraculously, even approaching 5 p.m., the M6 through Birmingham is free of traffic jams. Soon, the car is so far north that there is a danger of arriving almost an hour before the 6.45 p.m. kick-off, so I slow down and reflect that whilst on Boxing Day this route took four hours, today it's taken less than three. Naturally, this is because Leeds are playing Manchester City, not United. Everything about Manchester is better when seen through sky-blue-tinted glasses. The red youth team are also in action tonight, taking on last year's Youth Cup winners at Anfield, in a match that has been mentioned on Ceefax, with Anfield claiming it expects a 'bumper' crowd. Or perhaps they are just trying to drum one up.

The phone rings at the very moment I negotiate the M6/M56 roundabout and the distraction means I take the wrong exit while declining the offer of a drink in London. The unexpected detour through Altrincham facilitates a meeting with Leeds' Wallace Arnold team coach one mile from the ground. My attempts to serve as an escort/pilot vehicle are as unsuccessful as they are fanciful, and the coach cruises past unaware of our interest as I park right alongside the ground in Ebberslone Road. The Photographer is thirsty so we walk to the Park Inn and prepare to run the gamut of Man City fans irate at having their local despoiled by opposition supporters. But the pub, big enough to hold a five-a-side match in, is occupied by only eight men and a dog, all watching Sky Sports. Anchorwoman Gaby Yorath confirms that Leeds have lost another centre-back, Ramon Vega, to Spurs and that all (first-team) matches are off tonight.

Lloyd Street outside is as deserted as the pub, so if anyone is going to this match they are cutting it fine. In the chip shop opposite, The Photographer and I each order a tray of their finest fried potatoes swamped in curry sauce for just £1.20. Plus two pence for a plastic fork. This quaintest of northern customs is forgiven as we wander to the ground, past an elegant piece of graffiti suggesting in letters two feet high that 'Lomas is shit'. Manchester City's Steve Lomas presumably uses another road to the ground on matchdays.

Skirting the main stand and approaching the end where away supporters are traditionally billeted I am struck first by a very cold wind and second by the realisation that the end is closed. Retracing our steps we ask a Man City fan queueing to buy tickets for a first-team fixture where to go and, very politely under the circumstances, he suggests we try the main stand. There I ask a pretty blonde stewardess if there is such a thing as an away end tonight.

'Oh, no,' she smiles. 'There won't be any trouble tonight.'

'But we're looking to start some,' deadpans The Photographer.

She looks momentarily concerned, then recognises the joke.

'Just go in here, and sit anywhere,' she explains, helpfully.

For £2 each we do. Climbing the stairs into the main stand puts us in the company of less than a thousand people, none of whom appear to be followers of Leeds United. The other three sides of the ground are eerily empty save for half a dozen ball boys, and the bright floodlights give the ground a surreal atmosphere. In selecting a seat we are hugely spoilt for choice, but as Leeds are going to kick right to left, we wander round the back of the directors' box and choose two alongside it nearest the net which the Leeds team will hopefully soon be stretching. To our right sits Frank Clark, watching his first game as City's new manager. His hang-dog expression, so familiar from his days at Forest, has, I note, survived intact.

That Man City net, and perhaps Clark's hang-dog expression, is stretched even sooner than I might have hoped, when good work on the left flank by Tony Hackworth after just three minutes sets up Wesley Boyle on the edge of the box. Boyle takes the chance neatly and City keeper Michael Brown can only watch as the score goes to 1–0. The Photographer and I cheer and applaud, inviting the glances of several disgruntled City fans. More alarming, however, is the realisation that only about 20 other people are doing the same. Excluding Leeds' chairman Bill Fotherby and coaches David O'Leary and David Williams, whom I've just spotted sitting close to Clark in the directors' box, this suggests that everyone else in that minority is related to someone on the pitch. Which means that The Photographer and I have entered the realms of the Extreme. Perhaps even Very Extreme Indeed. Where is everybody else? An average of 33,000 people watch the first team play at Elland Road, 2,000 travel to most away games and it seems inconceivable that less than one per cent of the latter are here tonight. With the way the first team have been playing recently, wouldn't any unhappy Leeds fan be impressed and intrigued enough to be curious? Wouldn't the chance to see a star of the future before he becomes famous make the trip worth while? Both these reasons were enough for me – together with a sense of guilt at having missed the match at St James' Park. (Although this last idea may be something for which I should seek professional help.)

And so The Photographer and I tough it out and continue to encourage the team wearing all-yellow who, frankly, are making the home side look as inferior as possible without actually scoring any more goals. Just like the first team they place great store in the use of aerial advantage, with forwards Hackworth and Lee Matthews lining up alongside centre-back Jonathon Woodgate on the edge of the penalty area at every corner won. A second goal fails to materialise before half-time, but during the interval passage to the fourth round seems a near certainty.

With nothing else to do but keep warm I wander around the bars under the main stand and relish the chance to be the only one down there. The childlike temptation to explore the playground which is a near-empty football stadium is impossible to resist. But when the boarded-up food counters and toilets all begin to look exactly alike, I pass through the deserted Tony Book Bar and head back up the steps to the main stand. I re-emerge at the end a steward has managed to keep completely empty. He spots me and gestures his disapproval. I wave an apology but twist my ankle falling down a step in the process and have to limp back sheepishly to the seat next to The Photographer.

Manchester City start the second half in a far more positive mood with their captain Jeff Whitley in midfield and defender Steve Rimmer looking particularly promising as the team goes forward and Leeds start to lose their shape. The goal Leeds eventually concede is from the penalty spot after a particularly amusing dive from City's Whitley. All around City fans are smirking, and the referee appears the only one in the ground who saw a foul. After 65 minutes, Doherty's penalty represents only the home side's third shot on goal and Leeds indignantly redouble their efforts, replacing Tommy Knarvik with Andrew Wright, whom Wilkinson signed from Sheffield Wednesday at such great expense, and pushing forward patiently. Yet with around ten minutes to go there appears no sign of a goal and so coach Eddie Gray has a sub prepare to enter the fray. Before he can get on, however, Stephen McPhail completes a weaving run on the left wing by sliding in an inch-perfect pass to Hackworth, who sidefoots the ball into the City net. The would-be Leeds sub puts his kit back on and sits down.

Ten minutes later the final whistle prompts around 20 muted cheers, and then The Photographer and I file out. Every steward we pass smiles and politely wishes us goodnight. Leeds scoring twice and polite stewards: two more things equally unexpected in a Premiership fixture . . .

Saturday, 11 January: home to Leicester City

Given the first team's recent record it's hard to imagine anything less appealing than this fixture. At the start of the season this would have seemed like an easy three points, but these days Leicester at home can't even be relied on for that. The newly promoted team almost everyone said were certain to slip straight back down into the Nationwide League have made a far better job of staying up than half a dozen teams – including Leeds United. They've scored more goals, conceded fewer and picked up an extra point and there seems a real chance that the visitors will triumph today. All I hope is that Leeds tear up the form book, as Tim Henman did to win the Sydney Open, his first major international tennis tournament, in the early hours of this morning . . .

Ten minutes after setting off in the car, the phone rings and it's The Photographer saying he's running late. Again.

'About half an hour. I was just sitting around watching the telly and eating my breakfast and I just couldn't be bothered,' he explains matter-of-factly. I suggest he is supposed to offer an excuse.

'You don't mean that,' he laughs.

Actually, he's right. I hardly care either. Strangely, neither do Andys Big and Little, travelling with us today because in deference to the recent bad weather I agreed to leave a little earlier. But the weather has broken today and there is a big thaw, so The Photographer being late is no real problem.

We have much to talk about to pass the time. On Monday Howard Wilkinson was appointed the FA Technical Director and Tomas Brolin was refused permission by Leeds to train with Parma, his old Italian club who are reportedly keen to buy him back. On Wednesday, Kevin Keegan resigned as manager of Newcastle United. Then on Thursday, Leeds paid a reputed £1 million for an unknown Dutch defender called Robert Molenaar, previously captain of FC Volendam, a team I'd never heard of.

Clubcall made much of Molenaar's recent topping of a poll amongst ex-players voting for the Dutch league's 'Mid-season Player of the Season'. Praise indeed – or evidence that ex-players have precious little to do in Holland? Ironically, he was once interesting Spurs, before they took Scales and Vega from under George Graham's nose. Rather more amusing is Clubcall describing Molenaar as 'six foot one or two, blond, blue-eyed and likely to be a big hit with the ladies at Elland Road'. He is almost certain to play today as Leeds are missing six defenders: long-term injuries John Pemberton (who has seemingly spent the whole season commentating in the gantry above our seats) and Richard Jobson; international call-ups Lucas Radebe and Harry Kewell; and the suspended pair of Carlton Palmer and, mysteriously, Gunnar Halle (who must have been a referee's favourite whilst at Oldham Athletic as he has only played four games for Leeds).

Big Andy has brought along a cutting from yesterday's *Daily Telegraph* that, all other papers devoting page after page to Keegan's shock departure, inexplicably carries a huge quarter-page photograph of George Graham and Molenaar in the obligatory dumb here-is-the-club-shirt-and-here-is-my-new-signing-behind-it pose. The prospects for the ladies at Elland Road are not good. And, despite reports elsewhere that he may now be six foot four, he appears to be a head shorter than his new manager. 'Perhaps,' observes The Photographer, 'George is standing on a box.'

The M1 is almost clear and we move north almost as quickly as we agree that Keegan's achievements as Newcastle manager have been overrated. Give almost any other Premiership manager £60 million to spend and five years to rebuild, and that manager would have a picture of himself alongside some silverware. Hell, if Leeds had only bought back David Batty and landed Alan Shearer for, say, £20 million, the team would be up there with Liverpool at the top and Wilkinson would still be the manager. Instead there he was, in Wednesday's *Sun*, speaking up for Keegan and giving his first hint about what life was like during his last days at Leeds: 'There were times when I stopped and asked myself, "What am I doing?" I was driving myself into the ground. People told me ages ago I needed a change; now I realise they were right.'

I could do with a change myself but that's now in the hands of George Graham. Right now I am overtaking car after car containing Chelsea fans *en route* to their away game at Nottingham Forest. Every other Chelsea car is a four-wheel-drive designer jeep and The Photographer makes what appear to be 2–0 signs at each one to remind the occupants of the score in December. After the M6 turn-off we see no more of them and the road gets ever clearer. Even after a 15-minute break at Trowell Services, arriving more than an hour before kick-off looks likely and I am just preparing to point this out to any Andy who might care to listen when the car in front puts its hazard lights on and I almost run into the back of it. All three lanes slow to walking pace and I switch on Radio 5, hoping for some travel news. The news soon comes and it's bad. The M1 is closed between junctions 33 and 34 and northbound traffic is advised to leave at junction 32 and take the M18 and A1 north. Junction 32 is in sight – but only in the rear-view mirror, and so we crawl to 33, turn and head south again. The idea occurs to us all simultaneously that maybe this is our chance to miss the match and get home early, but instead, with 45 minutes to kick-off and Elland Road still over 30 miles away, I accelerate up the alternative route and we miss only the first minute of the match. We stroll to our seats just as Molenaar, who is indeed making his debut, makes a tackle from behind on Leicester's Emile Heskey that leaves the young forward in a crumpled heap. He's 19 today but as birthday greetings go, it's not one he'll cherish. Yet as a statement of intent it has me beaming like a proud father. The ladies in the West Stand seem to have got over the disappointment of their first look at Molenaar (who looks big and strong but also, tragically, sports a fleshy coloured egg in the nest of his short blond crop) and console themselves by craning their necks to watch Lee Sharpe (who looks hunky and cute but, tragically, sports a white woolly hat) when he gets off the bench for a warm-up with fellow sub Ian Harte.

Judging by the gaps in the Leicester-City-supporting contingent in the South Stand, many of them are still stuck on the M1. They are not missing much from their own team and little more from Leeds, but steadily the home side gains the upper hand. The half-dozen of us in row BB are in light-hearted mood and Graham, looking down from his vantage point somewhere above, is too. It is fully 16 minutes before the telephone in the dugout rings and this is duly noted as a new record. It's half an hour before the first real chance presents itself, to Ian Rush, who cannons his shot into the back of Leicester's stand-in centre-half Ian Marshall when it appeared easier to score. The *Sun* this morning made Rush 'Key Man' in its match preview and today's programme has a banner headline with the man himself proclaiming 'The goals will come in '97'. Presumably when he passes to someone else. Looking around the pitch, the realisation dawns that apart from Rush and Brian Deane up front and Lee Bowyer and Rod Wallace in midfield, everyone wearing a Leeds shirt today is a defender. God bless George Graham.

But just when it has become almost impossible to believe Leeds will ever score, Dorigo gets to the byline on the left and crosses long to Deane, who nods it back to Bowyer, unmarked ten yards from goal. Bowyer volleys the ball past Leicester keeper Kasey Keller, then celebrates his second goal of the season by running in front of the visiting fans suggesting they show their appreciation. They decline and he is lucky not to be booked for incitement. In the absence of Yeboah, the Kop adapts his three-syllable chant to fit the Leeds number 11's name: 'Lee-Bow-Yer! Lee-Bow-Yer! Lee-Bow-Yer!'

Just five minutes later, almost on the stroke of half-time, Deane and Bowyer combine again and the latter shoots from a narrow angle, only to see the ball rebound off the defender stationed on the line. Almost in slow motion the ball rises into the air a yard off the line where Rush, also in slow motion, rises to head it down into the net. The old codger has scored and I am very pleased for him. The Photographer is the only one standing still, attempting to take a shot of the electronic scoreboard bearing the scorer's name to record this rare event. But when he sits down again he is unsure whether he got the shot.

As the second half progresses, amused fatalism gives way to genuine appreciation. Leicester City are clearly having a very bad afternoon indeed but Leeds are actually playing rather well, and while it's too one-sided to register as exciting, it is at least entertaining to watch Leeds create a number of half-chances. There are sterling individual performances, too, notably from Dorigo, making darting runs down the left flank just like in the old days. His right-side foil Gary Kelly, plus Deane and Bowyer, are impressive also. Molenaar looks strong too, showing a nice line in cross-field passes with the outside of his right boot, and when he gets booked for yet another crunching tackle on Heskey, his new hero status is confirmed.

Better still, 15 minutes into the second half, his long ball out of defence finds the head of Rush, who flicks on to Dorigo. Dorigo miscues his cross as he slips on contact and Deane does something similar, taking the ball away from the onrushing Wallace but helping it into the path of Rush who hooks it in the Kop end net for his second. Delirium ensues. Rush salutes the crowd and, although it takes a while, they remember the song eventually: 'Ian Rush! Ian Rush! Ian Ian Rush! He gets the ball, he scores a goal, Ian Ian Rush!'

A small voice inside reminds me this is the same Ian Rush I have spent the whole season despairing over. Rush told the programme, in syntax as lousy as his shooting: 'If I am not scoring and we are in the relegation zone I am willing to sacrifice myself and maybe someone else should be given a chance.' Suddenly the talk is of hat-tricks and even I find myself willing the ball towards him.

There is a stirring in the Kop and a Mexican wave emerges. It rattles rather half-heartedly to the bottom left-hand corner and then heads south through the tiers of the giant East Stand. People at the front wave what look like Star Wars light sabres but are in fact the rather naff inflatable 'soccer sausages' handed out by girls working for the *Mirror*. But soccer sausages aren't the craziest thing happening on the far side of the ground. That prize goes to Leicester's Neil Lewis for the most entertaining throw-in of the season. Whether Lewis has a long throw remains unknown because in his apparent efforts so to demonstrate, he conspires to fall flat on his face and send the ball on a near-vertical trajectory, with it landing just a few yards in front of where his face is buried in shame in the grass. 'Let's all laugh at Leicester! Let's all laugh at Leicester!' chants the Kop, but because it was so funny and because the Kop waited so long, everyone already has.

At the final whistle, Leicester have got off lightly and Leeds have acquitted themselves well, albeit against very obviously inferior opposition. But that doesn't seem important as a glance at the scoreboard reveals it's still 0–0 at Anfield between Liverpool and West Ham which means that Leeds are no longer the Premiership's lowest scorers. Back in the car, Radio 5 says Leeds are up to 12th. It's flattering because three teams below have a game in hand, but it's a good feeling nonetheless. Good, too, to learn that Chelsea lost 2–0 to Stuart Pearce's revitalised Forest, which may explain that while there are many four-wheel-drive vehicles heading towards London south of Nottingham, none of them are displaying Chelsea colours.

I arrive home in a good mood which is only spoilt when my mother rings to offer her congratulations, followed by the inquiry: 'What happened? Did Leicester send a team from the blind school?'

Tuesday, 14 January: away to Crystal Palace, FA Cup third round

London matches are, for people who live in London, supposed to be easy to get to. But Selhurst Park isn't easy to get to from anywhere. In fact, Selhurst Park may be the hardest ground to get to in the world, no matter where you start from. According to maps, the ground is only six miles from where I work and a similar distance from where The Photographer lives. I leave work early to meet him at his home but it takes me longer to get to his place than it would have done to reach Luton and we have to leave straightaway. Selhurst Park is, he swears, just 20 minutes' drive away, but I don't believe him. Even opposite corners of Selhurst Park take more than 20 minutes to travel between. I know for certain that he's lying when he spends five minutes reading the A–Z, then pulls out into an ominously slow-moving snake of traffic muttering about this being the route the radio has just warned motorists to avoid. After 30 minutes of driving he admits that he did once get to his sister's house somewhere near Selhurst Park in 20 minutes – but that wasn't on a matchday or during rush hour.

The Photographer is very excited because of all the teams he has written to this season, Crystal Palace is the first to allow him a camera pass and he will be allowed to take photos from the edge of the pitch. He's excited because the report on the Leicester game in Monday's *Guardian* so offended him he has written in to complain. And he's also excited because Sky Sports carried a news item on Caspian's plans to redevelop Elland Road by rebuilding the West Stand (to increase ground capacity to 45,000) and joining it to an 11,000-seat arena for an ice hockey team. 'It's incredible. The model looks like something that has flown here from Mars,' he gushes.

But the main sports news stories concern Middlesbrough – who have today been docked three points for declining to play Blackburn – and Newcastle United – who have announced the appointment of Kenny Dalglish as the manager to replace Keegan. No matter what Leeds do, they always seem to do it on a day when something more important is happening . . .

We park and arrive at the ground only five minutes before kick-off. While The Photographer goes to collect his promised pass I hurry to entrance four of the Arthur Wait Stand alone. On entry, it's easy to see why so many matches here have recently been postponed due to ground frost: the street-level turnstiles lead through to entrances that are almost in the rafters of the stand, with the pitch 40 or 50 rows below. Apart from the impressive new Holmesdale Road two-tier stand to the left, this is not a great ground, as Palace chairman Ron Noades, in the *Daily Telegraph* last week, admitted. Noades complained that the ground was originally shortlisted as a Euro 96 venue on the condition that its capacity was increased from 24,000 to 30,000, but the local council wouldn't allow planning permission. Just as well, or people would still be arriving even tonight . . .

Leeds are impressively well supported for a midweek match, even a cup tie, with their fans filling almost half the Arthur Wait Stand and making plenty of noise. The Man From Birmingham is here somewhere but I forget to phone him when I bump into Big Andy, then spot The Photographer wandering casually behind the goal to the left. The electronic scoreboard suggests Leeds are fielding just seven players and using the same three substitutes as Crystal Palace – but I am still optimistic. And after all the hassles of my journey here, I feel relatively fortunate standing next to three men complaining bitterly about a journey obviously far worse – all the way from Leeds by train. I count my blessings and then add my voice to the cheering as the teams run out, Leeds all in yellow.

Leeds start strongly and play most of the opening exchanges pressing Palace back into their own half. In the third minute, Lucas Radebe takes a free-kick that misses its target, the head of Brian Deane, and drops instead to the Palace captain David Hopkin. But Hopkin mishits his clearance and gives it straight to Deane, who takes a step closer to the goal then lashes the ball past keeper Chris Day for a dream start. 'Deano! Deano! Deano!' comes the cry, and with it the idea that this is going to be an easy safe passage.

Three minutes later the idea evaporates. A high ball finds Palace forward Bruce Dyer well placed to head goalwards, but instead Paul Beesley, in close contention, appears to raise a hand and make contact with the ball. Referee Roger Dilkes points to the penalty spot and I am incensed at Beesley for thinking he might get away with it, then for compounding his idiocy by getting booked protesting his innocence.

The stage is set for Nigel Martyn, on his first return to Selhurst Park, to make a save at the expense of his former club. But he hasn't read the stage directions and dives right while Dyer puts the ball to his left for 1–1. Leeds counter with menace and Deane, who has spent most of the first seven minutes with the ball at his feet and Palace players in his wake, dribbles round another on the right wing and hits a ball that Rush will surely score from. Instead, however, Palace's Leif Andersen intervenes with a finish as clinical as any Rush might have hoped for to make it 2–1 with a peach of an own goal. Deane celebrates anyway, as well he might. He is a frustrating player, always giving 100 per cent but so often looking clumsy. Stuart Hall once described his passage down the wing as like that of 'a lumbering pterodactyl', but when Deano is on form, defenders hate him and Leeds score goals. Minutes later, Lee Sharpe is brought on as a substitute for the limping Dorigo who walks down the players' tunnel with his head bowed and a couple of thousand Leeds fans hoping the old injury hasn't flared up yet again.

Chances come and chances go at both ends, with Dyer and George Ndah looking ferociously quick for Palace and Rush and Bowyer are fighting hard – the latter almost literally – in every tackle for Leeds. But Wallace and Sharpe look woefully off the pace and I cannot feel comfortable with just a one-goal cushion. Fortunately Martyn is again in fine form, saving magnificently time after time. At the other end Wallace, in his most assured piece of play of the half, dribbles in from the right of the penalty area – but makes a vicious air shot at the ball at his feet. Another excellent opportunity arises right on the stroke of half-time when great work by Gary Kelly, forward on the far right, sees him harry a Palace defender into a mistake. Kelly skips around him and delivers an excellent low cross into the path of Deane – who follows Wallace's example and misses it totally. Stuart Hall take note.

The half-time whistle prompts the now-customary shirts-off 'We are the champions!' tomfoolery and makes me confident enough to sample the Selhurst Park catering. I regret it when the hot chocolate melts the stirrer and removes flesh from the roof of my mouth, but the Mars bar is reassuringly within its sell-by date.

Ten minutes into the second half two changes are obvious. Radebe is now man-marking Dyer and Palace are squeezing Deane out of the game. Leeds are thus less impressive going forward and Palace look far more composed. Frustration gets the better of Bowyer who is booked for the latest in a long line of fierce challenges and then finds himself the target for retribution from Palace's Kevin Muscat who, suggests one of the three men who came by train, should be playing second row for Dewsbury rather than football. The Palace supporters in the Holmesdale Road end clearly disagree. Bowyer is, they suggest, a young man well used to the practice of self-abuse. But their casual attitude to the pronunciation of the letter 'k' in the word 'wanker' prompts only hoots of derision from the Yorkshiremen in the crowd. The higher than usual proportion of Leeds-supporting southerners can only smile and keep their mouths shut.

Time ticks by and Palace slowly gain the upper hand. With 20 minutes to go Muscat wrong-foots Kelly and his cross is met by Carl Veart, who glances an excellent header just beyond the diving Martyn's fingertips and into the net for 2–2, an equaliser that had long been threatened. A replay looms and the Leeds fans are deflated. The players, though, try harder, and only a couple of minutes later Deane is free on the left with only the keeper to beat. Deane attempts a chip but the keeper gathers and Deane chastises himself furiously. No one around me is too pleased either.

Looking at my watch almost as much as the pitch brings relief only when the game finally enters its last minute. Then Dyer, racing towards the Leeds penalty area, gets goalside of Radebe when he slips and falls. One second later Dyer falls as well. Ludicrously, Palace fans appeal for a penalty but I only want to see Dyer booked for diving. Referee Dilkes bows his head and walks slowly towards the incident, either wondering, I presume, whether to show a yellow card or merely to escape the mounting protests. His interminable stroll ends on the penalty spot and the realisation dawns that he somehow believes that Radebe fouled Dyer. David Wetherall reacts fastest by sprinting over to the linesman begging for him to offer a second and better-judged opinion. Wetherall then runs back to Dilkes, surrounded by yellow shirts, who finally wanders towards the linesman. The yellow-shirted mêlée follows him like a swarm of bees and suddenly Leeds fans are all standing on the seats to get a better view. There is pandemonium in the stands and something almost as chaotic on the touchline. Only Wallace, continuing his form in the bulk of the match, is nowhere near the action. Kelly takes a turn as peacemaker, imploring his team-mates to back off and give the officials room to talk. But when they finally do so, the briefest of exchanges results in another of Dilkes's presumably patented slow walks back to the penalty spot. In a red mist, countless thoughts flash through my mind: Leeds are going out 3–2 . . . giant-killing headlines . . . phonecalls from a certain red-haired Palace fan . . . and – bizarrely, perhaps – Alan Green's voice going into overdrive on Radio 5.

As I perch with one foot on the back of the seat in front, I experience what I can only describe as a moment of premonition. I am absolutely certain that Dyer will place his penalty to Martyn's left once again. I yell dementedly at Martyn, forgetting that he can't hear above the incredible din. Leeds' furious players take an age to clear the area, with Wetherall the last to step back over the 18-yard line. Up steps Dyer, and sidefoots to Martyn's left, where the keeper leaps and parries. The ball rebounds to the taker who, with Martyn in a crumpled heap, lashes the ball wide of an empty net.

The save drives myself and every man, woman and child in the Leeds contingent over the edge. Two people to my left leap off the seats and fall heavily to the ground. I help one up then climb again on to the backs of the seats and experience the closest thing all season to an out-of-body experience. There is a man shouting four-letter insults through gritted teeth, both his fists are clenched and his heart pumps furiously. Every muscle in the man's body is straining with adrenaline, those in his face contorted into a mask of hate and fury. The man is as close as he has ever come to being a football hooligan. And he is me. It's not big, it's not clever, and it's not anything I'd want my mother to see.

I have not calmed down much when the whistle goes two minutes later and Ian Rush continues to remonstrate with Dilkes. David O'Leary sprints on to the pitch to drag him away and save Leeds' captain from himself. The rest of the Leeds players come over to the Arthur Wait to applaud their supporters, then turn back to the dressing-rooms. As they go I take a deep breath, count to ten and wander forward to meet The Photographer. I am human again. The replay is announced for Saturday, 25 January, and I only hope Mr Dilkes has better eyesight in daylight hours . . .

Monday, 20 January: away to West Ham United

Chris Evans decides not to turn up for Radio 1's breakfast show this morning but I must stick to the job in hand. Another week, another night match, another game in London. And while everyone in Yorkshire complains about the long journey south to take on cockneys, I leave work on time, meet The Photographer, hop on the tube and get out at Upton Park station 30 minutes later. This is more like it. As the train pulls into Upton Park there is even a recorded announcement advising passengers that this is the station to alight at if they are going to the match. Ahead on the platform, two Hammers fans laugh.

'Ha ha, bet all the stupid Leeds fans got off at West Ham.'

'Not all of them,' corrects The Photographer.

They hear him and turn, then laugh again. West Ham fans have a fearsome reputation but these days it's nonsense. These two are fine. And I was only notionally scarred when, at a Leeds match here in the 1970s, some herbert wearing a round-collared shirt and DMs suggested that my scarf would look better tied around his wrist than my neck. When I gingerly refused, the herbert laughed rather than battered me as I had feared, so I kept the scarf. The memory I've kept rather longer, and it resurfaces again now as I walk past fanzine sellers dropping 'g's and 'h's like the world's worst juggler playing Scrabble.

I'm wearing no colours anyway, because I'm meeting Tony West Ham for 'a sociable drink' in the supporters club bar on Castle Street. He even pays the pound to get me in. We go upstairs to a small bar called The Trophy Room. I bite my lip to hold back the obvious joke about how small it is. His friend and adjacent season-ticket holder is nowhere to be seen, so we go back downstairs. Here there's no carpet, a couple of people wearing Leeds shirts, Tony West Ham's mate, and a bar selling Yorkshire bitter. I order a pint, convinced I've made a statement. At the other end of the bar I recognise Kirk Blows, author of *Terminator: The Authorised Julian Dicks Story* that I bought as a birthday present for Tony West Ham two days ago. Blows edited the official Leeds United magazine for a time last season, but there are a lot of bodies between him and me and I figure he wouldn't want to be reminded of that tonight.

West Ham fans have much more on their minds tonight. Many here are watching Sky on the overhead TV screens but with the sound turned down. I can only assume their lip-reading skills are superior to mine. Tony West Ham and his friend, like so many others around us, are depressed about West Ham apparently declining Michael Tabor's £30 million takeover offer. They are even less keen on the rumour of swapping Slaven Bilic for Andy Cole.

As kick-off approaches, we finish our drinks, wish each other some less-than-sincere good luck and head for the door, passing on the way several Iron Maiden gold discs on the wall. The band's Hammers fanatic bassist Steve Harris runs a Sunday league side that wears an exact replica West Ham kit with Iron Maiden's logo over the club sponsor's. I played for a scratch side with him once and remember being seriously wounded by the look he gave me when I pulled on a pair of Leeds shorts. Lovely bloke, but I hope he's miserable tonight.

Inside the Centenary Stand, the Leeds team news is encouraging. Robert Molenaar, unable to play against Palace because of the FA's 'seven-day signing rule', is back in a defence West Ham have little hope of penetrating given their woeful scoring record thus far. In the bar, Tony West Ham's mate was laughing about Brian Deane, but West Ham would be twice as potent if they had him, and I am relieved that on Clubcall today Bill Fotherby is denying rumours of a £2.7 million bid from Sheffield United and insisting he is not for sale. More interesting is further news on Caspian's plans to redevelop Elland Road's old West Stand. The adjacent arena will also accommodate boxing, basketball, pop concerts and exhibitions but, insists chief executive Robin Launders, such activities would only raise money for the football club and the construction costs (anything upward of £20 million) would in no way affect the pot of money available to George Graham for use in the transfer market.

Ice hockey, boxing, basketball, even basket-weaving would have been more entertaining than the first half at Upton Park. At half-time, the Sky TV feed relayed on to the ground's two screens says Leeds had five attempts on goal but I can only assume they are counting any pass that didn't go astray. The shirts-off singalong begins even before the half has finished and gathers momentum when the screens reveal Sky are broadcasting it to the nation. I wander over to the corner where The Man From Birmingham, The Biggest Yorkshireman In London, Radio Rhys and a few more are moaning about their appalling misfortune to have paid for a seat facing the pitch.

'Shite, isn't it?' is all the conversation that the first half warrants, and we turn instead to watch the shirts-off loonies in the far-smaller-than-usual travelling contingent. TMFB and TBYIL are amused, but I've seen it before and am too depressed to enjoy it tonight. Instead I go under the Centenary Stand to buy a Twix and a hot chocolate. Tony West Ham phones from the other end of the ground but the reception is so bad it's two minutes before I realise I'm talking to him and not The Photographer, who is making use of his second photo pass in two games. Through the crackles I can tell Tony West Ham is as depressed by the match as I am. There's worse to come, I suggest, shuddering, then hang up and wander back to my seat.

Eight minutes after the restart things do get worse, but only for him. The excellent Bilic, who has had a virtual running battle with Deane all night, fouls the Leeds attacker 20 yards out, directly in front of me. Without any fuss, Gary Kelly steps forward and hits a curving free-kick over the wall and towards keeper Ludek Miklosko's right-hand post. Miklosko reacts well and parries the ball up on to the bar – but it bounces down, hits him on the back of the head and rolls into the net. Having just doubled his career goal tally, Kelly goes mad, sprinting away triumphantly towards the halfway line before leaping into the air with an agility that suggests he should be pushed forward to meet, rather than deliver crosses.

Kelly is forward again, 17 minutes later, when he fires in a shot from the right-hand side of the crowded West Ham penalty box. The ball is destined to miss the post but Dicks opts to clear it. From Dicks's boot, the ball goes directly to the chest of Lee Bowyer. The little midfielder, who has been our most menacing player given Bilic's ability to subdue Deane, reacts quickly to bring the ball under control and fire it back, goalwards this time and beyond Miklosko for 2–0.

I fear the worst when a cross at the far end reaches West Ham's Mike Newell, on loan from Birmingham City, but he misses from just five yards out. Soon after Molenaar gathers the ball inside the Leeds half and comes rampaging forward to just outside West Ham's penalty area. Unchallenged, the big Dutchman shoots just inches wide. The Leeds supporters go for broke and salute him with not one but two chants: 'Mo-lly! Mo-lly! Mo-lly!' and the rather less popular 'Ooh Ah Molenaar!'.

But the absolute highlight of the evening has little to do with football. It occurs when a West Ham player goes down injured and a dialogue, in cartoon speech bubbles, begins on the screens. 'Send for Super Sponge!' reads one caption, giving way to a graphic of a sponge with human eyes that spins à la Clark Kent and comes to a halt wearing a claret and blue cape with a big 'S' on its chest. Leeds fans guffaw and inquire: 'What the fuck? What the fuck? What the fucking hell was that?'

The West Ham physio runs along the goalline in front of them and the chanting gathers pace: 'Super, Super Sponge', 'There's only one Super Sponge', 'Super, Super, give us a wave' (boos when the physio doesn't) and 'We love you Super, oh yes we do'. West Ham fans groan with embarrassment.

When the whistle finally goes, Super Sponge has been immortalised but the match is instantly forgotten. Bilic and Deane embrace, shake hands and laugh in the centre circle, but as they walk off the West Ham fans are far less happy, booing and calling for the board, manager Harry Redknapp, or both to resign.

Five minutes later, with the ground almost empty, and watching The Photographer pack away his lenses, I discover that Tony West Ham has turned his phone off . . .

Saturday, 25 January: home to Crystal Palace, FA Cup third round replay

Anyone who thinks I got a little uptight over this fixture's original game at Selhurst Park is welcome to come around to my house and watch the video of the two penalties awarded against Leeds United. And that invitation extends to Crystal Palace manager Dave Bassett, who has said some very unkind things about Leeds in the press over the past few days.

Having watched the footage more times than I'm going to admit, both at normal speed and frame by frame, I *know* that neither kick should have been awarded. For the first, Beesley's arm, even if it did make contact with the ball, did so only because Dyer lifted it by raising his own arm and *Dyer* touched the ball before Beesley could have. No wonder the Leeds defender's protests were enough to get him booked. And for the second, happily fluffed, penalty, both Radebe's hands can be seen to hit the grass with Dyer's ankles still ahead of them. I know that, Dyer knows that, but twist my arm and I will admit that there is no way the referee Roger Dilkes could have known that. And so Leeds and Palace have to start over again today, when the FA Cup is scheduled to be at its fourth round stage. It's okay, everyone else go on ahead, we'll catch up.

Andys Big and Little have left an hour earlier than The Photographer and me, and as we're completely bored at five to two, five minutes after we take our seats in a near-deserted ground, I wonder what on earth the Andys have been doing since one o'clock. For season-ticket holders today's seats cost only £10, but not everyone would seem to have been impressed enough to take up the offer. Bored with our normal vantage point between the dugouts we have opted to sit in the Kop. We get prime seats dead centre that some other season-ticket holder is perhaps bored with also.

It feels odd looking down on our usual seats and at Helen The Ellie Fan, who is sitting alone wondering where the hell all her mates have gone. Time passes. Slowly. The PA asks us to welcome Palace mascot Eddie The Eagle as he/she/it wanders around with Leeds' own, frankly embarrassing, Ellie The Elephant. The Eagle is much better than Ellie and hams it up with the players as well as the fans. He even stops for a chat with Nigel Martyn as he warms up. Ellie, meanwhile, brings up the rear rather forlornly. But at least when he gets to the dugouts Helen, still all alone, is pleased to see him.

More time passes. I try in vain to get interested in the programme. When I read it at home, I know this will be a terrific magazine, but something about a pre-match atmosphere always makes it impossible to concentrate. Only a picture of the model of Elland Road's proposed new West Stand-cum-arena holds any interest and soon I give up on that and watch the distraction of Martyn and Beeney exchanging long shots.

When three o'clock comes around and the match finally begins, it produces none of the drama or passion of the first tie. Five minutes into the game, I am already gazing around the crowd in boredom. Halfway to the goalline in front and to my left, I spot a bare shoulder topped by long blonde hair. It looks odd. The shoulder raises an arm and that's bare, too, with long, painted fingernails. Very odd. Suddenly, I'm not the only one watching as the game is forgotten and 99 per cent of the Kop have realised their number today includes a tanned 'beauty' – she's facing the pitch but I give her the benefit of the doubt – doing just what the Billy Ten Bellies have been doing for months: going topless. The Photographer whips out his compact camera but everyone stands up and no one gets an eyeful. Five minutes later, to the accompaniment of considerable booing, a policewoman moves in and persuades blondie to cover up.

The game continues, but it's deadly dull. After a quarter of an hour we get a timely reminder of what the FA Cup is supposed to be about when the scoreboard flashes the news that Hednesford have just gone 1–0 up against Middlesbrough. At Elland Road, however, the world's most celebrated knock-out competition is having an off-day. Gunnar Halle, Mark Jackson and Lee Bowyer are all playing well, but collectively Leeds are about as menacing as Ian Rush. Or Ellie The Elephant.

Five minutes before half-time, Bowyer gets the ball in a 50:50 challenge but is fouled for his trouble and goes down just inside the Leeds half, where he writhes in apparent agony. His last touch sends the ball out to the right wing where it reaches Kelly. Dilkes, trying to keep up with the play, looks back over his shoulder and plays the advantage. Kelly, who has been belting passes into the West Stand or at red and blue shirts all afternoon, seizes that advantage by trying a backheel. I am about to swear at him when the backheel falls perfectly for Wallace, who has been useless all afternoon. And I am about to groan when he quite unexpectedly runs goalwards rather than to the byline, feinting and switching the ball from one foot to the other before belting it past keeper Chris Day's stretching fingertips and into the top right-hand corner from just outside the box. At last – a stunner! The Kop leaps to its feet, and I cannot recall so many people getting so much exactly right in such quick succession. I replay the goal in my head where it waltzes before my mind's eye like some sublime sporting ballet and looks like the best I've seen Leeds score all season. The memory bank tosses in Ian Harte's belter against Derby on the opening day but I'm in no mood for a debate. Instead I cheer maliciously and grin some more when I see Dilkes booking a Palace player, presumably for the challenge on Bowyer. My face has only just straightened itself out when the half-time whistle goes three minutes later.

The interval scoreboard shows that giant-killing acts remain in the balance at Middlesbrough – where Hednesford have been pegged back to 1–1 and Coventry, where the other non-league side, Woking, are holding their Premiership hosts at 0–0.

In the second half, Leeds remain poor but Palace are weaker, and a shadow of the side that ran their hearts out at Selhurst Park 11 days ago. Bowyer is still Leeds' best player but Jackson and Halle have faded. Dorigo and Deane are getting stronger but not enough. On the hour, an attack breaks down and as the players turn away the linesman raises his flag. Dilkes, who by now has given Leeds so many ludicrous decisions he has evened out the wrongs of the first match, ignores the flag and play continues. The ball reaches Carlton Palmer, who sees the Palace defence open up before he takes aim and scores –

but only because Day makes a complete dog's dinner of saving it. Palmer wheels away in delirium and Palace heads sink. But so does Roger Dilkes's, aiming its nose in the direction of where he now wants a free-kick for offside to be taken, having decided, what seems like five minutes later, to acknowledge the flag the linesman is still petulantly holding aloft. Of all the referees in the world that I don't like, and there are a growing number, Roger Dilkes is definitely the most recent.

With the left side of the Kop teasing 'Right side, right side, give us a song' and everyone waiting for this tedious game to end, the PA announces that the crowd is just 21,903. Leeds fans are either unimpressed by the magic of the FA Cup or are too tight to buy what amounts to a platform ticket to look at a train they expect to be derailed at Arsenal in the next round. They might have a point. With 80 minutes gone many begin to leave, perhaps afraid that 30 minutes of extra time should Palace equalise is more torture than they can bear.

On 90 minutes, the remainder are spared the torture and look instead to the scoreboard for light relief as they stand to leave. It shows West Ham and Wrexham are drawing 0–0, Coventry are beating Woking 1–0, and (to a chorus of boos) Man United are 1–0 up against Wimbledon. The strangely muted crowd files slowly out and the scores keep revolving. Short stuttering paces take The Photographer and me finally to the exit, where one last glance at the scoreboard shows three late goals have been scored since we left our seats: Woking have equalised, Wrexham have put West Ham out and, best of all, the Dons have got one back at Old Trafford. The emptying Kop chants 'Wimbledon! Wimbledon! Wimbledon!' and suddenly the departing crowd's mood lightens.

After saying goodbye to The Photographer at Luton, I drive alone across East Anglia to visit my parents, a journey that turns into a marathon by a fog thicker than I have ever seen. With rising excitement I await Wallace's goal on *Match of the Day* and when my viewing is interrupted by having to babysit my nephew because his father needs to rush my sister to the maternity ward I get a sudden reality check. A brand new life is a far truer measure of excitement. And when Wallace's goal is eclipsed by footage of Chris Waddle scoring from the halfway line for Bradford at Everton and Trevor Sinclair's sensational bicycle kick against Barnsley, the reality check is complete. Life 1 Leeds United 0 . . .

Wednesday, 29 January: home to Derby County

He doesn't say it but I can tell what Little Andy is thinking: 'I told you so.' Having delayed our rendezvous to the last possible minute – and then been half an hour late – we're not going to make it. Just north of Nottingham, a sea of flaring red tail-lights and a lane-closure sign bring our progress to a grinding halt. Ten minutes and about half a mile later the slim chance we had of seeing the kick-off has gone. When we finally dawdle past the flashing blue lights, the chief reason for the three-lane hold-up is yet again idiots rubber-necking at the crumpled cars who got there first but too fast.

As we pull off the M1 into Ardsley East we can't find Radio Leeds United so listen to Radio 5's commentary on Southampton versus Stockport in the Coca-Cola Cup, hoping against hope that there is no interruption by news (not even good news) from Elland Road. As we race into the car park the good news from the marshal is that (a) it remains 0–0 and (b) we can park right next to the ground and don't have to pay. With the window wound down we can hear the crowd noise as we drive into the glare of the floodlights high on top of the East Stand. Running the last hundred metres we are delayed another minute when one of the two other people in sight gets her handbag stuck in the turnstile, but by now it doesn't matter. We finally stroll into the ground with the clock showing 16 minutes played. Which, uncannily, is almost exactly how much of the fixture I missed the last time Leeds played Derby, on the opening day of the season.

Chesterfield Ken and wife Barbara confirm we have missed nothing. Mark Beeney is in goal as Nigel Martyn strained his back in training, but neither Beeney nor his opposite number Russell Hoult has been tested. The next 30 minutes provide absolutely nothing that even closely resembles entertainment and I am reduced to watching the grass grow. Except it doesn't and appears to be being replaced by large, muddy studmarks.

By half-time, being stuck in a traffic jam seems much more fun than watching Leeds United. Every team, even those at the top of the league, will sometimes produce games like this, but this season Leeds fans have had to sit through more duds than seems statistically credible in their search for a game of lasting memory. I'm starting to feel like a princess kissing frogs in a leper colony, and tonight we've even got a pitch to make the little green buggers feel at home.

I'm not thirsty but offer to make a trip to the John Charles Bar to kill some time. The queue for four hot chocolates takes more than ten minutes and so I watch the game restart on the TV monitor hanging in the corner. Elsewhere in the bar a dozen or so miserable souls clutch plastic glasses half-full of beer while apparently pondering whether to order another or merely go home.

Back in my seat I sip chocolate while sullenly watching the match. The at-least-partially structured tedium of the first half is, incredibly, unravelling and the 'play' is getting worse. But if the football is awful, the officials are even worse. The programme identifies the guilty man in the middle as Keith Burge, another so-called celebrity ref who appears no more gifted than any of the 22 players running around much quicker than he is. George Graham and

David O'Leary have noticed this too. 'Tony, Tony!' Graham yells at Dorigo. 'Tell the ref to stop blowing his whistle!'

Considering the wing-back is further away from the Leeds dugout than Burge, it would appear simpler for George just to tell the ref direct. Dorigo acknowledges the shout but opts to play football instead. George Graham gives up on the game and instead shouts at the fourth official, seated in front of us. The fourth official grimaces and stares at the match, avoiding the irate manager's gaze and perfectly reasonable appeals by making secret marks in his notebook. When Burge twice stops play to make Leeds retake a free-kick from what he deems to be the correct spot only five yards away, I hope he makes a mental note that involves the words 'needless' and 'pedantry'.

Graham gets bored berating the man with the notepad and starts shouting at his team instead, imploring them to do something, anything, that might lift this dreadful game out of the mire the pitch may soon become. 'Why *does* he shout so much during the game?' demands Chesterfield Ken. 'Doesn't he tell them what to do on the other six days of the week?'

To our left, Derby manager Jim Smith is experiencing his own frustrations, with Lee Carsley suddenly chosen as the target to relieve them.

'No, Carsley, no!' he yells, adding, as the young player turns apologetically to face his boss's wrath, 'Use your brain!'

'He hasn't got one!' cries The Photographer, clearly not cut out for a career in the Samaritans.

Smith's chin sinks to his chest but his right-hand man in the dugout turns and shouts to us.

'We fucking *know* that!'

Poor Carsley, still in earshot, looks embarrassed. Crestfallen, even. But what the hell, he's not the worst player out there. Only County's veteran stopper Paul McGrath has had what might count as a good game and for Leeds only Molenaar and Bowyer are worth a mention. Towards the end, two Derby substitutes combine on the right and the second, Darryl Powell, gets to the ball just ahead of Beeney who appears to have fallen asleep due to inactivity. Powell's shot flies over the Leeds keeper and hits the bar. Had it gone in I think I might have cried, but at the final whistle there are only groans of relief from myself and what's left of the meagre crowd.

Driving home, Radio 5 drones on and on about Stockport having come from behind to beat Southampton 2–1, and Man United doing the same at home to Wimbledon in the league. There's an almost full Premiership programme tonight and, even though the reports get progressively shorter as the station works its way through them, it still takes almost 20 minutes to mention the game we have just watched. When that mention comes it stretches to just eight letters. One bloody word. 'Goalless' . . .

Chapter Eight

February

Saturday, 1 February: home to Arsenal

By the time the room stops spinning it's too late to remember to wake up to the radio alarm. The answerphone reveals a baffling call from The Biggest Yorkshireman In London, apparently in Yorkshire today, about David Bowie and today's game. I'm still pondering this when the phone rings and The Biggest Yorkshireman In London, very definitely in Yorkshire, is asking me if I could give David Bowie's manager a lift back to London after the match. Like you do. But this makes some kind of sense as TBYIL works for Mr B's record company and Mr B's manager, an Arsenal fan, is going to the game today. (Although the exact whereabouts of the 50-year-old rock star are anybody's guess.) I weigh this all up, then stutter an apologetic no. Purely because I'm not driving today, as Lord Percy is driving Penelope Pitstop, The Photographer and me in his brand new Peugeot 406 company car. When Lord Percy picks me up and I tell him the news of the fifth passenger who never was, he spits feathers. In his brand new car are six cassette tapes. Four of them feature David Bowie.

But even that kind of obsession pales alongside Lord Percy's love of Arsenal. He lives in a house he has christened 'O'Leary's Web' in honour of his all-time favourite player and his nickname, Spider. Because I know my season ticket is within feather-spitting distance of the Gunners' former centre-back, I have bought tickets for the two adjacent seats. Just to watch Lord Percy's face.

After we park, Little Andy phones The Photographer to say Arsenal's Ian Wright has been relegated to the substitutes' bench because he is carrying a hamstring strain. This is an incredible fillip. Wright's tally of 24 goals is three more than Leeds United have scored collectively in the Premiership. And he's been suspended for a couple of games. (Then again, from where I've been sitting, Leeds haven't played in every match, either.) Now all we have to worry about is Paul Merson, John Hartson, Patrick Vieira — and where on earth Leeds might find a goal of their own at the other end.

When the four of us take our seats, all I can think of is how much I want Leeds to win. Not because Lord Percy will make my life a misery if they don't, but because I can do it to him if Leeds do. I deserve that after the shameful performance Leeds put up at Highbury back in October, losing 3–0. It's a tall order, but today's game gives Leeds the chance to recover some pride. It also serves as a dress rehearsal for the FA Cup match against Arsenal on Tuesday. And so 20 minutes later, while Lord Percy leans into the Leeds dugout and asks David O'Leary to sign an old Arsenal shirt bearing his old squad number and the name Spider, I say a short prayer.

Leeds start well and play much better than the rapidly deteriorating pitch. Happily, they keep their feet while slipping into their stride more quickly than Arsenal. In the absence of Wright, Radebe marks Merson and dutifully follows him all over the pitch. As befits a team playing three forwards (Rush has been recalled and plays up front alongside Deane with Wallace marauding behind them), Leeds look like they mean to attack and wipe away the horror of the performance against Derby in midweek. The game is scrappy but the better team is wearing the white shirts. Nigel Martyn, apparently fully fit again, makes two good saves from Ray Parlour but then Bowyer threads a long pass through to Deane on the far side of the Arsenal penalty area. As Deane receives it the referee David Elleray blows for offside but Deane rifles it in from a narrow angle past David Seaman anyway. I cannot see whether Seaman was beaten or merely let it go, but am content that it will make Deane feel good. Five minutes later Deane takes a pass from Rush and slips it past Seaman once again. And once more the 'goal' is disallowed for offside. Arsenal fans, packing not only both tiers of the South Stand but also most of the south-eastern corner block as well, jeer in relief. The irony of George Graham's new team getting caught out by his old team using a system he taught them is presumably not lost on them either.

At the other end, Martyn twice dives bravely at the feet of onrushing Arsenal forwards and although the visitors have had more chances, as the half-time whistle goes Leeds have come closest to scoring. They have looked good, too, and I notice Lord Percy is sighing with relief. Under pressure he admits that Leeds were the better side, 'probably'. Then the *Match of the Day* cameraman in front of us calls us over.

'Deane's first attempt was onside. He was just level, here, look,' he says, pointing to his viewfinder where a small-scale action replay is visible. He's right, too, Leeds should be 1–0 up. Lord Percy smirks while the news spreads backwards through the West Stand.

Leeds begin the second half as they ended the first. Deane fires a shot just over and later releases Rush who gets one ferociously on target – only to be met by an equally stunning save by Seaman. In the Leeds penalty area, Arsenal appeal for a penalty when a ball hits Molenaar on the hand but Elleray is unimpressed.

The Leeds side, with only the switch of keeper and Rush replacing the flu-struck Carlton Palmer, is unrecognisable from the one that played Derby and George Graham and David O'Leary seem thrilled to be getting this much revenge over Arsenal manager Arsène Wenger's team. As the *Match of the Day* camera swings towards them, they even wink at it.

On the pitch, Arsenal's John Hartson is the one player of the 22 looking off the pace. Ian Wright, who has been stretching and exercising in or around the dugout for the whole match, seems the inevitable replacement, but I just hope Wenger will wait a little while longer. Directly in front of us, Wright lies flat on his back while the Arsenal physio bends over him, putting weight on the forward's raised right leg. It looks like something out of the Kama Sutra.

'Isn't there a law against that?' asks The Photographer, leaning forward.

'Not unless you're into buggery,' grins Wright, his gold tooth gleaming.

But his wits are fitter than his legs and when he does replace Hartson, it's ten minutes before he gives me a scare – by an excellent through ball to Parlour, whose chip beats Martyn as he rushes forward but lands on the roof of the net. With just seven minutes to go it was Arsenal's best chance. I breathe a sigh of relief, thinking there would have been no way back for Leeds had it gone in. But almost immediately Deane, at the opposite end, rounds Tony Adams and forces in a cross that Rush has only to sidefoot in. He does and this time Seaman is definitely beaten. The net bulges and Elland Road erupts. But the bloody whistle has gone again and this goal, too, is disallowed.

Adding injury to the insult, Deane is poleaxed by an accidental but ugly clash of heads with Arsenal's Scott Marshall. As he is stretchered off motionless, the ground goes quiet. Andy Gray gets a rare opportunity as his replacement, but I'm more concerned about Deano. I'm still worried when the whistle goes but watch Graham and O'Leary shake hands warmly with everyone from their old club. Graham even makes a beeline for Hartson and gives him a big hug. And I do the same to Lord Percy, knowing that Leeds were for once good enough, and merely unlucky.

It's an opinion confirmed watching *Match of the Day*, which shows Deane was very unlucky and is, apparently, okay. At the end of the programme Lineker, Brooking and Hansen study the table which shows that Leeds, by virtue of Everton winning today, have slipped back to 11th place. Hansen, pondering the relegation candidates with optimism notably missing in his Littlewoods Pools TV ad, says: 'I think you can rule Leeds and Blackburn out of that equation.'

He's right, of course, barring unforeseen disasters. George Graham, I finally think I love you . . .

Tuesday, 4 February: away to Arsenal, FA Cup fourth round

The last hour at work is the day's longest by far. My stomach churns, the light fades and the heavens open, emphasising the sense of impending doom. Word has it that Carlton Palmer will return and Ian Wright will start. The omens are not good.

The Photographer and I get to Arsenal tube station and meet Little Andy as we leave the platform. I smile hello but am too tense to talk much. Winning tonight would mean so much but the odds are clearly stacked against Leeds. Relinquishing home advantage is one thing, but facing Ian Wright with Carlton Palmer is like trying to lasso a tiger with a string of spaghetti. As we walk to our seats in the Clock End and stand nervously watching highlights of previous Leeds vs. Arsenal FA Cup encounters on Highbury's screens, the statistics make the whole team's task look even more impossible. Leeds have only ever once beaten Arsenal in the FA Cup (at the 1972 final, won with an Allan Clarke diving header from a Mick Jones cross in the 53rd minute) in 11 attempts. The omens get worse.

After Saturday's game, Arsène Wenger was widely quoted as whingeing: 'The pitch was the worst I have ever seen.' In front of us, now the rain has stopped, Highbury looks as verdant as a snooker table and presumably better suited to Arsenal than Leeds. A few Arsenal players trot out on to it to warm up. Ian Wright comes out a little later and trots to the centre circle where, with his arms aloft making a jubilant 'Y' shape, he turns to accept the salute of the four sides of the ground now chanting his name. I like him. He's arrogant but funny. And very likely to score. I gaze at the electronic clock, willing the minutes away so that this match can be over and done with.

When it begins a fraction after eight o'clock, the Leeds fans are instantly confused by the shape of the team. Graham has dropped Radebe and brought in Palmer in place of Rush to play in front of a back three which has Gary Kelly swapping wings to play on the left alongside Gunnar Halle and Robert Molenaar. Dorigo plays wing-back in front of Kelly and on the right the wing-back slot is taken by Ian Harte. It looks unbalanced and performs worse. Palmer is paired not with Wright but the Frenchman Patrick Vieira, and although both are lanky and wear a number four shirt, the comparisons end there. Vieira is quick, elegant and skilful, whilst Palmer is slow, clumsy and gives the ball away – to Vieira, mostly. While The Photographer hates him,

I've always forgiven Palmer his many trespasses because he tries so hard. Tonight, though, my patience runs out. Regarding him from the same unsympathetic angle as The Photographer reveals him to be the very liability everyone is always telling me he is. I shudder at what I've missed and note his involvement in the three half-chances Arsenal have missed in the first ten minutes when Leeds have barely been out of their own half. The defensive uncertainty so recently banished has returned in spades. And Palmer is there shovelling it around like a navvy.

Then Halle underhits a pass to Harte and I fear the worst, but Harte races to the ball and instinctively sticks his toe in ahead of the Arsenal attacker. The ball skys goalwards, dropping somewhere near the 18-yard line with Rod Wallace in pursuit. He runs around the nearest defender while the first bounce strands David Seaman and the second wrong-foots Martin Keown, now on the line after sprinting back to cover. But the ball hits the post and bounces back to Wallace, the first person to actually kick it for what seems like hours, who lashes it into the roof of the net even as he falls over.

The scoreboard reads 0–1 and shows 11 minutes played. The goal came from Leeds' first shot. The next 79 minutes stretch before me like the road to hell, but somehow the goal galvanises the Leeds defence who have to cope immediately with Arsenal racing towards the Clock End with furious intent. Ian Wright is everywhere and seems certain to equalise with a close-range header until Martyn parries it brilliantly to his left. Wright shakes his head in disbelief and pats his one-time Palace team-mate Martyn on the back. As he does so, some oik behind me yells at the striker to leave the keeper alone. Within minutes, Martyn has another Wright effort to stop. This time his parry falls into a scramble between Halle, Kelly and Wright who, although flat on his backside, pokes the ball free to Merson who thunders in a drive that Martyn pushes right even as he dives left. It is a magnificent save, but only seems to delay the inevitable equaliser that will wipe out all his efforts. Suddenly Wright is free again, but again Martyn saves Leeds, rushing out to dive at his feet.

I look up at the clock which shows only 20 minutes played and can think of no way I can survive the next 70 without tearing out my hair.

The rest of the first half passes as an agonising blur, Leeds fans spending most of it on their feet to get a better view of a heroic rearguard action. Eventually no one bothers to sit down again. I watch the clock, I stamp my feet, I turn to see hundreds of anxious faces contorted in worry then glance at the pitch and up at the clock again. Halfway through the first half I tell myself the ordeal is 25 per cent over, but half-time takes an age to come.

When it does, I watch the replays on the screens and marvel at Martyn's saves, sigh with relief, then move to my right to speak to a man I saw at West

Ham. I introduce myself and he tells me his name is David Wilson and he comes from Wakefield. He says he has been to all the games since West Ham and will go to every one until the end of the season. He has been following Leeds United since 1964 and has travelled to matches all over Europe including the 1975 European Cup final. This is remarkable enough, but even more so because David Wilson is blind and has never seen Leeds United play at all. At Elland Road his trannie is tuned to Radio Leeds United, but tonight can find commentary only of Wimbledon versus Man United. He could have sat in the disabled section but prefers to be here, with a friend who gives his own running commentary, because he loves the atmosphere. I am so moved by the idea of David Wilson's dedication that I can utter nothing but dumb admiration. I splutter some more then return to my seat in awe.

As the teams re-emerge, I ponder the idea of Leeds hanging on to their advantage. But at the restart John Hartson comes on as substitute and the siege starts again at the far end. Within minutes Arsenal have forced a corner which Hartson heads against a post. The distance between my vantage point and the action in front of the North Stand only intensifies the ache of the tension. From my low vantage point it is impossible to judge distances and trajectories and every ball forward seems to herald a goal. Vieira skips away from Palmer yet again and volleys magnificently on to the bar. Turning to my right I seek out a pair of Arsenal-supporting eyes to see in them some reflection of the agony I am in. Mainly, though, I am jealous of Vieira, the epitome of what Leeds are missing. To kill some time I fantasise about George Graham ordering Palmer into the Arsenal dressing-room. In the confusion that results when he inevitably trips over and falls into the bath, O'Leary will throw a sack over Vieira's head and bundle him on to the Leeds bus. A straight swap. No one need ever know . . .

The word goes around that Wimbledon are 1–0 up against Man United but I refuse to believe it until I get confirmation from David Wilson via his friend and commentator to my right. It won't last, of course. Just like Arsenal, Man United are bound to spoil everything and equalise, but as every minute passes and the score remains 1–0 at both matches, there is always hope. More fine work from Martyn racing to deny Dixon on the byline and Wetherall coming on as substitute for the limping Bowyer kills a little more time, but every second is torture.

When Leeds finally counter-attack, it is Deane who bears menacingly down on the goal in front of us, shrugging off red-and-white-shirted challenges with uncommon ease. He nutmegs Bould but with just Seaman to beat he pushes the ball too far and the half-chance is cleared. In what proves to be Leeds' only other serious attack on goal of the half, Wallace has a similar run that leaves him one-on-one with Adams. Uncharacteristically the defender backs away offering no challenge. Wallace shoots from just outside the box but the ball goes straight into the grateful hands of Seaman when the chance to kill the tie seemed begging. Nevertheless, on seeing him turn to run back, a crazy thought offers hope a good omen at last. The last time Leeds beat Arsenal (an Allan Clarke diving header from a Mick Jones cross . . .) the scorer wore a number eight shirt just as Wallace does tonight. I share this thought with The Photographer, who passes it on to Little Andy. In times of darkest need, hope springs eternal. But Wallace is substituted by Rush shortly after – which cocks the plan up rather.

Then comes incredible news that at Wimbledon, where the match kicked off 15 minutes earlier than here, Schmeichel has had a last-minute equaliser disallowed for offside. The excitement generated by this news distracts me from clock-watching until The Photographer points to it reading just 59 seconds, 58, 57 . . .

Five minutes of injury time follow the zero during which Arsenal force two corners. From one of them Hartson heads on to the roof of the net for what I first fear is a goal. But then the referee blows time and Leeds have won.

The pain of suffering evaporates in blessed relief that leaves all around me looking as exhausted as they are elated. Leeds have beaten Arsenal and Ian Wright and their fancy pitch and their home advantage and their enigmatic French manager. Leeds are in the fifth round and Man United are not. Leeds fans are going mental – and so is Alan Brazil, leaning over the balcony of one of the Clock End executive boxes above my head. The former Ipswich and Scotland striker applauds and waves at the Leeds fans like the Queen at Buckingham Palace looking down The Mall. It's a surreal sight.

When we finally troop out of the ground, still singing and still delirious, I briefly regret not having a phone with me but am instantly consoled by the knowledge that every Arsenal supporter I know is chewing his lip waiting for his to ring . . .

Saturday, 15 February: home to Portsmouth, FA Cup fifth round

After dumping Arsenal anything seems possible, although Lee Sharpe's insistence in an interview in today's *Sun* that Leeds are just three games from Wembley and will soon be pushing for a place in the top six does sound a bit like tempting fate.

Because the Premiership has missed another weekend to make way for England's 1–0 defeat in the World Cup qualifier against Italy at Wembley, Leeds have had 11 days to recover from the cup tie at Highbury. But not the rejuvenated Paul Beesley, who moved to Manchester City for £500,000 a week ago. Strange, but I'm actually sorry to see him leave. Tony Yeboah has been busy, too, scoring twice for the reserves in two consecutive games against

Liverpool. Last week he used a Clubcall interview to send a message to George Graham: 'The manager says I need match practice but reserve games are not the same as the Premier League. When he picks me, I'm ready.'

And when the manager's ready, he'll pick Yeboah. He is not expected to play today.

This is some comfort to the two guys sitting in my back seat as I pull on to the M1 at junction 11. They are friends of The Photographer and supporters of Portsmouth who, although they talk about their team's run of five wins on the bounce, are hoping against hope to get a draw and a replay. They know Leeds have kept five consecutive clean sheets and can only laugh nervously when The Photographer and I moan that George Graham thinks he can afford to leave out Tony Yeboah and Lee Sharpe, the latter banned this week from a Leeds city-centre nightclub for alleged 'exuberant behaviour' – which sounds unlike anything he's produced on the pitch of late.

As we reach Elland Road, it's hard not to feel patronisingly smug as they gasp in amazement at the size of the car parks that may or may not be replaced by an ice hockey arena. This week Portsmouth were bought out by Terry Venables for just one pound, half the price of a car-park ticket. Welcome to the Premiership, 1997. The Photographer and I escort them to the United Fisheries, the best chip shop on Elland Road, and introduce them to Andys Big and Little, who have been wandering around the ground doing God knows what for at least an hour and will chauffeur them back to London after the match. Then, as it's 2.30, The Photographer and I say farewell and head off to meet The Biggest Yorkshireman In London. He's here in Leeds today with Russ The Boss, an East-Ender into lager, lager, lager, shouting and Leeds United. Not always in that order. This is his first game of the season as he now works in Spain selling time-shares and doing very nicely, thank you. But it'll all be a lot nicer if Leeds can play better than the last time he flew back to watch them, which was against Aston Villa in last year's Coca-Cola Cup final. They will, of course; nothing could be that bad again.

We meet by the matchday ticket office (an overgrown garden shed, actually) and enjoy something of a party atmosphere. The sun shines, the air tastes good and maybe Leeds *are* just three games from Wembley. With TBYIL, his brother and Russ The Boss is Radio Rhys, whose new job producing Radio 1's *Mark Radcliffe Breakfast Show* begins on Monday. Even The Man From Birmingham has broken his vow of abstinence and decided to come along. There is much gung-ho talk of a Leeds versus Chelsea final and we arrange to meet after the game and discuss the prospect at length. The Photographer and I leave them and head into the Kop, convinced we are in the best place to watch a cup run.

But as we take our seats, two sights undermine our optimism. The first is the South Stand and the south-eastern corner packed with Portsmouth fans. There must be 5,000 or more of them and they are making more noise than the rest of Elland Road put together. The second is the pitch. From the Kop, it's easy to see exactly what Arsène Wenger was complaining about. The goalmouths look like duck ponds and there are balding patches along the touchlines, the corners and through the middle. The entire playing surface looks more yellow than green and seems to be under a layer of sand, recalling the bad old days two seasons ago when the Hunslet rugby league side used to play here too. The Photographer points to an item in the programme about Hunslet Hawks having returned for a one-off cup tie last Sunday. I hope they got a good stuffing just like the pitch.

Radebe is well again and replaces Ian Harte (in the Ireland squad last week alongside uncle Gary Kelly), with Deane and Wallace up front, with Rush once more on the bench. Lee Bowyer plays despite aggravating an ankle injury against Italy in the England Under-21 side in midweek, and so does Carlton Bloody Palmer, as captain. Vieira still plays for Arsenal. Sharpe is presumably at home reading the *Sun*.

When the teams come out the South Stand disappears behind a curtain of confetti, but happily the rest of Elland Road wakes up and there is a very expectant buzz as the game gets under way. The expectancy takes only five minutes to turn to frustration as Leeds underhit passes, kick clearances skywards and fall over. The pitch, it seems, is surprising Leeds more than their opponents who, coming from a coastal town, presumably feel more at home on a beach. Playing wide left, Paul Hall looks particularly at home and would appear to have time to beat Gary Kelly and go back to build sandcastles if he wanted. Also dangerous is the Swede Mathias Svensson and Lee Bradbury. In fact, everyone in a blue shirt. Leeds look desperate and I'm not surprised to see a seventh-minute cross from Bradbury headed past Martyn by the unmarked Alan McLoughlin for 1–0. The Kop is stunned first to silence, then to an impressive round of swearing followed, finally, by chants of support. The band, exiled to near the security tunnel in the West Stand corner, reckon this is their moment to strike up but they succeed only in inciting a torrent of abuse, their performance even more offensive than the team's. But, either impervious to criticism or stone deaf, they beat the drum a little while longer and only cease due to lack of interest rather than a proper sense of shame.

None of this has inspired the team, who seem unable to raise their game. Particularly risible is Carlton Bloody Palmer, who today could not complete a pass or win a tackle if his life depended on it. Why the captain's band adorns his arm passes all understanding. Portsmouth, on the other hand, are confident and positive and put the home side under frequent attack. On 20 minutes, when Leeds finally force a corner, Portsmouth kill the momentum by signalling a substitution. McLoughlin limps slowly to the bench, only to change his mind when he reaches the halfway line and limp back. The crowd are furious and Portsmouth survive.

Deane is trying hard and I predict to The Photographer that Leeds will equalise and go on to win 4–1 – but aside from a rising Kelly volley that is well held by keeper Alan Knight, most of the action is at our end. Martyn saves well a couple of times and Kelly heads off the line from a corner. He does it again on half an hour and I breathe a huge sigh of relief when a Portsmouth player, from close by the post, rifles the follow-up into the crowd rather than the net. When referee Paul Alcock disappears in a cloud of white shirts, I assume he has given a corner. But worse, he is pointing to the penalty spot and signalling handball by Kelly, soon booked for dissent.

Nothing in the world would persuade me to swap places with Portsmouth's Fitzroy Simpson as he waits to take the kick. In front of him stands Nigel Martyn, and about five metres behind, 5,000 incensed Leeds fans howling and screaming through a primordial red mist. Simpson hits it low to Martyn's right where Martyn dives and saves it. Elland Road erupts. All control is lost. With goals in such short supply, a Nigel Martyn penalty save has become the zenith of a Leeds United supporter's matchday experience. This is just like Crystal Palace all over again. And still 'England's, England's number one!' can't get into Glenn Hoddle's national squad. Hoddle was in the stands at Highbury 11 days ago but in Seaman's absence still preferred to name Blackburn's Tim Flowers, Tottenham's Ian Walker and Liverpool's David James.

The shock of the save and the ferocity of the crowd's reaction knocks Portsmouth back on their heels momentarily and Leeds step up a gear. But even though McLoughlin does finally limp off, adding to the atmosphere of discontent, there's a horrible irony in the fact that at half-time Leeds still trail 1–0 and the man running the show in Portsmouth's midfield is former Arsenal/George Graham midfielder David Hillier . . .

Portsmouth are nowhere to be seen when the Leeds team trot out for the second half and the crowd grows increasingly restless. Molenaar does his best to raise some support and justly gets even more for himself, but there is no sign of opposition and Elland Road voices its disapproval loud and long. When Portsmouth do run out, the Kop applauds the approaching keeper, and as he trots into his new penalty area he looks up and applauds in return. As he does so 4,999 people stick two fingers up and yell, 'Fuck off!' I hope nobody notices me forgetting to swear because, until the last second, I thought the Kop was being sporting.

The second half is only seven minutes old when neat interplay between Deane and Wallace lets in Lee Bowyer who coolly sidesteps Knight and plants the ball into the net for an equaliser that evokes such a roar of relief it is all Bowyer can do to walk into it, fists in the air, to receive the salute of the Kop. At the restart, the predictable southbound chant of 'You're not singing any more' has me shifting in my seat, preparing to watch the match begin in earnest. There are 38 minutes left and now surely Portsmouth will crumble and Leeds will progress to the quarter-finals. By winning 4–1, I pray.

Portsmouth, however, have other ideas. They continue to play with the kind of assurance Carlton Bloody Palmer can only dream of. Behind me a Geordie voice demands Palmer leave the pitch. Immediately. The Geordie has spent the entire match screaming blue murder but now seems on the verge of a heart attack. I dare not look around, even though the view in front of me is so frightening.

With 23 minutes remaining, a pass from Hillier finds Svensson, running away from goal, who switches direction, leaving Molenaar for dead, and shoots past Nigel Martyn for a peach of a second goal. Given that it took half the match to force their first equaliser, Leeds are in serious trouble. Just how much trouble is demonstrated by the increasing number of Kop voices calling for Ian Rush to come on. With 15 minutes to go he does – replacing Jackson, not Palmer.

Rush looks different. Rush looks *sharp*, laying off balls that Wallace and Deane come close to making something of. Close but no cigar. Then, as Wallace runs menacingly towards the goal beneath us, I sense something special. An equaliser, even. But horribly, something miserably ordinary manifests itself in the shape of Palmer, arms aloft, begging for the ball five metres to Wallace's left. Wallace, in one of those moments during which planets turn and unseen forces do things only they can understand, opts not to take on the last defender but to slot an inch-perfect ball into Palmer's path. But Carlton Bloody Palmer, in one of those moments during which planets turn and Leeds captains do things only they can understand, misses the ball entirely. I want to break down and sob.

When Portsmouth hit a third with three minutes left, the result of some spectacularly inept Leeds play on the halfway line, there is a groan and a rush for the exits, and for the second time in years I consider joining them. But I don't. I sit there, numb with disbelief, and watch Leeds attack with vigour for the first time in the match. But when an unmarked Bowyer grabs his and Leeds' second in the 90th minute with a header there is no celebration anywhere, just a little hope. The referee gives Leeds more by playing three minutes of injury time, but for most of this the ball is nowhere near Portsmouth's goal. When the whistle goes the away fans in the South Stand go wild and the Portsmouth players perform a celebratory conga. But everywhere else there is silence save for the occasional jeer. The Leeds players hurry off. Only Martyn wins any lasting applause from the home contingent.

Losing a league game is one thing: there is always next week. But after losing today there is no next week, only next year. It's been 24 years since Leeds last reached an FA Cup final, and although the unhappy voice whose owner is filing out behind me declares 'I hate London, anyway', it's painfully clear that he wanted the chance to go there, to Wembley, and to be able to complain about it first-hand. This year Leeds really might have gone all the way, but have spurned the opportunity like it meant nothing to them.

Outside, The Photographer and I say nothing. When we meet Russ The Boss he is distraught. He feels like a jinx. He arrived in the country last Wednesday and even England lost, to Italy. The Biggest Yorkshireman In London asks quietly who scored Leeds' second, as they were among the hundreds who walked out when Portsmouth scored their third. With the four of us in my car, the journey home begins in brooding silence. The day's other 'shocks' – defeats for Nottingham Forest away to Chesterfield and Birmingham at home to Wrexham – make none of us feel any better. The truth is, today was not so much a giant-killing as an act of suicide. As the car speeds south, we gradually feel able to speak about it – but do so gingerly, introducing players' names and opinions like a bomb-disposal expert snipping wires. Nothing goes off but we are all agreed that Palmer should have done. Paul Ince's name is placed at the top of the midfield wish-list.

A phone rings and TBYIL answers it.

'No, we lost 3–2. We were terrible.'

There is a pause.

'No, it was just fucking awful. Er, sorry.'

He hangs up and explains. It was his girlfriend asking how his day had gone.

'She's great, but she does ask stupid questions. After I told her the score she wanted to know if I'd had a good day anyway, seeing you lot. She just doesn't understand . . .'

Wednesday, 19 February: away to Liverpool

Astonishingly, my boss didn't bat an eyelid when I announced rather than requested I'd be taking the afternoon off to drive to Liverpool. But now the prospect looms, I almost wish he had insisted I work all day.

Yeboah is rumoured to be fit enough to join the squad and there is, of course, no way the team can play as badly as it did against Portsmouth, but catching Liverpool on an off-day and spoiling for a goalless draw seems to be the very best George Graham can hope for. And the weather is appalling: extremely heavy rain and gale-force winds.

Before I leave work, The Photographer phones to announce he has just

Some day, son, all this misery will be yours

At least George has sorted the defence out

Woolly hats at Elland Road

Mad hats at Stamford Bridge

Even 'England's number one' needs a little help sometimes

Cheer leader

Pause for thought

*Carlton Palmer (centre) gets the
run-around. Again*

Celebrating alone or a cry for help?

Derek Lilley sees his first 'goal' disallowed, away to Forest

Derek Lilley sees a path to goal, away to Villa

That's my boy

Synchronised warm-up

First Leeds outings for substitutes Derek Lille
and Pierre Laurent, home to Blackburn

Deane gets the better of Colin Hendry.
For once

The faithful live in hope

Pierre Laurent still signs autographs after his eight-minute debut

Nigel Martyn, player of the season. By a mile

Heads up, away to Wimbledon

Pierre Laurent

Laurent speeds up, away to Wimbledon

Rubbish on the pitch, home to West Ham

*England Under-21 international
Lee Bowyer*

*Glamour in the stands, away to
Tottenham*

Elland Road stewards try the hands-on approach, last game of the season

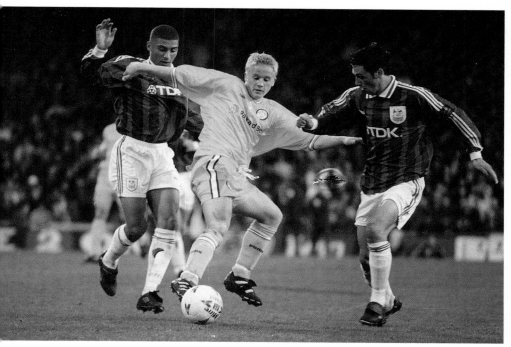

Tommy Knarvik races through Crystal Palace, FA Youth Cup final, second leg

Leeds United's double-winning youth team races to salute the visiting support

The all-conquering youth team. New heroes and new hope

Will the last one out please turn off the lights

been gesticulated at by former Leeds striker Lee Chapman, outside whose house in Wandsworth, south London, he has just parked. 'I couldn't believe it,' he continues excitedly. 'Of all the people I could have blocked in. I had no idea he lived there . . .' I hear The Photographer's wife, in the background, say she cannot believe he is phoning me to tell me this 'news'. Ah, but she has no idea how interested I am. The Photographer and I arrange to meet at 4 p.m. and he hangs up, but not before remarking how Leslie Ash has also been seen in the vicinity, jogging around Wandsworth Common and distracting the cloggers playing Sunday league football.

Whether Leslie Ash was jogging along the Finchley Road at 4 p.m. is unlikely, but the traffic there is at a standstill. This is very bad news both for The Photographer, who is stuck among it, and myself, parked and waiting at the Luton Gateway. The next half-hour passes agonisingly slowly, interrupted by progress reports that get less and less encouraging. I'm slowly getting closer to the end of my patience, and when he finally arrives at 5 p.m. I've got the engine running and pull off before he has done up his seatbelt. Apologies are made but the conversation is clipped and by the time we hit Birmingham it's rush hour on the M6 and there may just be steam coming out of my ears. The bumper-to-bumper crawl reaffirms my belief that the M6 entry ramps should all be blocked off, freeing the carriageways to tourists like myself to drive speedily through. Andys Big and Little, who must already be in Liverpool, once showed me a short-cut but I can't remember it and so soldier on, switching lanes just in time to join the slowest moving one. Again and again. At 7 p.m. we're only just leaving Walsall and the match kicks off in 45 minutes. Long resigned to missing the kick-off, the chances of seeing any of the first half dwindle rapidly. Radio 5 then broadcasts news that has me seriously considering turning off and returning home: Yeboah will start the match on the bench. The Photographer is equally appalled. Has George Graham gone mad? Has he not watched that Yeboah video yet? And why is he ignoring the fact that Yeboah has scored three times in three matches for the reserves, including two in two matches against Liverpool themselves? Radio 5 then returns to blathering on about China's Deng Xiaoping, who died today. For some reason, this chiefly sports station is giving over airtime to eulogise a man whose human-rights record is worse than Leeds' goalscoring.

North of Birmingham, the traffic clears slightly but the rain belts down harder and the car swerves alarmingly in the gusting winds. A sign announces Liverpool is still 55 miles away. A glance at the clock reveals my Ford Orion diesel needs to average 220mph if we are to see the kick-off. 'If only I'd left the house an hour earlier,' announces The Photographer with a quite uncanny degree of understatement. I consider steering with my knees and strangling him with my bare hands, but another ferocious gust knocks the car on to the cat's-eyes.

As we reach the M62 and head east, Radio 5 says more nice things about Deng Xiaoping then offers fresh hope: all over the country kick-offs are being delayed while pitches are spiked and squeegeed. A handful of games were called off earlier and now the match at Upton Park between West Ham and Newcastle has been cancelled with 20,000 people already in the ground. Perversely, I decide I would rather arrive and discover Leeds' match to have been cancelled than go all this way and see only half the game. But the game kicks off without me and only five minutes later than planned. Worse still, Radio 5's commentary game is at Highbury where Arsenal take on Man United. But at least Deng Xiaoping is put on hold.

Even with my foot flat to the floor, the head wind reduces our progress to a frustrating 60mph. Arsenal have their foot flat to the floor also, but are being frustrated by deflections and Peter Schmeichel. At last Alan Green hands over to Marcus Buxton at Anfield. No goals but Liverpool are in command. At eight o'clock they interrupt the Arsenal game for live coverage of the recently introduced midweek National Lottery as if it's more important than football. When the numbers are known, Radio 5 returns to the Premiership, but to Anfield not Highbury, and replay a piece of commentary that features the names of ominously few Leeds United players.

'Collymore to Fowler, 1–0.'

Thank you God. We reach Liverpool and hurtle along the broad dual carriageway of Queens Drive Road so fast I miss the left turn into Utting Lane. While I U-turn through one of those incredibly dangerous-looking gaps in the central reservation, Collymore makes it 2–0. This is horrible, but at least the floodlights are visible now and the roads are clear. I race towards the ground and turn the radio off as I approach the Priory Road car park. Although I can see space to park a bus in, the attendant says it is full and won't let me in, suggesting instead we try further along. As he does so there is a huge roar from the stadium behind him. That must be a third goal. I don't even consider the possibility that Leeds scored it. No, Leeds are 3–0 down and I haven't even parked the car yet. Swapping places with a minibus by one of the gates at the foot of Stanley Park secures the best parking space in Liverpool and The Photographer and I have just to run across the park in a howling gale to reach Anfield Road. When we reach it, it is deserted except for one copper whose radio crackles with the news that the half-time whistle has just gone as we walk past him.

It starts to rain. The rain turns to hail. I pause and pay my respects to the Hillsborough monument then sprint to the first turnstile. Four Leeds fans spill out, cursing the weather and their team. It was obviously a cracker of a first half. Getting drenched in the few seconds it takes to climb the steps into the Anfield Road End is no fun but at the top a marvellous sight awaits. Millions of crystals of icy rain swirl in the white haze of the floodlights while 3,500 Leeds fans are chanting and clapping and bouncing up and down like it was their team who had scored three goals without reply. I know I'm late, I'm sure I'm mad but right now there is enormous consolation in the fact that I'm not alone. Mass insanity is alive and well and rampant in the visitors' enclosure. The ground is packed and all attention is on the lunatics waving scarves, flags and once again the shirts off their backs above their head. I keep my four layers in place as The Photographer and I walk down to the front, get drenched some more and then go up the central aisle to take our places in a prime seat just above and behind the goal. Nothing needs to be said. We just join in, with a topless Billy Six Bellies holding one corner of a blue, white and yellow Union Jack to our right, and a woman perhaps in her forties and her elderly father to our left. It's an awesome feeling and only the emergence of the teams for the second half can spoil it.

They spoil it soon enough and then some more. Graham has made no changes and both Yeboah and Rush are still tracksuited. I ask the woman beside me how bad the first half was.

'Bad,' she says. 'Very bad.'

'And he still won't give Yeboah a game.'

'Will he ever?' she responds, miserably.

When the game restarts, Leeds are instantly useless, chasing red shirts all over the pitch, misdirecting passes, never threatening. Wallace contrives a halfway decent run but caps it with a shot that goes feebly wide, and after 20 minutes mumblings of discontent become louder. Yeboah's appearance warming up on the touchline is hugely appreciated but chants of 'Georgie, get Yeboah on' fall on deaf ears once more.

Things get so bad that when Leeds finally get the ball there is an ironic cheer, repeated with every touch by a player in a white shirt. After as many as six cheers (meaning three players have successfully managed both to control and to pass) the ball reaches Carlton Bloody Palmer. As he traps it, the Leeds fans boo. He sidesteps, they boo again, until finally he kicks it away and everyone cheers with relief.

'He's going down! He's going down! Carlton's going down!' sing not the Liverpool, but the Leeds fans.

Nigel Martyn saves magnificently from a close-range Steve McManaman volley, although the flag is up and it wouldn't have counted. Another attack from the home side ends safely gathered in Martyn's arms.

'One player, we've only got one player.'

'Super Leeds! Super Leeds! Super Leeds!'

The team might be shite but the supporters are dynamite. One lousy at football, the other brilliant at irony.

With a little over 15 minutes remaining, there is finally real activity on the Leeds bench as yellow number boards are gathered up. Leeds are making not one but two substitutions. Excitement mounts. Then on come Rush and Harte. Off go Wallace and Jackson. But Yeboah's backside is still on the bench. Given the truly appalling nature of Leeds' performance I wonder if it isn't a mercy that Yeboah is left where he is, not needing to lower himself by becoming involved in the débâcle unfolding before us.

At the far end, the Liverpool Kopites roar their approval at the introduction of Rush, their erstwhile hero, chanting his name in a wonderfully sporting gesture. But Leeds fans are in no mood for romance.

'What the fuck? What the fuck? What the fuck is going on?' they chant in disbelief.

'Yeboah! Yeboah! Yeboah!' they mantra, to no avail.

'Why is Tony on the bench?' they plead exasperatedly.

'Are you Wilko in disguise?' they wonder facetiously.

Suddenly it's all going horribly wrong for George Graham. Three and a half thousand Leeds fans are at the end of their collective tether. Five minutes later the changes have made so little difference that Liverpool manager Roy Evans takes pity on Leeds and substitutes both his strikers, Collymore and Fowler. One of their replacements, Patrick Berger, continues the charitable gesture by firing over when it would have been easier to score. The other replacement, Mark Kennedy, follows suit when Molenaar inexplicably takes a throw-in that lands right at his feet, unmarked, in the middle of a yawning gap between the last two defenders. It's such a surprise that Kennedy lets it run and Kelly tidies up. A little.

With three minutes of misery left, a joker behind remarks that at least Leeds have kept a clean sheet this half and almost immediately Liverpool win a free-kick 25 yards out. Leeds are too stupid to form a wall so Jamie Redknapp just belts the ball into the net unopposed while Martyn screams helplessly at a defence that would be in serious trouble if officers enforcing the Trade Descriptions Act were suddenly to raid the Leeds penalty area. They are, in the immortal words of Terry-Thomas, an absolute shower.

When the whistle goes, tonight briefly seems like an improvement on last year's 5–0 defeat – but for much of that match Leeds were down to ten men. Tonight nobody got sent off and the scoreline flattered not the home side but the visitors. As the team trudge dejectedly off the field, only two seem to care. One is Molenaar, who runs towards us and applauds, shrugging his shoulders in what looks like a gesture of apology. The second is keeper Nigel Martyn, who gathers his glove bag and heads not for the dressing-room but the front of the Anfield Road stand where he shakes hands with those who chant 'England's number one!'. Without him, God only knows what the score might have been . . .

'I thought George Graham had sorted the defence out?' asks a scouser in disbelief as The Photographer and I curse and swear and mutter all the way back across Stanley Park.

Back in the car, listening to Radio 5, Danny Baker appears to be getting in on the Deng Xiaoping act.

'It is my sad duty to impart,' he announces reverentially, 'that at 8.45 this evening the Andy Cole joke died. Yes, listeners, the Man United forward played well for the entire first half of the match against Arsenal and even scored . . .'

Saturday, 22 February: away to Sunderland; home to Scunthorpe United, Northern Intermediate League

Highlights of the Liverpool game on *Sportsnight* revealed that Rod Wallace had fluffed a sitter when it was only 1–0. So George Graham had watched that, and still left Yeboah on the bench.

'I'm not afraid to make unpopular decisions,' said the Leeds manager when asked at the press conference why Yeboah had been left out. 'He's the one taking his time to get match fit.'

Yeboah, on Clubcall, expressed a different view, claiming, 'To be fit for the Premiership means I have to play in the Premiership. Playing for the reserves is not the same thing.' As reported in the *Guardian*, Graham remained unmoved. 'I'm still trying to make decisions for the good of the team and the club,' he stated. 'You take the plaudits when it goes well so you must take the flak when it doesn't.'

There will be plenty more flak if he makes the wrong decisions this afternoon at Sunderland, and although he has vowed not to be influenced by the chants from the terraces, The Photographer and I don't believe he will be so stupid as to ignore them again today.

Neither Big Andy nor Little Andy is going today, the latter having bottled it at the 11th hour, saying he can't face the drive. But I'll be at the wheel so maybe he just can't face my company. Setting off I ponder this. All my friends think I'm crazy driving to and from this fixture in a day, but I think it's all relative. In Barnet on the way to the M1 I see an old woman walking along the roadside, pushing a trolley and opening and closing her mouth like a goldfish. This is crazy. Going around the M25 I see a coach full of Essex Reds – Liverpool fans – bound for Anfield that must have left Essex even earlier than I got up this morning. This is crazy, too. No sane person would travel that many miles confined to a coach. I overtake it and leave it for dead, noticing in the rear-view mirror that the driver and his mate are pointing and laughing at the Leeds sticker in my back window. Bastards.

Luton has never seemed so pleasant: the sun is shining, the breeze is crisp and The Photographer is on time. To the second. The M1 unfolds before us like clockwork, traffic parting as if I were Moses, and soon the M1 has led to the M18 and thence to the A1. We are making fine time and are likely to be ludicrously early to meet my Makem mucka, Dekka. It's a mouthful and no mistake. Then a sign to Wetherby racecourse gives me an idea. The Photographer is immediately on the phone to his wife who finds herself putting down the baby and rummaging under the coffee table for an old Leeds programme.

'Yes . . . Doesn't matter which match,' he says, with mounting anticipation. 'Now, towards the back on a right-hand page . . . green panel.'

The Photographer glances at me and winks conspiratorially.

'Got it?'

There is a pause during which I swear I can feel my heart rate quicken.

'Scunthorpe United . . . At home . . . GREAT! . . . Er, how's the little lad?'

The little lad is crying, apparently, because his mum – while rummaging under the coffee table for an old Leeds programme – has dropped the phone handset on him. He will survive and we will drop in at Thorp Arch and watch the all-conquering Leeds United youth team play Scunthorpe United. Fabulous.

We have missed the kick-off but no goals, perhaps because today's team includes only around half the stars we have watched earlier in the season as the team must play a tougher fixture against Barnsley in two days' time. Worse, a week ago today the side suffered its first league defeat of the season, a 1–0 reverse away to Barnsley, ending their run of 20 league games unbeaten. This is very upsetting news, much more upsetting than that from the club photographer who cannot give me a team sheet today because of problems with his computer.

'It's not printing "a"s and "e"s,' he says apologetically.

'A bit like that old typewriter in Stephen King's *Misery*,' I suggest.

'Hmmmm,' he says, smiling awkwardly, seemingly not having the foggiest idea what I'm on about.

The game is beautiful: fast and flowing, with every ball that goes out of play instantly replaced by another for a quickly taken throw-in. If the Premiership really want to increase the amount of time the ball is in play they could save a quarter of an hour a match by following this example. The ball boys today include several first-choice players, presumably being rested for the return fixture with Barnsley. Looking around these – and the players on the pitch – I am struck that perhaps these are youngsters after all, and not the all-conquering troupe of supermen my imagination has built them up into.

They play well but the goals are not forthcoming until after Scunthorpe's keeper is sent off. Then goals from Matthew Jones and Andy Wright see Leeds into the break 2–0 up. Scunthorpe return to the dressing-room but Leeds, obviously made of sterner stuff, gather in a huddle around Paul Hart and Eddie Gray. When the huddle breaks, one of the team, Andy Quinn, a little ginger-topped midfield dynamo, trudges over towards us, a little disconsolately. The woman to our left speaks to him.

'You've done well, son,' she glows. 'You nearly scored.'

'He's just given us a right rollicking,' he scowls in reply. 'Says we're not trying. Bloody hell.'

He trots back again, determinedly, and I wonder what he's given up to get even this far.

Quinn and his team-mates start the second half better for three minutes until an offside trap goes disastrously wrong and Scunthorpe's number nine, a piece of string in a football kit I'd hitherto complained looked nothing like a footballer, pulls one back. Five minutes later another from Jones makes it 3–1 and that's the score when we leave to complete the 70-odd remaining miles to Sunderland.

Once again the roads are clear, and we make the outskirts in good time. Skirting to the west we approach up the Wear valley and encounter a spectacular first sight of Sunderland's new stadium, still under construction. It clings to the valley edge like a castle and, as The Photographer notes, has ingeniously located its tallest stand on the side that backs on to the river. 'That way, they won't lose so many balls when Carlton Palmer plays there.'

Traffic and parking nearby, therefore, should be their only worries. We crawl past the new stadium and on to Roker Park, parking in one of the many streets of well-kept red-brick terraced houses that surround it. The ground, which will close at the end of this season, appears as a grand old-fashioned affair, never likely to be called a stadium, never likely to have wanted to be. Floodlight towers stand at each corner and red and white painted signs sit flaking over narrow turnstiles. No one carries a rattle or wears a rosette, but it looks like the fashions have only recently been abandoned.

Dekka is waiting for us in a pub called The Cliff which, he promised me, everyone would know. But no one does and as we head towards the sea, we are an hour late. A greying, cheerful policeman has suggested we try a pub on the cliff that has recently changed its name. Dekka isn't in it but half the world's Sunderland fans are and as I squeeze out again, like a cork from a champagne bottle, I look up at the sign to see if the pub is indeed now known as The Black Hole of Calcutta. A helpful chap drinking, more sensibly, outside on the pavement directs us to a pub that is still called The Cliff and five minutes later The Photographer and I are in it. Along with the other half of the world's Sunderland fans. Dekka is among them and with the time at 2.45 offers me the dregs of his pint and an escort to the ground. In exchange I give him a leaflet handed to me earlier for a 'Sunderland Loyalty Blanket', a rug worn Superman-cloak-style by another of those identikit beauties who always give away things outside football grounds.

As we walk back to the ground he stops taking the mickey long enough to adopt a serious tone.

'You know how the modern game is supposed to have improved its image? Well, I'm gonna show you something now that will make you realise it's all a big con.'

We approach a corner and I wince, expecting to be confronted by a burnt-out car or some gruesome piece of racist graffiti. But instead he merely reaches into his pocket and waves his season-ticket book at me.

'Look at that, man, it's obscene, isn't it? Have you ever seen 'owt like it?'

The book is an amusingly effeminate shade of pink. I have to admit I haven't. And laugh. We arrange to meet after the game and he ducks into the main stand. It's five to three as The Photographer and I squeeze through the turnstiles and up to the back of the ancient-looking Roker End stand.

As we go in, the Tannoy announces the teams. George Graham has not bowed to pressure from the terraces but has dropped Mark Jackson, Rod Wallace and Carlton Palmer, bringing in Lee Sharpe, Ian Rush and Tony Yeboah. Discounting Yeboah's false start at Old Trafford in December, this is what Leeds fans everywhere have been waiting for all season. It seems almost tragic that he now has at most just 12 games to play, but the mood among the supporters is ecstatic as we enter the ground and watch the players lining up. There are only 1,000 away supporters allowed into Roker this afternoon and all of us are enjoying one final chance both to visit Roker Park and to stand on terracing at a Premiership fixture. There have been murmurings in recent weeks about allowing grounds to take out seats once again but it's hard to imagine many clubs wanting to. And so The Photographer and I push our way into a mass of bodies, hear the noise subside as we duck down beneath each old crush barrier, and trip over countless tiny concrete steps as we jostle for position a little higher up. It's a strange feeling, almost like stepping back in time, and a glance around Roker Park seems to confirm it. The stands look tiny and the ground as a whole like a decrepit antique. Only the absence of the famed Roker Roar seems to indicate this is 1997. The terracing at the opposite end is supposed to be making most of that roar, but is strangely subdued. It looks odd, too, with a gaping hole off-centre at the back and a ridiculously high roof that looks like the lid of a giant hamburger box perched on a number of oversized cocktail sticks.

As the game kicks off, the wind is gusting but the Leeds fans are in ebullient mood, chanting 'Sit down if you hate Man U' within seconds. The joke brings many smiles and Yeboah's presence brings many more. An early miss suggests that he is, as George Graham has insisted, far from match fit, but he is nonetheless instantly exciting and seems to imbue a feeling of confidence in the whole side. It strikes me that the 11 players on the pitch are the best Leeds United could pick from their current squad and are hereby recorded for posterity: goalkeeper Nigel Martyn; defenders Gary Kelly, Tony Dorigo, Lucas Radebe, Gunnar Halle and Robert Molenaar; midfielders Lee Sharpe, Lee Bowyer and Ian Rush; and Brian Deane and Tony Yeboah up front. It's Leeds United's 34th game of the season, the 27th in the Premiership, and this is the very first time the team has been anything like full strength.

But just to make things interesting there's Carlton Bloody Palmer warming up on the touchline. Wearing a white bobble hat and white socks pulled up to his knees over his tracksuit bottoms. It is a relief when he sits down again.

On the pitch, Sunderland's early attacks peter out with poor passes or lightweight shots, and when Sharpe skips around half-hearted challenges to hit a long drive at the far end, it seems Leeds will not have a difficult afternoon. Yeboah, although slower than of yore, is no less exciting and his distribution is once again a joy to behold. On 20 minutes he slots an inch-perfect ball into the path of Rush who gives it full-boot-and-laces towards the top right-hand corner. Sunderland keeper Lionel Perez launches himself and makes a magnificent save.

It's all going so well that I pessimistically expect something to go wrong. Sure enough, two minutes later Dorigo limps off yet again. Ian Harte, who played for Eire in the friendly against Wales 11 days ago, comes on as substitute. Ten minutes later Sharpe intercepts and races forward with Deane ahead of him to the left and Yeboah ahead to his right. I can imagine Sharpe thinking, Deane or Yeboah? Yeboah or Deane? He opts for the crowd-pleaser but Yeboah needs one touch too many and Perez rushes out to save with his legs. A fully fit Yeboah would have buried the chance – and then made it two minutes later when an almost identical shot and save follow a through ball from Bowyer.

At half-time it remains 0–0 but all the near misses have given Leeds much hope. The shirts-off ritual is therefore rendered with a little extra enthusiasm, with a variety of Billy Six Bellies taking turns to balance on crush barriers. Another, who goes on the pitch for a penalty shoot-out against a Sunderland fan, is made to put his shirt back on, but he still loses because the keeper makes only half-hearted attempts to save the home fan's spotkicks. Back in the Roker End, this injustice has gone largely ignored because on one of the barriers stands a man in a Yeboah mask. Stewards, police and Sunderland fans look up with a mixture of amusement, confusion and shock.

As the second half approaches, the penalty shoot-out goal is carried off the pitch once more and the Leeds taker removes his shirt before rejoining the crowd on the terrace. With the pitch now clear and the teams due out any second, I watch as a single steward, fancying himself as something of a vigilante with a mission to stop people enjoying themselves, decides to enter the enclosure. The steward had been pointing to a fan standing on a barrier five yards to my right and presumably he now intends to eject this fan. Quite how he expects to do it alone is a mystery but he wades into the crowd nonetheless.

There is much booing as his bright orange jacket goes over the fence and down in among the Leeds supporters whose angry shouts turn to cheers as everyone closes ranks and forces him back. But the cheers are short-lived as a line of around eight policemen try where he failed. They get further into the crowd but long before they get anywhere near the fan sought by the steward, things get a little ugly. No punches are thrown but the police are trapped in a crush of outraged supporters who can see no sense in the arrest of someone who has been entertaining rather than harming others. One by one, the coppers have their helmets knocked off and these are passed back down the line and placed on top of Roker's wheelchair enclosure. The scene is rapidly becoming farcical: the police cannot move, the fans won't back off, and the man they are looking for has long disappeared from view. In the midst of all this the game has restarted but few in the away enclosure have noticed.

Almost as soon as I turn to pay attention, with Leeds fans barracking the police by chanting 'You don't know what you're doing', a long clearance reaches Deane, who heads the ball down to Bowyer. Perez races out to cover but Bowyer has seen his chance and takes it, slotting the ball into the net then wheeling towards us, looking for all the world like he too wants to leap in and knock off some copper's helmet. Joy supplants the mood of anger and the situation is further diffused by one policeman, the only black man among them, following his comrades in and ordering them out. He is not their senior, just a well-intentioned and eminently sensible copper who can see the futility of the situation. One by one, the other policemen take heed and leave the terrace, collecting their helmets as they go. The black policeman remains and argues nose-to-nose with one incensed Leeds fan until all the hostility is gone and he shakes his hand. A triumph of common sense over nonsense.

And so attention returns to the match, where the home fans are becoming increasingly dissatisfied with Sunderland's poor performance. Leeds might be thrashing them off the park but seem unable to score again. Yeboah comes close with an overhead kick that hits the bar but would have been disallowed for an infringement anyway. Minutes later he directs a free header over the bar from the edge of the six-yard box. But then, with the wintry sun breaking through and shining directly into everyone's eyes, the Ghanaian almost wipes out an entire season's memories of humdrum forward play. Almost. Racing across-field 40 yards out, he is first to a loose ball that he hits left-footed into the air. At first it looks a toe-poke to nothing but a second later, peering under hands shielding eyes from the sun, everyone sees what Yeboah knew instantly: Perez is off his line and the goal of the season is waiting to be scored. The lob sails goalwards with the mounting sense of anticipation propelling it ever closer. It gathers speed and dips viciously beyond the furiously back-pedalling Perez . . . only to clip the top of the bar. So near and yet so far. So inspired and yet so unlucky.

When the whistle goes a little over ten minutes later, Yeboah's shot is still being talked about. He should have had a hat-trick today and might even have grabbed five, but we would have settled for just that one. When we meet him, even Dekka and his mates are raving about it and so, because the shot has filled me with the warmth of human kindness, I offer them a lift back to Newcastle, even though it is eight miles to the north. Walking back to the car I spot the copper who sorted out the mess at half-time. He is genuinely shocked when I tap him on the shoulder and congratulate him for a job well done.

Eight miles looks like being a long journey in queueing traffic and I begin to regret offering the lift. One of Dekka's mates asks him if he has mates that support every team in the Premiership and the general consensus is that every football fan does – although they don't always enjoy talking to those mates at certain times of the season . . .

Crossing the high-level Tyne bridge, dropping off our three passengers, then swinging around the roundabout and back over the Tyne again means The Photographer and I have spent around 90 seconds in the fine city of Newcastle – which goes only a small way to making up for the 90 minutes we missed on New Year's Day.

The long drive home is made no more pleasant when a hysterical female Sunderland fan calls David Mellor's 6.06 phone-in and totally misrepresents the events among the Leeds fans at half-time. The Photographer instantly calls the show to complain and explain – but while his call is logged, a man called Howard goes on air and Mellor gives him time and space to tell the truth. The strangest truth of the day, however, is that Leeds are now ninth in the Premiership, the highest position since the day Howard Wilkinson was sacked . . .

Tuesday, 25 February: away to Everton (please)

No match today, but returning from the pub I check Teletext as usual and see rumours that Everton want to buy Carlton Bloody Palmer. For money. The

Photographer has left a message and it's obviously about CBP, but it's too late to call him and I'm too drunk to risk dialling an 0891 Clubcall number that might involve a call long and boring enough to send me to sleep before replacing the handset. Instead I write a note to myself to remind me to save a fortune and phone Clubcall from work tomorrow. Then fall asleep. Doubtless grinning hopefully . . .

Chapter Nine

March

Saturday, 1 March: home to West Ham United

After three days, I'm getting used to the idea that the Carlton Bloody Palmer story was a hoax. A dream, even. Today's reality is: The Photographer wants to raid the club shop and so we will leave early enough to travel in Big Andy's new Big Red Car. Although the colour is a little unfortunate, it seats four of us – including Little Andy – very comfortably. Because I'm about to replace my car, today was to have been the last time the old Orion went to Leeds. Instead it gets its last day off and retires gracefully basking in my warm appreciation and the cool shadow of the Luton Gateway. I park it near a white van which has two mini Man United kits hanging from the rear-view mirror and half a ton of dirt coating its rear doors. In this dirt I write the word 'Yeboah' with my fingertip. Because I can.

Yeboah is a word on everyone's lips as we drive off. The Photographer is able to recount in detail his every strike at Sunderland, but because none of them went in he is concerned that George Graham might drop him today. After the game Yeboah was quoted in the *Independent* as saying: 'I know the fans like me but the important thing is whether the manager likes me. I always play with confidence . . . I want to do something extra but I want to do it for the team.' The striker even has the crazy idea that he needs to fight for his position because 'Leeds are a very strong team now'. Presumably he has seen some top international strikers recently purchased by Leeds United that have been kept secret.

Until they are revealed, Leeds may need to rely for goals on Lee Bowyer. The midfielder has been in the news this week, and not for any laddish behaviour, either. Big Andy brandishes a copy of this month's *Total Football* magazine quoting Howard Wilkinson on its cover: 'If Lee Bowyer were an animal I'd have had him shot!' Further investigation reveals that this is not some hard-line disciplinary stance adopted by the FA's new technical director but a reference to the demands put upon young players these days. When Wilkinson bought him, Bowyer was 'fresh' from a season of 70 games and weighed less than ten stone. Shooting him, argued Wilkinson, would have been like putting a lame horse out of its misery. On Clubcall, George Graham spoke on a similar theme: 'Lee Bowyer will go on to become a very good player. He has a lot of learning to do, though . . . And we've got to build him up. We are working on all aspects of his build but particularly his upper-body strength so he can't be pushed off the ball so easily. But Leeds have had some great midfield players, like Billy Bremner, who were small . . .'

It's a tough life, especially when you're not quite tough enough. But with six goals this season Bowyer is Leeds' top scorer bar Rod Wallace, four of whose seven went in against lower-league opposition in the cups. Swapping statistics and reading the same team news in half a dozen newspapers passes the miles as the Big Red Car heads northwards. Putting one paper down for a second, I gaze out the window at an aeroplane, then at the road ahead and quickly back at the plane again. A quick bit of mental geometry enables me to plot the point of landing at about a mile ahead. On the central reservation. A sign by junction 24 suggests half a mile further west at the East Midlands Airport would be safer, and I point this out to my fellow passengers. Everyone stares in disbelief as the plane, a four-engined turbo-prop of unidentifiable airline, continues on a trajectory unmistakably bound for the M1. We all recall an aircraft doing just that a few years back. Given the choice, I'd rather hit a swan. With barely 400 metres separating our mutual point of impact, the pilot realises his error, lifts the nose sharply and in a great black plume of exhaust smoke soars skyward again, lifting his undercarriage. And all Lee Bowyer has to worry about is getting knocked off the ball.

Although he might also worry about being replaced by, for example, a Paul Ince clone. No one pushes Incey off the ball and as of this week the possibility exists in the real world and not just in the arena of science fiction. Dr Ian Wilmut has unveiled a sheep called Dolly grown from a single cell's worth of DNA. Avoiding the moral high ground I venture that sheep all look the same and doubt if they score very highly on the soul-o-meter. Far more interesting are the possibilities to revolutionise Leeds United. Should we round up the survivors of Revie's old team and take samples? But if we start now won't we have to wait another two decades for the clones to reach maturity? Is it possible, instead, to get some original '70s DNA and speed-clone a perfectly finished article? Surely there's a ginger hair floating around some forgotten

Elland Road corner that once grew out of the head of Billy Bremner? Or perhaps in an attic somewhere there's an old pair of Liverpool hard man Tommy Smith's boots that have Allan Clarke DNA on the studs . . . The rest of the journey passes in a fantasy world until we park and walk into the Elland Road 'superstore', just over an hour before kick-off.

Outside the ground itself, few places in the world are as exciting to the football fan as the club shop, each one a glorious temple decorated in club colours and laden with images of current players, past glories and future hopes. Leeds' shop is bigger than most but is otherwise no exception. I always enter swamped by a surge of adrenaline and euphoria. Normally reasonably sensible with money, just being inside its doors fills me with a flagrant disregard for the most basic notion of financial common sense and I move around in a daze touching, feeling and just itching to buy. Replica kits and training wear by this season's kit sponsors, Puma, fill around a third of the store, but I always get stalled at the front, where the Ellanique brand of clothing tries hard to mix casual fashion with club loyalty, and, rather unfortunately, falls flat on its face between the two. I want desperately to buy something but don't want to go down the pub in something that will look about as cool as that duffel bag with a generic footballer on it you got many Christmases ago when all your mates got zip-top Adidas hold-alls.

Deflated, I walk past the hideously inaccurate Corinthian caricatures of David Wetherall and Richard Jobson, dismiss the urge to buy a Tony Yeboah fridge magnet, then trudge dejectedly out of the shop bypassing even the Leeds United jelly babies and after-dinner mints.

Because the shop is so big and so busy, we have gone our separate ways and have arranged to meet later. To kill some time, I opt to sit on a bollard outside The Peacock pub, read the programme, get some fresh air and eat a tray of curry and chips. The programme boasts Leeds will be the first club in Britain to have its own TV station, the fresh air is cold and the curry and chips not a patch on those available in Lloyd Street near Maine Road – but here the plastic fork is free. The Biggest Yorkshireman In London phones from nearby on the M621 and I arrange to meet him and his brother at the West Stand ticket office in ten minutes. When he hangs up the curry and chips have gone cold in the wind.

In one of the quieter West Stand bars I fill them in on the 'rumpus' at Sunderland and Yeboah's near misses. Then the great man's name booms over the Tannoy: today he starts his first game at Elland Road for almost exactly a year. Everyone in the bar and the stand above cheers, we down the beers and make our way to our (separate) seats. Next to mine sits The Photographer, who has spent £99 in the superstore on a training top for him and three romper suits for his son. Looks like I got out just in time.

The seats to my left are empty and I think of Tony West Ham, currently sunning himself in South Africa. I bet he's not thinking of me. The Hammers went mad last Monday and beat Tottenham 4–3 but West Ham and Leeds remain the Premiership's two lowest-scoring teams and the narrowest of 1–0 wins seems inevitable. To get it, however, both teams must find their way around a pitch that is steadily improving but seems to have been the venue for a bit of impromptu fly-tipping overnight. The triangle of pitch between the Kop end goal and the West Stand halfway line is ankle deep in sweet wrappers, crisp bags and hundreds of pieces of paper. The joke about rubbish on the pitch is just aching to be given an airing. The Photographer duly cracks it. And so does everyone else.

With the game under way, the players impersonate the crisp bags by eddying around ineffectually. Although not as fast. In front of the dugouts, a Homepride bread bag has inflated like a balloon and spins around like a terrier chasing its tail.

Helen The Ellie Fan has come with her dad and her five-year-old nephew Ashley. It is Ashley's first game and I'm sure he finds the litter more interesting than any of the players Helen insists on identifying for him. Ashley's now-tragically-blighted life as a Leeds fan is only a few minutes old when he sees his first moment of genius from the one outfield player he may never forget. A lobbed pass brings Yeboah dashing towards the touchline to our right, where West Ham left-back Julian Dicks advances menacingly close to him. But Dicks may as well have been on the other touchline tying his boot-laces because Yeboah controls the ball with his ankle, deftly flicking it on in the same action, leaving his marker for dead. The attack peters out but the sight of Yeboah even trying such a trick is consolation enough. Oh, how we have missed him.

Sharpe looks good but lacks direction. Howard The Student seizes the initiative and yells his name, then steers him in one. Sharpe, thinking the voice belonged to O'Leary, turns and waves acknowledgement. A whole vista of possibilities opens up before us. Interactive soccer, virtual reality, fantasy football. Here is an opportunity to lift the team, to direct them to unprecedented heights of entertainment and progress. Trophies and glory await. If only we knew what the hell to shout.

Bowyer looks good, too, and avoids being pushed off the ball by anyone in a West Ham shirt for several minutes, during which he chips a pass over the Hammers' defence which Yeboah volleys first time into the South Stand. But at least it came close. At the other end Nigel Martyn has little to do until Iain Dowie, a man whose twisted visage surely offers conclusive proof that aliens are among us, outjumps his marker and sends a looping header curling to nowhere in particular. Suddenly, however, nowhere in particular sets up a forwarding address on the Leeds United crossbar and I watch in agony as the woodwork saves the back-pedalling Martyn's blushes. It's the closest anyone has come to scoring when the half-time whistle blows two minutes later.

During the interval, the groundstaff poke and prod with pitchforks but no one comes on with a pointy stick and collects the rubbish. For the second half, Leeds bring on a bit more in the shape of Carlton Bloody Palmer, replacing Bowyer who had finally been pushed off the ball and had twisted his ankle.

Two minutes into the second half, Harte threads a ball through the paper storm and into the penalty area ahead of Deane. Dicks, who has been having a nightmare game after his triumphant midweek performance, shields the ball for keeper Ludek Miklosko. But Miklosko leaves it to Dicks, and so Deane charges into the gap between them. I wince as he and Miklosko go down in an unsightly heap while the ball pops out to the left. A foul on Miklosko, surely. The ball, meanwhile, rolls to Sharpe who – still following Howard The Student's instructions to the letter – controls it and shoots neatly into the unguarded net despite the acute angle. It won't count, obviously, and yes, the linesman's flag is up.

'He's disallowed it,' says Helen's father, like me confused as to why so many people think Leeds have scored. But there is no downturn in the clamour, no cheers turning to disappointed groans, no corresponding roar of 'Nyaaah!!!' from the West Ham fans in the corner. I am sitting down but the goal stands. I have missed the moment and to me, it still feels like 0–0. Although the scoreboard reads 1–0, Leeds will need to score again before I can feel like I have taken part. This is horrible.

West Ham do their best to make it worse but the best entertainment of all is coming from their dugout. Bethnal Green-born reserve keeper Les Sealey, his chin jutting into the breeze, yells incessant encouragement in his irrepressible barrow-boy cockney accent. He stops just short of trying to sell anyone five parns o' 'taters but makes more noise than the rest of the West Ham bench combined. Harry Redknapp looks like what he is, a beaten man, occasionally calling half-hearted instructions but seeming crestfallen, lowering his eyes as he talks to players who, like me, can't wait for this dull match to end. Ashley is getting fidgety, too.

Leeds raise the tempo a little in the last ten minutes but West Ham kill it with ineffectual substitutions. Yeboah does his best by trying another flick which this time misses its target. When O'Leary admonishes him by yelling 'Twat!', any lingering doubts that he and Graham might like the team to play with flair are banished once and for all. Leeds win 1–0. And have still scored fewer goals than West Ham . . .

Saturday, 8 March: home to Everton

After getting up early to watch the Australian Grand Prix qualifying session on video I am almost late leaving to meet The Photographer at Luton. Football and Formula One have long been twin obsessions, although I can see no obvious connection, except perhaps the way I sometimes drive to get to a match. Today, however, a connection presents itself with perfect timing: Damon Hill's Arrows-Yamaha's major sponsor is Danka, the same company that sponsors Everton. Damon and his underperforming blue racing car qualifies by the skin of his teeth. I take this as a good omen and hope that manager Joe Royle and his underperforming blue football team struggle likewise.

Elsewhere teams in blue are fairing better, for this is FA Cup sixth round day, and Leeds' fifth round conquerors Portsmouth are at home to the dreaded Chelsea. The Photographer brings a cutting of the 'Fan's Eye View' column from last Saturday's *Independent,* written by south-London-based Leeds supporter Yannis Andreas. It adds further weight to my anti-Chelsea grudge by suggesting that the Ian Hutchinson throw-in from which David Webb scored the winning goal only reached Webb because it had been punched onwards by a Chelsea player. The handball went unpunished and the goal stood.

Thoughts of the FA Cup resurface at Woodall Services where, having made such good time on an almost-deserted M1, we stop for a Little Chef breakfast. There, hordes of Middlesbrough fans *en route* to their quarter-final at Derby mix cup fever with bacon and eggs. The Photographer orders the biggest vegetarian fried breakfast ever assembled and not even the two of us can finish it. Unfortunately, this gluttonous plate-clearing attempt puts us well behind schedule and Mortgage Terry is left standing alone outside United Fisheries for over an hour. He doesn't punch either of us and emits only a small whimper when paying The Photographer £21 for the ticket, despite having five minutes earlier been offered one for £4.

The three of us buy a programme and beam enthusiastically at the cover photograph of 'United's Striker – Tony Yeboah' (so captioned, presumably, lest we have forgotten him). We enter through entrance four. As we come up the steps into the paddock, several stewards and two policemen with big side-handled coshes marshal us in, but instead of the normal pulse-quickening euphoria at the first sight of turf, today my heart only sinks. I'm back again. The fun has gone.

But there is more to football than football. Such as the extended family who only ever meet behind the dugouts in the West Stand Lower Paddock. Passing acquaintances united by one terrible love. Here today are Ian The

Moustache and his new girlfriend Niki, Helen The Ellie Fan, Chesterfield Ken (and his pockets full of chocolate), Chesterfield Barbara, Howard The Student and Kay From Blackpool, each one suffering just like the man in the Cellnet ad trudging disconsolately through New York after his wife phones from home to tell him the score: Leeds 0 Rotherham 3. At least together we are all similarly vulnerable . . .

*　　*　　*

Reluctantly, I turn my attention to the team news. Happily, Yeboah plays again, but suspensions rule out Kelly and Radebe so in come Wetherall and Harte in defence. Bowyer is fit again and plays but so does Carlton Bloody Palmer, ironically, considering Everton were the side rumoured to want to buy him. I can but hope he uses this match as a shop-window.

The atmosphere is subdued, the Kop strangely quiet. Even the now-traditional 'Stand up if you hate Man U' chorus fails to materialise. The most noise all afternoon is directed at the band when it tries to lift the mood. 'Stand up if you hate the band' is quickly deemed too polite, and replaced by a variety of expletives that have the desired effect.

The match is uninteresting, with Yeboah subdued. Martyn saves well from Terry Phelan and the lanky Duncan Ferguson, who is menacing in the air but nowhere near as good with the ball at his feet. A bit like CBP, who is his usual embarrassing self. 'It's all right, Joe,' Howard The Student lies to Everton manager Royle. 'He's usually a lot better than this.'

Ex-Leeds hero Gary Speed is booed at every touch, but not by the girls. He is booed a little louder after being booked and pointing the finger at Halle, as if to indicate that the Norwegian had faked the incident. And so things drift pathetically along until, with almost half an hour gone, a Bowyer corner is met by the head of Robert Molenaar and loops into the South Stand net beyond Neville Southall's grasp. As Molenaar celebrates his first goal for Leeds, both arms thrust skywards, I thank God for Dutchmen. Yeboah aside, it couldn't have gone to a more popular bloke.

Royle is late back to the dugout for the second half and arrives looking thoroughly miserable.

'Cheer up, Joe, give us a smile,' yells Ian The Moustache. Royle turns around and eyes his tormentor, scowling for a second and then breaking into a huge grin. He gets a cheer for his efforts, then sits down. But there's not much on the pitch to encourage him or anyone else. After 15 minutes he substitutes the almost-invisible £5.75 million striker Nick Barmby who trudges off in a daze, perhaps wondering what it was he used to do at Tottenham that made him an England international. Deane is booked for chipping the ball over Southall after the whistle has gone for offside, and his look of tired disbelief says it all. His is the third Leeds name in Martin Bodenham's book this afternoon, bringing Leeds' season total to a magnificent 70, excelling all other 19 teams in the Premiership with Arsenal a close second. But, come the end, that's all there is. Everton rally in the closing minutes and are clearly worth a point, but instead are denied by another stunning reflex Martyn save, in the last minute, from a Gary Speed header.

And so we file out and go home, neither pleased nor relieved, just able to cross off one more fixture . . .

Monday, 10 March: home to Lowestoft

At work today I get the news I've been dreading, and football is the furthest thing from my mind. My father, who has been fighting a brain tumour for the past two and a half years, now has just days to live. All season I've mixed watching Leeds with visiting him, but after spending much quality time talking and joking with him yesterday and Friday, I now face the fact that a short time is all we have left.

Much of the south-east is tonight blanketed in thick fog. This morning three died and 60 were injured when 90 vehicles were involved in two pile-ups on opposite sides of the M42. Tonight motorists are advised not to travel, but this is one journey I cannot postpone whatever the weather. On the A12, nervous motorists drive perilously close to one another in timid nearside lane congas, but feeling safer alone I hurry past, concentrating hard on what may lie ahead of me both on the road and in my life. Football only enters my mind when a cassette runs out and Radio 5 cuts in with the familiar voice of Alan Green announcing that Liverpool are 3–0 up against Newcastle. At half-time the news bulletin includes a report that a high-ranking Roman Catholic in the Vatican has condemned football as a destroyer of family values, a game for which fans sacrifice all sense of priority. On tonight of all nights this is an ironic suggestion. Love of a football team can be a powerful force, but it is nothing compared to the love for a family. I continue to drive into the dark wall of fog, straining my eyes in anticipation of my headlights picking out another road-user while mulling over that bulletin. Time devoted to Leeds United has often meant that I have been away from my family but not that I care less about them. Football fans know this and their families, by and large, understand it. Leeds United are important to me but a mere distraction compared to the loss I must soon endure, and I really wish I had remembered the name of the man whom Radio 5 has quoted so that I might tell him how wrong he is. I want to explain to him that even on a night like tonight I can listen to a match on the radio, and will recall forever the moment when

Fowler snatched a last-minute winner for Liverpool after Newcastle had pulled back to 3–3, but still have a full and proper sense of priority. This season I've been hurt by football many times and in many ways, but at no time has the pain compared to what I am feeling now . . .

Saturday, 15 March: away to Tottenham Hotspur

My father died yesterday evening, little more than an hour after myself, my mother and his two grandchildren had sat around his bed wishing he might awake but knowing that he wouldn't. Today I go to a football match not because the official in the Vatican was right but because there is no more that can be done. And I go not because everyone in my family has told me I should and that he would have wanted me to, but because as I sat alone with my father yesterday lunchtime I explained to him that I would be away for one day and would return to see him tomorrow.

In his working life he had been a steel erector, and in the '70s had worked at White Hart Lane, helping build a roof over one of the corner stands. I always longed for him to do similar work at Elland Road so I might join him on site, but he never did and I had to be content with a brief visit to Ipswich Town's Portman Road instead, where on another day he told me he met and chatted to the team's manager, Bobby Robson.

Ground developments at Tottenham since those days have replaced his monument, but it seems heavily ironic that this afternoon I will sit in a corner of Tottenham's ground with a roof over my head, watching a game from a vantage point where he once worked beneath the jib of a crane. That this fixture in this of all grounds should fall the day after his death inspires me as I drive back home to London. I am heavy-hearted but hopeful that Leeds United will bring some small measure of happiness to the sadness I now feel.

*   *   *

White Hart Lane is an uninspiring 40-minute walk from my house but because it is the one fixture in the season that I can walk to, I do. The sun is unseasonably warm and I have to carry my jacket, checking directions with someone in an Arsenal shirt whose eyes light up when he sees my Leeds top.

'How's Georgie getting on up there?'

'Pretty well, I guess, but boring us all to death.'

He smiles and promises, 'You'll be all right, just you wait and see.'

I smile back and walk on, not wholly convinced. In midweek I missed a game at Elland Road, a 0–0 draw with Southampton that newspaper reports suggested was the very worst of the season.

Bird shit is lucky, my mother insists, and yesterday a flock of seagulls used my new Rover for target practice. As I approach the Tottenham High Road I spy a Lottery sign outside a newsagent's, remember my mother's advice, and walk inside to test the omen. Having grown accustomed to unfulfilled hope with Leeds United, I rarely find the optimism to enter the National Lottery. But today I feel I deserve some luck and happiness so grab the pencil on a string and do the numbers: Yeboah's age (30); Yeboah's three shirt numbers (21, eight and nine); Yeboah's fee (£3.4 million, make that 34); and my own lucky number, four (Yeboah's first goal for Leeds was scored on his fourth appearance as substitute, but that's stretching a point).

With the Lottery ticket in my back pocket alongside the match ticket I enter The Two Brewers, a great little pub about five minutes' walk from the ground. Already there are The Biggest Yorkshireman In London, The Man From Birmingham, Radio Rhys, and – drinking for Spurs – Mad Perry and Xavier. All have heard my news and one by one pick a quiet moment to offer condolences. I tell them why White Hart Lane is special and they agree this is fitting and toast my father and an away win in his memory.

The pub is full but the beer garden isn't so we take our drinks outside and sit in the sunshine. One free trestle table will accommodate us all, but first we must negotiate several strategically placed dog turds, several of which sit shrivelled and white, in defiant contradiction of several stand-up comedians' routines. The perpetrator of the turds remains nowhere to be seen. The colour of the turds suggests that said perpetrator may have been dead some time.

Mad Perry and Xavier whinge about their season, then have a go at Arsenal. The rest of us whinge about our season and then have a go at Man United. There are some things all fans can agree on. TBYIL says the game I missed against Southampton was a crushing bore, but he at least left the ground (early) with some new Elland Road trivia.

'The front three rows in the West Stand hold 1,000 people,' he reveals without prompting.

The Man From Birmingham nearly chokes on his pint and the rest of us stare in disbelief.

'Good game, was it then?' cackles Radio Rhys.

Things have clearly got very bad indeed if Leeds United fans would rather count seats than watch the team play football. But at least today the sun is shining and there's a beer to hand. The two combine to put everyone in a first-day-of-the-season frame of mind and optimism resurfaces briefly until the talk turns to this afternoon's likely line-ups.

The Photographer, late again but somehow right on cue, walks into the beer garden, glances at the turds surrounding the table and says: 'I see the Leeds team are here in strength this afternoon.'

For that he deserves a drink and although it's nearly ten to three and the others all want to take their seats in the ground, I buy him, Xavier and myself one more for the road. As we drink he shows me a fax from Elland Road. General manager Alan Roberts wants to meet us to discuss this book . . .

*　　*　　*

Irrespective of the part my dear departed dad played in its history, I like Tottenham's ground a lot. Its continuous roof and filled-in corners make White Hart Lane a natural cauldron – although Tottenham fans have neither the wit nor the voice to fill it with the atmosphere it deserves. This afternoon, even before the kick-off, all the noise is coming from the South Stand's western corner and the Leeds fans which fill it. Across in the East Stand a Tottenham fan with a drum is trying to lead the home fans in some kind of response but the travelling fans merely adopt his rhythm and chant louder for Leeds United.

As the teams line up and the mascots leave the pitch, Sharpe is in but Wallace is apparently unfit and Yeboah plays again. In fact, with Carlton Bloody Palmer not even on the bench, Leeds have the same line-up that started at Sunderland and the signs look good. The game gets under way, I say a quiet word to my dad, and I take a deep breath.

Everything goes wrong almost immediately. In the first minute Martyn has to make a save of outstanding quality when the left side of the Leeds defence opens up and a cross finds a Tottenham player unmarked in the penalty area. I rise to my feet in disbelief and awe and all around do likewise. The Spurs striker can't believe it, half the Leeds team can't believe it, and most of White Hart Lane doesn't want to believe it. The Leeds fans' chant of 'England's number one!' has rarely been so fervent and becomes more justified with every match he plays. The rest of the team, however, struggle to string passes together and make any impression even on a Spurs team that is sometimes worse. The chances of them scoring a goal look a lot slimmer than Yeboah, still off the pace, getting no service and apparently not bothered enough to get involved. Deane looks keen, but the best player on the pitch is John Scales, making a rare appearance since ditching his chance to become a Leeds player and opting to join Spurs in December.

Leeds go nowhere, and on 25 minutes the inevitable happens when Teddy Sheringham reaches the byline in the opposite corner of the ground and crosses to the unmarked Darren Anderton who bests Martyn with ease. Leeds' supporters groan then respond but the team can't match them. Don't deserve them.

At half-time I trudge disconsolately to the toilets, meeting TBYIL on the way back. My face must tell a story.

'If it's any consolation, they were much worse against Southampton.'

Re-entering the upper tier shows Leeds fans split 50:50 between standing around looking miserable and jumping around with their shirts off looking crazy. Looking at the latter group at least cheers me up but when a steward asks me to return to my seat the view of the pitch only serves as an unwelcome reminder of the misery soon to continue. My dad, if he's watching, is shrugging and asking how Norwich are getting on.

The second half brings more of the same dismal football. George Graham is unimpressed and orders Ian Harte to get ready to come on. I assume his appearance will be a straight swap for the left-sided Lee Sharpe, still apparently some way off full fitness and the weakest link in a very poor chain. As play stops, Sharpe appears to assume this too and with head bowed walks towards the touchline. But then a board bearing the number 21 is raised and Leeds' miserable season reaches a new low.

Yeboah, seeing his number held aloft, tears off his shirt and starts to stride the 40 yards or so to the touchline. Reaching the touchline, he throws the shirt in the direction of the dugout and without acknowledging Harte disappears down the tunnel. As my mouth drops open in shock, the man in front turns, shaking his head slowly and speaks the thought everyone is consumed with: 'Well, that's his last game for Leeds . . .'

After almost an entire season spent aching for his return and barely a handful of games, almost an entire season's worth of hopes and dreams have just disappeared in one moment of petulance and a flash of yellow shirt. For a few seconds The Photographer and I are speechless, then dismay gives way to anger.

Ironically, in the remaining ten minutes or so Leeds make a belated effort and Harte, playing in Yeboah's position on the right side of attack, actually gets some service. But where Yeboah might have turned and scored he can only hold the ball up and look for support. There is little forthcoming and the game ends 1–0. I glance up at the roof over my head, hope that my dad wasn't here, then leave, feeling bewildered and betrayed . . .

Saturday, 22 March: away to Sheffield Wednesday

All week, the tabloids have been like sharks in a feeding frenzy reporting Yeboah's very public protest and his seemingly imminent departure from Elland Road. Monday's *Sun* honed in on Leeds season-ticket holder Kevin Morgan who threw his own shirt at the Ghanaian as he left the ground to board the team bus. On Tuesday the same paper broke the shock news that it is backing Tony Blair in next month's general election, while backing George Graham in the campaign for the vote at Elland Road. Leeds old boys Peter Lorimer and Allan Clarke were canvassed and duly criticised Yeboah's actions as an embarrassment to 'himself, his manager, his club and its fans' (Lorimer) and showing 'a total lack of respect for his manager' (Clarke). The paper also delved into the background of the conflict in a story claiming Yeboah had earlier expected Leeds United to pay his wife's medical bills and that she herself called George Graham to ask him to replace her gardener. Whatever the truth, the effect is plain. Yeboah has been discredited in the eyes of many fans and without their support his current form is simply not good enough to allow him to remain at Elland Road.

I am first to Luton and sit there pondering all this and more. The *Sun* did allow Yeboah a single column inch on their double-page spread in which he was quoted: 'I am so very sorry for my actions. I hope the fans are not angry with me. I love the Leeds supporters; they have been fighting to get me a chance in the team. I was very frustrated on Saturday, but I hope they realise I was not looking to offend them or the club.'

Leeds' company secretary Nigel Pleasants told Clubcall that Yeboah would be fined 'about two weeks' wages' (around £20,000 according to tabloid guesses), and Graham said he has told Yeboah to get himself back to playing fitness by losing 'just under a stone'. Yeboah then proclaimed himself unfit for this match against Sheffield Wednesday with a hamstring injury that none of the medical staff at Elland Road can detect . . .

The mystery injury is the first thing we speak about when first Little Andy (Big Andy has bowed out, opting to earn money refereeing a match rather than lose it watching one) and The Photographer get into my car and we head off. It's hard to conclude anything except that Yeboah has gone too far. Although Graham has clearly spurned the chance to rejuvenate a very special talent, it is best to recognise the end of an era, close the book of dreams, and not dwell any longer on what might have been. Besides, there is good news after so much bad: last Tuesday Carlton Bloody Palmer asked Leeds for a transfer.

Ceefax told the news with a juicy quote from the manager: 'I told him to put it in writing and I will put it before the board of directors with my recommendation. I am not surprised by his request. Some people who are out of the team will try to fight their way back in and others will ask for a transfer.' Palmer responded by announcing he would issue a statement 'through his solicitor'. The timing cannot be good for the lanky number four, as I've been reliably informed by a West Bromwich Albion supporter that a Baggies fanzine has just published an All-Time Worst WBA 11 that includes Carlton Palmer – as captain. If his agent draws a blank perhaps Palmer could try advertising his services in *Exchange and Mart* . . .

With Yeboah out chances of a goal today seem slim. But with Palmer out chances of a clean sheet are improved and it takes about five seconds to agree on a prediction: Leeds to lose 1–0 or a 0–0 draw is the best we can hope for. The Photographer then interrupts our reverie. 'Look!' he screams. 'It's a peacock! A bloody peacock on the M1!'

Following his outstretched finger just north of junction 16 I see he is not hallucinating, for there, grazing on the grass of the embankment, its electric blue plumage glinting in the sunshine, is a peacock. I'm past caring whether this is an omen but cherish the memory while considering the notion that, increasingly, the M1 is providing far more entertainment than the football.

We got horribly lost last season after leaving the motorway so today take extra care to follow the directions in Little Andy's book of football grounds. Double-checking with the AA road atlas reveals there are two junction 34s on the M1, which explains a whole lot about getting lost last season. This time I am more confident and cruise past the steelworks lining the Don Valley, then turn right over the River Don near the floodlight pylons of the Don Valley Stadium. This is an education to Little Andy, who thinks that the stadium was named after a famous South Yorkshire runner. We forgive him as the queue of slow-moving traffic suggests we are close to the ground.

We are, three miles later, so park the car and walk down the hill of Herries Road, passing under a magnificent sandstone railway viaduct that gives way to our first view of the ground. Once again we have approached Hillsborough from the wrong side and, because it is police policy to block off the terraced streets that would otherwise provide a handy short-cut to the Leppings Lane end, have a further half-mile detour before we reach the turnstiles. It's frustrating but at least it takes us past a chip shop without a queue to speak of. We indulge, get a free wooden fork, then eat our chips standing outside the turnstiles.

Beside us, an overweight Leeds fan is crouching, apparently struggling for breath, and I find myself trying, but failing, not to think about what happened to the Liverpool fans here in 1989. But this guy is okay, and smiles grimly as his mate delivers a familiar complaint about George Graham's Leeds United: 'He'd rather win 1–0 than 5–4; we've just got to put up with it.'

As I stand there jealously eyeing The Photographer's curry sauce and regretting ordering fish cake when I meant cod roe, I spy a youngster, perhaps 15, clutching a plastic bag filled with a packed lunch of apple, tinfoil-wrapped sarnies and regulation chocolate biscuit. As I point him out to The Photographer and Little Andy, the youngster is joined by a dozen friends, perhaps two dozen, with anxious-looking German-speaking adults in their midst trying to organise them all. On Leppings Lane behind stands a coach still spewing kids and packed lunches. The lettering on its side indicates they have travelled here from somewhere called Bad Kissingen.

I am appalled. Surely no one in their right mind would travel all the way on a bus from Germany to watch Leeds United? Is this a sick joke perpetrated by some Fagin-like character with a fleet of air-conditioned buses? The youngsters look vaguely confused and some wear Leeds scarves they have obviously just bought. It may already be too late to help these kids. I shudder at the thought and perch my chip tray atop the nearest overflowing bin. Time to go in.

Just like at the post office, one turnstile queue is longer and slower but I join it because it bears the number 21, which I touch for old times' sake as I reach it. God knows, we'll see no one wearing that shirt for Leeds this afternoon. Or the rest of the season.

Inside, the kids from Bad Kissingen are lost somewhere among the top half of the stand that is packed with Leeds fans. Having travelled here from London, the significance of this as a Yorkshire derby has been lost on me until now, with those around me chanting 'One team in Yorkshire, there's only one team in Yorkshire' and 'Shit ground, no fans'. Neither of these statements is true, of course, but I do believe we have a point about the ground. Like Roker Park, it's quaint but old-fashioned. It has been restored since the disaster of 1989 but not significantly improved compared to others in the Premiership. It does, however, have one bonus – the seats in the upper tier of the Leppings Lane end are made of wood and make a noise when they fall down. They make a *loud* noise when *slammed* down. And, best of all, if the larger portion of perhaps 4,000 Leeds fans all slam them down at once, they make a most spectacular din. The trick is to do this not once but repeatedly, in a cacophonous tattoo that at once inspires your own team and annoys the hell out of the home supporters. To do so requires leaning forward, raising both buttocks and grasping the seat in a hand positioned between the legs. From there, the seat is at its occupier's mercy and even those with the most rudimentary sense of rhythm cannot fail. The sight of many hundreds of people doing so is as mad as anything Vic Reeves, Bob Mortimer or the Masons could devise, and reduces me to gales of helpless giggles. Even before the match has started my spirits are undeniably raised.

At two minutes to three when the teams run out, Sheffield Wednesday strike a cruel psychological blow by bringing only one ball on to the pitch and keeping it for themselves. The Leeds players stand around sheepishly, stretching and running on the spot and pretending not to notice. Saddest of all is the sight of the young Leeds mascot, clad all in yellow although the team wear white, standing alone on the penalty spot with nothing to do, his big day ruined by some Wednesday tightwad. He does, however, get to bask in some of the glory enjoyed by Nigel Martyn, who was finally granted a token of the recognition his form this season has warranted when he was drafted into Glenn Hoddle's England squad for the friendly against Mexico a week today.

'England's, England's number one!' we chorus for the umpteenth time. He claps those big gloved hands at us and waves in acknowledgement. Inspired, Leeds fans run a short roll call: 'He's here, he's there, he's every fucking where, Molenaar, Molenaar!' The big Dutchman knows the routine, waves and is cheered again. 'Deano! Deano! Deano!' brings a similar response from the number ten, but the other eight have to settle for being overlooked.

At the kick-off Leeds opt not to belt a long ball down the left wing to Deane and I am so shocked to see them try something different I almost miss a promising opening move. It breaks down but within minutes they've conjured another – only for Wallace to give the ball away in his own half and set up a swift Wednesday counter. For a few minutes Leeds look good going forward but shaky at the back and particularly vulnerable to the probings of Benito Carbone on Wednesday's left wing. Kelly, in particular, appears mesmerised by his Kermit-coloured boots.

But, at the other end, Deane and Wallace look as sharp as Sheffield steel and their interplay soon sets up Bowyer. Unfortunately keeper Kevin Pressman saves his shot easily, but with ten minutes gone I am overcome by a strange emotion. It takes a while to identify but finally I recognise it as happiness. Leeds are playing exciting football and are actually entertaining me. I sit back in the seat for the first time and feel the pain of the wood dig into my spine. This reassures me I am not dreaming and I turn to The Photographer and Little Andy. They both grin back.

'This is amazing!' laughs The Photographer.

'I can't believe what I'm watching!' gasps Little Andy.

The only nagging doubt is that despite all the unfamiliar flair and fluency, the darting runs, the short one-twos, the accurate passing and the attacking intentions, Leeds have still failed to get the goal they deserve – and Wednesday might have scored themselves. Sharpe, apparently recognising my worry, takes matters in hand in the 17th minute, swerving through the Wednesday half to the edge of the penalty area where he strikes a low drive into the net. It's a great goal and I'm only sorry it was scored down the other end.

Three minutes later, the Leeds defence, apparently recognising my minor disappointment, give me a rather closer view of a goal as they opt not to mark David Hirst, who turns a Carbone corner past Martyn with lightning speed. A sense of injustice fires the Leeds supporters into a particularly impressive chanting/seat-banging combination, and within a minute Bowyer wriggles free of a challenge then feeds the ball to Wallace, who jinks and retraces Sharpe's earlier footsteps before forcing the ball under Pressman from just inside the area.

The sun beats down but it's raining goals. This is truly unprecedented.

Perhaps George Graham is on holiday. But no, within minutes on the touchline is his now-familiar figure, arms aloft, appealing to the referee. Today the long navy winter coat is rested and he wears a light brown mac in deference to the sunshine. It is perfect weather for a Leeds display which, judged against the rest of the season's performances, ranks as samba soccer.

'And now you're gonna believe us, we're gonna win the league!' is the Leeds fans' prediction. It's already a mathematical impossibility, but no one cares.

'The kids from Bad Kissingen don't know how lucky they are,' laughs The Photographer. And in truth, only 2,000 of us poor bastards who have wintered and summered this team, home and away, since August can truly appreciate it. And appreciate it we do. Bowyer is everywhere, Rush is inspirational in midfield, Sharpe is as good as I've ever seen him, Deane rattles the bar with a powerful header . . .

Last season in the corresponding fixture, Wednesday scored with almost every shot on target. Had Leeds done so today they might have been 6–1 up when referee Paul Danson blows for the end of the best 45 minutes of football I have watched anywhere, including on TV, all season.

The second half fails to match it, of course, but is still several cuts above what any Leeds fan might dream of. Six minutes into the half, Sheffield Wednesday get an equaliser when Carbone beats Halle on the right then finds Andy Booth, who cleverly beats Martyn from close range and a narrow angle. Leeds continue to play well but fail to restore the lead their earlier dominance so deserved. Gradually, Wednesday come back into it and the game becomes a thrilling end-to-end tussle. With 13 minutes to go Kelly, still struggling a little, is replaced by Wetherall – who misses the mood completely, tonking the ball forward at every opportunity rather than passing it as everyone else does – but even he comes close with a header. The excitement flows free and while Danson does his best to ruin it by booking seven players (only one from Leeds, miraculously), I can't help but feel everyone here today has seen a match they will never forget. The best £13 I've spent all season without a doubt.

Upon leaving the ground, I notice the Bad Kissingen coach awaiting its presumably jubilant cargo and ponder that back in the late '60s just such a game made me a Leeds fan for life. But I only saw that on TV; these German kids watched it in the flesh. They are now part of the family. I just hope they don't expect it to happen again. If only they knew what they have let themselves in for.

Back in the car, Radio 5 says Graham actually told the Leeds players that, with enough points to avoid relegation, they should go out and enjoy themselves. I'll believe that if they play the same way for the rest of the season. But the day is complete when at Tollington services I meet a Leeds fan who couldn't make the game. He is anxious to know if the first half was really as good as Radio 5's half-time report had suggested. That depends what they said, I suggest.

'They said it was as if Leeds United hadn't turned up and they sent along Real Madrid instead.'

I muster all the objectivity at my disposal and we both go home happier men . . .

Saturday, 29 March: England's Number One

. . . is not even on the bench when England play Mexico at Wembley. There is, more predictably, no place on the bench either for Lee Bowyer, promoted from the Under-21s to the injury-mashed senior squad in midweek. But Martyn's absence is particularly galling as Glenn Hoddle has given the ridiculous polo-necked England keeper's shirt to David James of Liverpool. I watch The Wolves Fan's TV in disbelief as the team comes up on the Sky caption and thank God I didn't go. The phone rings just before kick-off and Scrapping Kid Brother, the most die-hard Liverpool fan I know, is on hand to remind the four of us in the room just how many Reds are in the frame today. I tell him how much we are looking forward to seeing James flapping at crosses and making an arse of himself and inform him that in this one room The Wolves Fan, Arsenal supporter Lord Percy and Tony West Ham all think Hoddle has got it wrong. Nigel Martyn should be in goal.

With only one shot on target to save all afternoon, David James doesn't let his country down. But in England's 2–0 win he doesn't let me down either by dropping two crosses, failing to stop a back-pass header going out for a corner and colliding with a post . . .

Chapter Ten

April

Monday, 7 April: home to Blackburn Rovers

As if turning into Real Madrid at Hillsborough wasn't enough, today Leeds fans face the prospect of something even more uncanny: Leeds United unveiling not one but two new signings. Two *young* signings who aren't defenders. The first was the hitherto unknown French winger Pierre Laurent, bought for a nominal £250,000 from French club Bastia. Then, 24 hours later, on transfer-deadline day, Graham made it a double-whammy by nicking Greenock Morton striker Derek Lilley for £500,000. Lilley, also attracting interest from Crystal Palace, scored 23 of the struggling Scottish First Division side's 35 goals this season and although described by Graham, rather impolitely I thought, as 'a squad player', may see first-team action sooner than expected.

Yeboah, two days after missing the Hillsborough game with his mystery hamstring injury, declared himself miraculously fit within minutes of his selection by Ghana. George Graham, mustering all the sympathy at his disposal, immediately ordered him to play for the reserves away to Birmingham City Reserves at Wednesford Town's ground. Birmingham won 3–0, leaving Leeds' second string bottom of the Pontin's League Premier Division and in serious danger of relegation. Laurent and Lilley are in the squad tonight. Yeboah, who presumably played against Sierra Leone in Ghana's World Cup qualifier yesterday, is not.

Playing on a Monday means another half-day off work but ensures that The Photographer and I will always remember where we were when another chapter of sporting history was written. The chapter has, of course, nothing

159

to do with Leeds United and we are merely in my Rover on the M1, but today is the day the 150th Grand National is being run, two days late after IRA interference led to the race being cancelled on Saturday. I've forgotten to check which horses are running in Leeds colours and have not placed a bet; nevertheless Radio 5's sense of occasion is quite touching. Talking of donkeys running in Leeds colours, I remind The Photographer that Carlton Bloody Palmer will be put out to graze tonight due to suspension. It's a cheap shot but oh how we laugh.

George Graham might allow himself time to smile, too, knowing he's achieved his first aim of getting Leeds clear of relegation, but with Europe a concept the team should regard only as a holiday destination, it's easy to forget that nine places above them sit Man United, followed by Arsenal, Liverpool and Newcastle United, all still battling it out for the title. The closest Graham gets to the battle this season is on Teletext, where he has joined in the Man United-fuelled debate about extending the season, taking the side of Arsenal's Arsène Wenger and Liverpool's Roy Evans in offering sympathy but not support for whingeing Alex Ferguson's proposal that his team be allowed to play its final game after the rest of the league programme has been completed. Like his side won't win it anyway.

Strangely, none of the managers involved in the struggle to cement a position of mid-table mediocrity have asked for an extension. Instead, Blackburn's caretaker manager Tony Parkes, whose team has played one less league game than Man United, is quoted on Teletext as saying he regards tonight's fixture as 'a chance to get the points they need to secure their Premiership future'. I trust he'll be equally as calm if Leeds impersonate Real Madrid again.

The Photographer is still laughing at the idea when the phone rings and The Biggest Yorkshireman In London calls to ask me to buy him a programme so he can see what Laurent and Lilley look like. He'd buy one himself but he can't be there as he's having dinner with someone who used to be in Take That. I've forgotten the name seconds after he's dropped it and berate him for being a lightweight. But at least he sounded like he'd rather be watching Leeds.

The Photographer and I get to the ground early, to wander around freely taking pictures thanks, finally, to special permission from Leeds United in the genial form of general manager Alan Roberts. He introduces us to chief security officer Tony, who apologises that we may be stopped many times due to increased vigilance after the IRA's Aintree interference, then leads us into the stadium through the players' tunnel. Billy Bremner is nowhere to be seen this time and I concentrate instead on looking professional and unemotional while Tony predicts that tonight's will be a small crowd, around 27,000.

Explaining we are to stay clear of the tunnel and dressing-rooms he leaves us free to wander around the near-deserted stands and concourses, which I do tingling with childlike excitement. Stewards check our ID then want their picture taken; several ask who won the National. From the dirt track round the perimeter, I can tell the pitch is vastly improved from its condition two months ago, but chiefly I look at the ground. In fact I ogle it lasciviously from every one of the 360 degrees around the centre spot, dwelling longer than is strictly necessary directly behind the goal nets and in the corner where Nigel Martyn, Mark Beeney, Ian Harte and coach David Williams are already going through their pre-match keeper-testing exercises. Today I posted a player of the season voting card with Martyn's name on it but resist the temptation to tell him so. Instead, as The Photographer snaps away, I walk on, round the pitch and finally back to my seat, my status as a fan restored the minute I leave the perimeter track and set foot in the West Stand.

*   *   *

Even with less than an hour to kick-off, the ground remains unusually empty. Helen The Ellie Fan breezes in complaining how she has 'missed her fix' since her last game here, almost a month ago. Howard The Student arrives with two friends from college, presumably unlikely to pass their courses if they're not smart enough to decline his invitation. Unless, that is, they came for his Carlton Bloody Palmer story, which he shares within seconds of my mentioning that the lanky number four is suspended tonight. 'Bloody hell! You should have been here for Southampton! In the second half George Graham was yelling at him, really yelling, and Carlton just came striding over towards the dugout and told him to "Fuck off!". Everybody heard it.'

Everyone agrees this is A Good Thing that has hopefully helped grease Palmer's exit route. And so we watch the teams file out at five to eight feeling much happier.

This feeling does not last long and after kick-off has evaporated altogether. The new signings are on the bench. Wetherall and Jackson are in for Radebe and Molenaar, which means this is the same attacking line-up that thrilled us so at Hillsborough – but Real Madrid are clearly back in Spain tonight and we have to watch Leeds United. So do Sky viewers, and I shudder to think of anyone broadcasting this in the name of entertainment. The Sky camera and monitor in front of us offer an instant replay facility but there's absolutely nothing worth watching twice. Blackburn sit back and wait for a counter-attacking opportunity while Leeds hit balls forward that all seem to come down on the head of Colin Hendry. A slip by Graeme le Saux lets Rod Wallace in with a run on goal, but his driven cross is cleared for a corner. That is the absolute highlight of the first half until, with 17 minutes to go, a Blackburn clearance loops lazily over the west touchline towards row CC.

It is the opportunity I have been waiting for all season, and before Howard The Student can react I have snatched the ball from behind his seat and hold it in my hands. It is cold, slightly wet and the focus of attention for everyone in Elland Road and, I imagine, the millions watching on television. The noise of the crowd fades away from my consciousness, my heartbeat rises deafeningly in my ears, all of my life-force balances on this fulcrum in time. Then I am suddenly aware of Howard The Student trying to snatch the ball from my hands and the crowd noise rushes back in like a tidal wave. I shrug him off and see the face of Gary Kelly on the touchline beckoning me to give him the ball. Standing up, I throw it quickly and expertly, directly into his hands so he may catch it easily without stooping or stretching. He throws it back into play just as quickly and sprints off. He has no time to thank me, but I am not offended. Instead I glance at the crestfallen Howard and sit down, my face the very definition of smug, my mind drowning in a sea of contentment.

I do my best to hide all this, of course, but force it into the first line of my conversation with The Photographer, who has come back to his seat after dozing through the first half sitting near the South Stand goalline. 'I touched it *twice*,' he scoffs, with an emphasis that is, frankly, irritating. 'Must have been on the telly, too!' I don't rise to his bait and instead take far more interest in his story that one of the newspaper snappers beside him gave up and went home after 20 minutes, confident of a goalless draw, simply too bored to continue.

Blackburn's Kevin Gallacher (who scored twice for Scotland last week) directs a header beyond Martyn's fingertips on to the bar 15 minutes into the second half, but the newspaper snapper's prediction still looks reliable. At the other end Deane has a chance, but his run towards goal is pure Buzz Lightyear, as he doesn't so much dribble as 'stumble with style' before hitting his shot straight at keeper Tim Flowers.

I laugh, a little, and the game returns to the frustrating pattern of long periods of nothing happening followed by a hopeful punt forward that Hendry gets on the end of. Bowyer runs long and hard in midfield but Leeds are running out of ideas just as the crowd are running out of patience. 'Come on, George, put the new guys on,' comes a cry from behind. The idea quickly gathers support and disgruntled murmurs spread around the ground. Stubbornly, George Graham ignores them and the substitutes remain on the bench while the manager waits for some signal that he has won and the crowd recognises his absolute right to decide when to change the team.

On the pitch, a Blackburn back pass is completely misjudged by Flowers, who slices it not into the West Stand to his right but into the Kop behind him, falling quite spectacularly arse over tit in the process. The Kop responds instantly.

'England's, England's number four! England's number four!'

'Dod-gy kee-pah! Dod-gy kee-pah!'

Flowers is not amused, and gesticulates and yells insults at the crowd behind him. The rest of Elland Road is enlivened by this, and momentarily distracted from their barracking of the home team. Seconds later Graham seizes the opportunity and tells Laurent and Lilley to get their tracksuits off as number boards for Wallace and Sharpe are held aloft. They have just seven minutes to play . . .

Lilley goes for it like a bull at a gate but loses his footing at the crucial moment. Laurent looks more impressive but his turn of speed down the left wing takes even his team-mates by surprise. The Frenchman's best touch prompts a rousing welcoming chorus of 'There's only one Pierre' – although, as Helen The Ellie Fan rightly observes, in France there are 'bloody millions of them'.

In the end, neither substitute can rescue the match and it ends as it began with the scoreboard reading 0–0. Many of the crowd, uncannily just 264 more than Tony had predicted, boo both teams off the pitch.

Because we can, The Photographer and I go to the post-match press conference, which is delayed while Graham tips Arsenal for the title on Sky's post-match interview. When he enters the room he has a strange grin on his face, avoiding eye contact until he looks up from behind his table to crack, half apologetically, 'Well, this shouldn't take long, should it?' The assembled journos laugh and try to think of something to ask. But there isn't anything, and all Graham adds to what everyone has just watched and taped on hand-held cassette recorders off the Sky monitor in the corner is 'No, I don't think I should have put the new guys on any earlier.' The conference breaks up and The Photographer and I head off, pausing only to watch as Laurent and Lilley – showered, changed and homeward bound – get mobbed by young autograph-hunters.

Our journey home is in near silence because, just as in the press conference, the game prompted no conversation. The M1 is empty and dull, comet Hale-Bopp can't be seen tonight and only a badger scuttling from the central reservation to the hard shoulder near Nottingham offers any variety. He certainly moved faster than anyone except Pierre Laurent tonight . . .

Wednesday, 9 April: away to Luton Town, FA Youth Cup semi-final first leg

At work today three people whinge to me about how boring the 0–0 draw against Blackburn was on TV. Arsenal fan Duncan Donut had the nerve to complain he had to leave the pub after an hour because he couldn't stand it. Nice Guy John, a Sheffield Wednesday supporter, suggests it was the only match he'd ever seen that could have been played without goalkeepers. And The Dawser calls from LA, where he watched it on cable, and describes it as 'the worst game I've ever seen in my life'. Tough luck all of you; I had to drive there and watch all 90 minutes. Besides, the goalless draw against Derby in January was infinitely worse.

Such complaints only stiffen my resolve to watch the youth team, even though The Photographer phones to say he's not going. Instead he meets me at lunchtime, mumbles something about being tired, then presses his terrifyingly expensive and nowhere near as simple as it looks compact camera into my hand, promising to phone the minute Borussia Dortmund score. Ah yes, while Leeds United pulses quicken at the thought of consolation glory courtesy of 'the kids', the rest of the football world thinks tonight's big match is a European Champions Cup semi-final featuring Man United.

After work I take the train from King's Cross to Luton and on it read an *Evening Standard* that only mentions Luton versus Leeds at the bottom of its fixture column – although it has a whole page on the match in Dortmund. I have no interest in golf whatsoever, but read about Nick Faldo instead. It has come to something when Leeds United's season has been so disappointing that I travel alone to support the youth team while inwardly cheering on a team in Germany.

Alighting at Luton it seems odd not to be anywhere near the Gateway Hotel. Outside the station I catch a glimpse of the Kenilworth Road floodlights and walk down the hill towards them, but speak to a man in a business suit to check directions. I walk with him a while, and he tells how Luton are only in this semi because they beat Watford away, on penalties, a week ago. The look of relish in his eye reminds me of the tales in *Everywhere We Go*, the book written by two Watford-supporting former football hooligans. It seems certain that my guide is no hooligan but his dress and manner underline that book's argument that there is no such thing as a typical football fan.

Inside the ground is further evidence. There are lots of teenage girls – and why not, with 22 teenage boys on the pitch? – and plenty of small children enjoying a night out with mum and dad. The main stand is the only one open and it's not full but well on the way to containing 800, perhaps 1,000 people. It's a good turnout, and unlike at Maine Road in January, there are several Leeds fans here. As the teams trot out I recognise the married couple I met in The Balti Hut half an hour ago. He told me there that he used to coach the young Leeds keeper Paul Robinson. It feels strange being at a match alone, so

I'm grateful when three men with Yorkshire accents sit down beside me. With five minutes to go to the 7.30 kick-off Paul Hart and Eddie Gray join the players on the pitch, and I watch in awe as Gray begins juggling one of the balls, finally balancing it on his boot-laces. He stares at it and holds it there, perfectly balanced, for several seconds, perhaps thinking of glorious days two decades earlier, then points his toe and lets the ball go, as if it were some butterfly alighting from the palm of his hand, and the spell is broken.

When the match begins, it is almost two minutes before Luton even touch the ball. To my left someone yells, 'Come on Luton!' To the right comes a response: 'Come on Leeds!' And directly in front a small boy cups his hands and calls 'Come on Dortmund!' before giggling cheekily at his dad. Dad smiles back in pride. From some way above and behind comes what must be the most unique chant of the season: 'Luton, Luton, Luton . . . I'd rather be in Luton than . . . Dortmund.' There are clearly a number of Leeds fans in the upper tier.

Leeds are quickly in control, passing the ball short with speed and fluency, like Liverpool with a sense of purpose, and I'm desperate for someone to discuss this with. Right on cue my phone rings and The Photographer asks for a report. It's 0–0 in Dortmund too and Man United are under the cosh. This beautiful evening just got better. Leeds bamboozle me and Luton with a deliciously worked free-kick and I share my admiration with the tyke to my left. He forgives me my accent, tells me they often use that in Northern Intermediate League games, and a bond is made. The rest of the half passes goalless, and even though Luton improve as it progresses, particularly through their captain Matthew Upson and centre-forward Gary Doherty, Leeds still look well on top. Midfielder Kevin Dixon, just 16, is in outstanding form. Left-winger Andrew Wright is keeping the opposition right-back busy and forwards Lee Matthews and Tony Hackworth look constantly menacing whether used as target men or, more commonly, brought into play at the sharp end of intricate attacking movements. Marvellous.

At half-time, the noisy guys in the upper tier remove their shirts and chant: 'We are the champions! Champions of Europe!' They introduce themselves with a blue, white and yellow flag as the Aylesbury Whites. Luton supporters look bemused but one of them takes his shirt off too. At the catering kiosk I bump into Bald Andy, a friend of The Man From Birmingham, and through the noise of the Aylesbury Whites he adds his voice to the growing chorus that this side is better than the first team. Luton fans are soon chanting 'Going up, going up, going up!' and it's an altogether livelier Kenilworth Road that greets the teams for the start of the second half.

The Luton youngsters respond and with barely two minutes gone score a quite magnificent goal with a 30-yard belter from Matthew Spring. The

Luton fans go wild and I feel conspicuous among them. Five minutes later, good work by Dixon lets in Matthews to score an equaliser and I stand to make myself even more conspicuous. Behind me the loudest and most clueless Luton fan in the world has stopped predicting a 3–0 win and is urging the young Hatters to score again. But instead, Leeds captain Alan Maybury undoes them on the right flank and his ball into the six-yard box is turned in by Hackworth to make it 2–1. I call The Photographer to let him know the good news. Engaged. He doesn't phone back until Dortmund have put one past Man U's stand-in keeper Van Der Gouw, but by then I already knew. A man behind with a radio to his ear has spread the news. I know he is a Luton fan when he says, 'Never mind, I'm sure they'll win back at Old Trafford.'

Both teams at Kenilworth Road survive late scares and the score remains 2–1 at the final whistle. I move to the barrier, applaud the team and shout congratulations to Eddie Gray. He turns, looks at me and smiles. I wish I could think of something else to say. Like, please teach me how to do that trick with the ball. But thankfully he's walked off before it occurs to me . . .

Wednesday, 16 April: away to Wimbledon

I have to admit I *like* that weird look people who know nothing about football wear when I tell them how many matches I go to. They think I'm mad and I'm happy to let them believe it. I like it even better when they ask why, so I can burble on about the sense of loyalty and belonging, of gaining strength through suffering and immeasurable joy in celebration, blah-blah-blah. If they survive that and ever ask again I may call their bluff and offer to take them to a game. So it is that Curious Of Croydon finds herself glancing around nervously as I lead her through unusually deserted south-London streets toward Whitehorse Lane while pointing out the worryingly large number of pubs I have visited while attending matches at Selhurst Park. None of the pubs look very inviting tonight and at least one of them is boarded up. She looks grateful we don't have time for a drink and nervous of the smattering of shaven-headed and pot-bellied football fans around us.

A vague arrangement to meet The Photographer has evaporated as we are even later than I predicted he would be, and so Curious Of Croydon and I go to the ticket office to spend £30 on a pair of the Arthur Wait Stand's finest. Curious Of Croydon accepts gratefully and points out that we could get into the Royal Albert Hall on a proms night for a fifth of that. I explain she has not come here for an evening of cultural entertainment but for 90 minutes of dour and meaningless Premiership football that may answer some of her questions as to the game's long-term appeal. She smiles but I'm not sure she is impressed.

At the gate, the larger portion of the ticket is returned and the lock on the ancient iron turnstile released as a cheery male voice in the darkness tells us we can sit where we like tonight. 'Sit where you like' echoes like a mantra from every orange-jacketed steward we meet, but I ignore the one at the entrance to the stand to turn and watch Curious Of Croydon as she catches her first glimpse of the arena before her. Just like the young Paul in the film of *Fever Pitch*, her face lights up. She smiles and offers, rather unpoetically but with due sense of occasion: 'Ooh . . . it's so . . . green!'

But there is hardly any crowd and no atmosphere whatsoever. Embarrassed, I lead her down the steps to a prime seat close to the front where we can see the Leeds squad warming up by running in a line towards us. Curious Of Croydon recognises none of them and, already regretting my decision to bring her here, I try to cheer things up a little by pointing to various players and explaining their roles, character and temperament. The crowd is so sparse that individual voices ring out like cheers from a Sunday league touchline, and so when someone calls to Sharpe for an autograph and he ignores them, one wag's muttered comment of 'Try telling him you're a hairdresser!' may have reached the player himself. But the only one on the pitch who seems to be listening is Nigel Martyn, who leaves his goal to sign autographs for a clutch of young fans in the corner.

The Photographer has been granted another pass and wanders along the touchline looking for us. We spot each other easily and Curious Of Croydon and I wander down to the barrier to chat with him. 'Have you brought your alarm clock, then?' he asks her. 'It's going to be another thrilling night's football with an atmosphere to match . . .'

Looking around the ground, listening to sporadic shouts, then casting an eye back into the Arthur Wait, I hazard a guess that Curious Of Croydon is destined to be part of the smallest Premiership crowd of the season. The irony seems lost on her but The Biggest Yorkshireman In London agrees when he wanders down out of the stand to say hello. As we talk, a steward wanders over to ask The Photographer to move as he's obscuring an important hoarding. Incredulously, I point out that the cameras are above us and the game is 15 minutes from kick-off. 'Ah, but this is a very important hoarding,' he winks, 'and they have cameras everywhere.' We lean over and see the FA Carling Premiership logo. Something about the impending attendance figure suggests this may be one they'd rather hide from sight.

Curious Of Croydon fails to grasp the significance of Gary Kelly being dropped to make way for Radebe's return while Wetherall keeps his place, but she recognises Wimbledon's Vinnie Jones and seems to understand that the huge response he gets from the Leeds supporters when his name is announced at 7.44 is a rare mark of respect. A minute later, to the tune of *Mission:*

Impossible, the teams run out and she starts to laugh. I am annoyed, until I notice the small boy in front who is dancing to the music as if a spot on *Stars in Their Eyes* depended on it. It's an impressively athletic and entertaining effort and, I have to admit, the chances of the game topping it are slim.

Both left-backs, Halle for Leeds and Alan Kimble for Wimbledon, show good touches, but up front little is happening at either end. Deane screws a shot wide where it looked easier to score and I sit down with my head in my hands while Curious Of Croydon does her best to look sympathetic. I take out my frustrations on Wetherall, who is solid but horribly uninventive. He seems unable to put his foot on the ball and pass to a team-mate, preferring instead to kick every clearance up in the air or into the stand. I check my watch in disbelief as he spends almost four minutes out of the game while retying his boot-laces. And then, on 18 minutes, while shepherding the ball out for a goal-kick, he cocks up and Dean Holdsworth nips around him, steals the ball and scores from a narrow angle past Martyn. Curious Of Croydon, uncertain how to react, takes her turn to look embarrassed.

I swear under my breath, but when after a peach of a through ball from Bowyer, Sharpe screws his shot so wide that it trickles to The Photographer positioned halfway to the corner flag, I swear aloud. Colourfully. The Photographer, clearly happy to have something to do at last, bowls the ball back to the Dons' equally unemployed keeper Neil Sullivan. Soon after, Sullivan's opposite number Martyn nonchalantly catches a long cross one-handed, prompting a grateful 'England's number one!' chant, but at half-time I can only apologise to Curious Of Croydon and – to spare her the trauma of so many people around her removing their shirts – take her to the kiosks to buy her a coffee and a big bag of Opal Fruits.

The second half starts in a much livelier fashion, with Vinnie Jones getting himself booked for trampling on Bowyer then substituted about a minute later by his worried manager Joe Kinnear after diving into another challenge on the same player through a red mist. Then Sharpe misses his second sitter of the night and the action sweeps to the other end. Jumping high, Wetherall takes a blow to the head and collapses in a heap. Kelly, the only defender on the bench, warms up, but after several minutes of treatment Wetherall gets unsteadily to his feet and gestures that he is okay to continue. His judgement, however, is clearly impaired and he resumes the game apparently believing he is a centre-forward. The first chance he gets, Wethers charges forward – with the ball – and shoots from 40 yards. He then stays in the Wimbledon area for some time, turning in the most impressive display of goal-hanging seen since my old school playground. At this point, he can probably even tie his laces. But with 15 minutes to go, a Neal Ardley cross produces a ferocious header by substitute Stewart Castledine and although Martyn miraculously stops it, the joy is short-lived as Castledine is on hand to nod in the rebound. The Tannoy gives us a burst of James Brown's 'I Feel Good', but no one in the Arthur Wait Stand does. Leeds are 2–0 down, Graham has seen enough and brings Kelly on to replace Wetherall.

The Leeds fans try to lift the team but few can be bothered to join in.

'Why am I the only one singing?' asks one trying harder than most.

'Because the rest of us are asleep,' replies a near neighbour.

My attention passes to an apparent fan of *The Fast Show* who insists on yelling 'Suits you, sir!' whenever Sharpe comes close, even though he may not have the ball. It's all a little weird, even for tonight, but is proving the most entertaining part of the evening for Curious Of Croydon.

At the other end, Rush misses from close up, but I've grown accustomed to that and am far more concerned when with ten minutes to go Deane takes a heavy blow to his ankle. He goes off behind the goalline for treatment but is still limping and clearly in pain when he comes back on. Insanely, it's several more minutes before Graham does the decent thing and brings on Derek Lilley to replace him. In fact, he does a double decent thing and brings on Pierre Laurent, too, in place of Sharpe. Instantly, Laurent is the fastest and keenest player on the pitch, but, unsurprisingly, in their allotted five minutes neither he nor Lilley can make an impact, and the match ends with a whimper.

The PA announcer declares that inside Selhurst Park tonight were just 7,979 paying customers, saluting us as 'Small in number but big in heart'. We are so small in number that by the time The Photographer has packed up his cameras, he, I and No Longer Curious Of Croydon are the last ones out . . .

Saturday, 19 April: away to Nottingham Forest

Big Andy's Big Red Car contains Little Andy, The Photographer and me as it pulls away from the Luton Gateway. We speak with pride about the fact that in the FA Youth Cup semi-final second leg at Elland Road, Leeds beat Luton Town 1–0 and so will play Crystal Palace over two legs in the final. A date for the second leg at Selhurst Park has not been arranged yet, but we all agree to go. With no stop for services we arrive with unseemly haste in Nottingham and park in the tarmacked grounds of a civic building across the road from Trent Bridge cricket ground. Though sunny, the weather is deceptively cold and the few hardy souls arriving for the cricket must be cursing the effect the start of their season has had on the hitherto improving spring weather. The pub on the corner is teeming with Forest fans and a few spill out and gaze with amusement through one of Trent Bridge's gates at the men in white out on the grass. The sight reminds me that the end of the footie season fast approaches and the long, dull summer of transfer speculation is about to begin.

On something of a roll since Leeds United granted him a photo pass two weeks ago, The Photographer wanders over to collect one for the City Ground, then bids us farewell while we three amble around to take our seats in the Bridgford Stand. But it's so cold that once inside we don't sit down but huddle by one of the bars and chat to some friends of Andys Big and Little who kill time with football trivia questions. Failing miserably to name the mere 11 black players who have ever worn a Man U shirt, we all buy a charity scratchcard from a man whose 'one-in-five chance of winning' sales story is stronger than our will to resist. He is long gone by the time we realise that of the five of us, no one has won. I manage to remember most of those who have played for both Leeds and Man United, but have forgotten which two teams share the record of being the lowest-scoring (non-relegated) team in the top flight this century. It's a record that Leeds, barring a goal avalanche in the final four fixtures, are about to steal. We all laugh and agree that this season cannot end soon enough.

The cold and the beer take their toll and so I slip off to the gents. Perched above the urinals is a butterfly, also apparently surprised by the sudden cold snap. It looks out of place in this grim concrete and chrome place where against another wall a voice ends a whinge about how few goals Leeds are scoring by declaring: 'Still, it's nearly over . . .'

I go outside at five to three in time to take my place behind the goal and hear the boos when Carlton Bloody Palmer's name appears in the subs list. Panic-stricken faces say he wasn't out there warming up. Surely this is a mistake? But when the teams trot out, the scoreboard is proven correct. Palmer is a sub (more groans) and Molenaar has been dropped. So too has Rush – making room for Laurent's full debut – and Wallace – letting in Lilley to partner Deane up front.

With Forest rooted to the foot of the Premiership only a win today will do them any good. Ironically, Leeds United Reserves played Forest's second string here facing a similar ultimatum ten days ago (on the night the youth team won 2–1 at Luton). Then, with Laurent and Lilley playing their first full game in Leeds colours, the underdogs triumphed and went a long way to ensuring their survival with a single goal from Ian Harte. This afternoon, the news that player/manager Stuart Pearce is unfit has surely not helped the seniors' morale but has certainly boosted my confidence.

Six minutes after the kick-off this is momentarily dented when a Forest attack is insufficiently cleared and the ball drops at the feet of their recent signing from Celtic, Pierre van Hooijdonk. He is so clearly offside, however, that even though he belts the ball into the net I merely join in the chorus of jeers at the celebrating Forest fans and look to the linesman for the flag. Van Hooijdonk does the same, but as neither he nor I can see one, he raises his arms and peels away in celebration. I am appalled and attempt to deny the goal has been scored. It's an interesting experiment in mind over matter that collapses only because the electronic scoreboard doesn't mind and my opinion doesn't matter. A volley of chants are launched in response:

'Cheat! Cheat! Cheat!'

'They're going down, they're going down, Forest's going down!'

'You're scabs and you know you are!' – just to prove the scars from the miners' strike will never heal.

Winding up the Forest fans livens proceedings no end, however, as their number extends through the top tier of the Bridgford Stand and their noise is reflected down by the asymmetrical roof. For a while, the home supporters get cocky and bait Leeds with some impressive self-deprecation:

'We're shit, and we're beating you!'

Leeds fans are so impressed that it takes them almost half a second to think of the response:

'We're shit, and we're staying up!'

On the pitch, the Leeds team is underlining the point, consistently underperforming and giving Forest plenty of room and plenty of hope. Van Hooijdonk is a constant threat and his fellow countryman Bryan Roy is playing out of his skin, never better than when he runs at the fragile-looking Leeds defence before unleashing a ferocious dipping shot that looks set to be goal of the month – until Nigel Martyn's fingertips push it out from under the bar and over for a corner. I am still applauding open-mouthed when Forest take the corner, having been so impressed that I forgot to join in with the 'England's number one!' chorus that inevitably followed.

At half-time I give up on the on-pitch entertainment (billed as 'Nottingham's answer to the Spice Girls') and meet up with The Man From Birmingham, who phones to ask if I'm anywhere nearby. We talk, we whinge, we look forward to the end of the season and then the cold drives me back to the gents where a voice sighs, 'Never mind, only three games to go' before adding, more cheerfully, 'and in three months' time we'll be saying "Only three weeks to go".' The most annoying thing is, he's absolutely right.

As the players line up for the second half, Carlton Bloody Palmer stands on the halfway line as a substitute for Sharpe – which seems dangerously like madness. Within minutes, however, it makes perfect sense as it becomes clear that George Graham has reorganised to drop Radebe back from midfield, switching from a flat back four to three central defenders, using Palmer to mop up in front of them while full-backs Kelly and Dorigo push forward. Palmer seizes his opportunity and doesn't put a foot wrong, forcing at least one of us in Row J to choke on humble pie and marvel at Graham's foresight. He hasn't, however, been clever enough to predict the weather, and is presumably shivering just like the rest of us and regretting he opted for that navy blazer rather than his recently preferred long mac.

Thoughts on the manager's sartorial shortcomings are rudely interrupted when Leeds' new-found attacking ambition wins them a corner to our right. Someone throws a toy football on to the pitch that referee David Elleray insists Bowyer removes before he takes the corner. Unsure where to put Bogus Ball, Bowyer turns to the Leeds contingent and kicks it to them. The corner itself is less well directed and Forest are soon attacking. Bogus Ball is used for an impromptu game of volleyball before it is tossed back on to the pitch, just behind Forest keeper Alan Fettis. The keeper is unnerved by its presence and wants to kick it away, but sensibly keeps his eye on the match ball, currently up the other end at the feet of one of his team-mates. Double-checking it's safe to do so he takes his eye off the game for a second, then, still watching play, moves to stand in front of Bogus Ball and backheels it away. But not on to the cinder track. Instead, with an accuracy that any forward would have been happy to emulate, he has sent Bogus Ball trickling over the line and into the net. Leeds fans cheer. Forest fans in the corner of the sexily named Executive Stand respond immediately: 'What's it like? What's it like? What's it like to score a goal?'

To shut them up, 11 minutes into the second half unlikely hero Palmer pushes down the flank in front of them in another of his ungainly, but for once controlled, forays. His low drive towards the box may be going nowhere but Chris Bart-Williams is taking no chances and tries to clear. Instead he slices his interception on to Fettis's right-hand post from where the stranded keeper can only watch helplessly as the ball trundles across the mouth of goal and into the path of the onrushing Deane, who manages not to fluff the tap-in from almost nine inches out. Leeds fans laugh. Leeds fans cheer. Forest fans scowl. And 'Deano' celebrates alone while his team-mates opt to mob Carlton Bloody Palmer. It's a funny old game.

It gets a little funnier when Deane's shirt starts flapping around his neck, ripped in some forgotten challenge. The tear down the front gets longer and longer while he divides his time between chasing the ball and gesturing to the bench for a replacement. When it finally arrives, the forward's predominant shirt colour is the navy blue of his undershirt and he looks less than amused at the indignity he has suffered. To make things worse, when his hard work sees the Forest defence begin to crumble, it is the debutant Lilley who gets the better chances and even looks to have stolen the glory – but his 'goal' is disallowed and he looks distraught. If he could hear the guys behind me, he might also be distraught to learn the nickname of 'Dennis', presumably after the 1970s Australian pace bowler, is fast catching on.

At the final whistle everyone has to settle for a single point. For Leeds it is meaningless, for Forest almost certainly the end. But although the home crowd's reaction suggests it was no less than they expected, I take little pleasure in knowing they will be relegated because Stuart Pearce deserves so much more than that.

For the journey home Big Andy cranks up the heater and introduces The Photographer and me to Baker and Kelly United on Talk Radio rather than 6.06 (with Alan Green still standing in for David Mellor due to the impending election). The two Dannys turn in a 90 minutes far more entertaining than those we have just paid £18 to watch, as they let a few honoured callers get the occasional word in edgeways while they discuss pitiful Tannoy announcers and the lack of women doing the job, get one punter to read the day's lower-league results based on sponsors not team names, and take the piss out of Chris Eubank. Long after saying goodbye to the Andys, I drive into London with Eubank continuing to bear the brunt of their assault. And then a London taxi-driver calls in to say he had the boxer in his cab while listening to the show and that he, Eubank, was planning a visit to the radio station just as soon as he had finished his meal at the restaurant the cabby had taken him to. At least if I ever meet Carlton Bloody Palmer on a dark night, I know I'll be able to outrun him . . .

Tuesday, 22 April: home to Aston Villa

I take the afternoon off work with a heavy heart, all but certain that Leeds will not score and the best the team can hope for is a 0–0 draw. The sports news this morning is all about snooker player Ronnie O'Sullivan making a maximum 147 break in just five minutes 20 seconds. That kind of scoring prowess is something that Leeds United can only dream of. The club's miserable total of 27 goals in 35 league games makes them the least-prolific scorers in English football. But at least Leeds are still top of the bookings league, their total of 76 now just one ahead of Arsenal. Then again, the Gunners played last night . . .

Journeying up the M1, The Photographer and I pass football fans who have something *real* to celebrate. North of junction 29, the entire population of Chesterfield appears to be *en route* for Sheffield, where their team tonight play Middlesbrough in the FA Cup semi-final replay at Hillsborough. Everywhere we look are cars trailing blue and white flags or scarves, and coaches packed with happy smiling faces and people waving banners. I sound the horn and we both wave as we pass each one while people in blue-and-white facepaint or wearing blue frightwigs acknowledge our support and wave back. It's great fun and exactly what the FA Cup is supposed to be about, and I can't help thinking that the town's ancient non-luxury coaches, plus one particularly rickety-looking double-decker, seem to complement perfectly

Chesterfield's status as devil-may-care Second Division underdogs. At junction 33, where they queue up to peel off, I take one last longing look in the mirror and wish The Photographer and I had something half as exciting to look forward to.

I park up and we walk through the car park, arriving at the top of the short flight of wooden steps down to the back of the West Stand just as a blue Porsche pulls up at the bottom of them. At its wheel is Lee Sharpe, leaning over to talk to someone he's recognised just ahead of us – or someone just ahead of us he's sure will recognise him (perhaps a hairdresser) – before zooming off to a parking space nearer the players' entrance. At the start of the season I'd have been excited to see him, but tonight I'm only concerned how my season ticket is subsidising his high-performance motoring and that his brilliant performance against Sheffield Wednesday was all too rare for a player who cost Leeds United a club record fee of £4.5 million.

In the seats between the dugouts, Ian The Moustache and Niki announce they expect to hear the pitter-patter of tiny Leeds booties in November, but Ian The Moustache seems just as proud to announce that Nigel Martyn and Lee Sharpe drink and eat (sensibly and moderately, he stresses) at the pub where he and Niki work. I've found a bunch of £1 refreshment vouchers that came with the season ticket to buy teas and Twixes (at Elland Road it is always best to eat sensibly and moderately), then turn to watch the warm-up. My earlier hostility towards Sharpe evaporates when I notice he is spending the warm-up swapping long balls with Ian Harte and knocking them ever closer to an oblivious Ellie The Elephant who is on the pitch and looking much livelier than of late. Such liveliness might be useful if the mascot wants to avoid taking a 40-yarder up the trunk. Sharpe comes close enough to suggest he's merely holding off and trots back to the dressing-room grinning broadly.

But when the team-sheet circulates, it's hard to see why Sharpe could be so happy. The starting line-up is the same as that which finished at Forest and so Palmer is on from the start with Sharpe, like Molenaar, once again keeping the bench warm. Just before kick-off I spot The Man From Birmingham and The Copper who have bought seats just behind us and are desperate to get a ticket for the last away game of the season at Chelsea. Why they should be so keen to go when they've missed so many others and suffered the Forest game, I can only put down to a lapse in sanity.

Leeds United are clinging grimly to theirs when Graham Barber's whistle gets things under way. The first 15 minutes are as shaky as they've been all season. Villa pour forward and the by-now godlike Nigel Martyn is called upon to make save after save – admittedly a task made rather simpler because Gareth Southgate (twice), Ian Taylor, the hopelessly one-footed Savo Milosevic and Ugo Ehiogu mostly hit the ball straight at him. Luckily,

Radebe is ensuring their top scorer Dwight Yorke has little room to move, let alone shoot.

Leeds are desperately looking for a way back and Kelly's enthusiasm provokes him to steal a few yards when he gets the ball for a throw-in near the Leeds dugout. Referee Barber signals him back and he does so but then, like a naughty schoolboy, he scampers forward some more. Barber immediately blows for a foul throw but when Villa retake the throw they take it even further away. Barber says nothing and play continues, while Leeds coaches O'Leary and Williams berate the fourth official in front of us about inconsistency and double standards. The fourth official ignores them stoically.

Once again Leeds are offering nothing of menace up front and it is to the defence that I find myself looking for heroes. Radebe and Halle are playing very well. So too, much to my annoyance, is Carlton Bloody Palmer, whose tackling and interceptions are excellent and who even looks menacing going forward. It's a relative term, though he's certainly a lot more menacing than Laurent, making his full home debut but looking very much out of sorts and out of position in the middle of the field.

Kelly, however, is full of running. In an interview in tonight's match programme he answers the question 'What change would you most like to see in football?' with a heartfelt plea: 'Full-backs not allowed to go past the halfway line!' But here he goes, haring down the right flank, beating Alan Wright and putting in a brilliant cross that Rush flicks on to the underside of the bar. It's the best bit of football I've seen from anyone in a white shirt in weeks and I decide immediately that if it ends 0–0 it was worth coming to see just that. O'Leary may even agree with me, yelling 'Well done Gary!' at the full-back as he trots back and recrosses the halfway line, with as much gusto as if he'd been telling him off.

Another attack sees Rush hit the South Stand end side netting – which at least proves he remembers what the goal looks like – although he should really have scored or at least dragged the ball back into the path of the increasingly desperate Lilley. All in all, when half-time comes, I have to admit I've been entertained.

The electronic scoreboard spoils the feeling a little because Chesterfield are a goal down to Middlesbrough. Southampton are leading Sunderland 1–0, too, and it's beginning to look as if Leeds and the other Premiership clubs won't get to play in that superb new stadium being built to replace Roker Park.

As Niki passes around tea from her flask, a small ceremony on the pitch by the tunnel and a Tannoy announcement go almost unnoticed: the name of Leeds' owning group Caspian's new ice hockey team will be Leeds Lasers. I think again of the plan to demolish the West Stand to make way for a giant replacement and its indoor arena that the Lasers may call home. On such trivial moments, history hangs . . .

As the second half begins, a wide-eyed little boy and his dad move forward to sit in the empty seats beside me. We smile at each other and I make a mental note to try not to swear. For the benches, however, it's business as usual. When a Villa player gives a free-kick straight to an 'unmarked' white shirt, a stream of expletives escapes the visitors' bench. From the Leeds fans behind, the noise is mostly ironic cheers, with a lone voice yelling 'Nice one, Brian!' at Villa's mild-mannered manager Brian Little, who is staring at the ground, hands in his pockets, unsure whether to believe what he just saw. Little pauses a while, looks for his tormentor, then calls back: 'It worked last time we used it.' He turns away grinning. Already a likeable man, Little seals it when he applauds as Martyn makes yet another world-class save. The fourth official does likewise but he's not off the hook yet for not making a note of that foul-throw incident.

In the Leeds dugout, Graham is working himself into a lather yelling at everyone except Martyn – but especially Dorigo and the still-useless Laurent. With an hour gone the manager puts the crestfallen Frenchman out of his misery and substitutes him with Wallace. As is his wont, Wallace comes on like a train, his 60-odd minutes of inactivity making him appear the fastest footballer on earth, never mind the pitch. This is an illusion Leeds fans are accustomed to, however, and the trained eye can also spot that very little of his energy is released in any meaningful way like, say, a shot on goal. The best one of the night ironically comes from Dorigo, who comes the closest to breaking the deadlock when he hits a dipping, swerving shot that nearly catches out the Villa keeper Mark Bosnich. But that's it and although Leeds finish slightly stronger, they are not strong enough and my 0–0 prediction has come to pass.

The scoreboard reveals that goals have gone in everywhere else tonight and that three from Middlesbrough have put paid to Chesterfield's (and everyone else's) FA Cup final dream. The Photographer and I say our 'Goodbyes' and 'See you at Chelseas?' to everyone and head for the exit. While he has a pee I watch Ravanelli on the TV in the John Charles Bar, so obviously relieved that he's going back to Wembley even though everything else has gone wrong for 'Boro this season. Feeling depressed for Chesterfield, I check the Ladbrokes figures on the board and see that 0–0 was 7–1. So was a one-goal victory for either side. This gets me thinking. Leeds have become so predictable that maybe I should take up gambling. I could have punted a fiver on my instincts, taken two options and *still* left the ground quids-in. The Photographer and I are still weighing the pros and cons of this potential extra misery when we reach the car and tune into Radio Leeds United 1323 AM, where a voice neither of us recognises is talking about close-season transfer activity. It seems the clever money is on 'big' changes, with many players joining as well as leaving the squad. But the talk has a hollow ring to it and smacks more of trying to drum up enthusiasm for season-ticket renewals. The radio reception fades to unlistenable at the M62 and we give up, making grudging promises to renew our season tickets anyway.

On the M1 we see just one Chesterfield bus, its banners taken down, its occupants sitting quietly dreaming – like us – of better luck next season. Behind a broken cloud the moon shines and sends out rays like the sun through smoked glass in an old black and white film's 'night' shot. It's uncanny. Over to the east I see a strange flash of light and suggest that after all the wildlife, maybe it's time to see a UFO. The road does strange things to a football fan. The Photographer gazes again at the moon, then over to the east before delivering a sage-like if tardy reply.

'Perhaps. It's certainly touch and go which we'll see first – an alien or Leeds scoring again.'

Friday, 25 April: away to Ghana

The small-print in the papers this morning reports that Leeds United beat Crystal Palace 2–1 in the first leg of the FA Youth Cup final at Elland Road last night, but chiefly they are still bleating about Man United's exit from the European Cup after losing not once but twice to Borussia Dortmund. Last night Liverpool exited the Cup-Winners Cup, going out after winning 2–0 against Paris St Germain, but did they get any more sympathy? No, actually.

This evening, however, Leeds United fans have something far more tangible to get upset about: a headline on Ceefax that reads 'Yeboah out'. It's the last thing needed after a hard week's work. I hastily tap the buttons and wait for the page to scroll up. When it does, things aren't as bad as I feared – yet. Yeboah is merely 'out' of the Ghana squad to play Gabon this weekend after having had a row with the national coach about being substituted in the previous match. It's little comfort to know that George Graham is not the only manager the striker can't see eye to eye with . . .

Chapter Eleven

May

Saturday, 3 May: away to Chelsea

Due to another break for international matches, it's been almost two weeks since Leeds have played a game. If pushed, I'd have to admit I haven't missed them. I've filled in the hiatus by discovering the Internet. Okay, I didn't actually discover it – it's been there for years, apparently – but I have taken to using it. Concerned at wasting my time and my employer's phone bill listening to Clubcall, I've been wasting rather less of each and using an office terminal to check out the Leeds United AFC official web site. Matchday programmes have long been trumpeting the joys of www.lufc.co.uk but I've refused to get involved, stubbornly preferring to believe, as someone once said, that the Internet is 'CB radio for the '90s'.

It may well be, but where else would I have learned that on 28 April, Robin Launders resigned as a director of Caspian and as chief executive of Leeds United Holdings PLC ('Leeds United')? Or that his departure prompted the appointment of Caspian's finance director Jeremy Fenn as managing director of Leeds United? Or that, according to Leeds United director Peter McCormick, 'Things have not gone well, or been delivered, over a period of time, leaving the board gravely concerned'? Unfortunately, continued McCormick, the exact circumstances of Launders's departure cannot be made public due to an agreement, signed that morning, between him and Leeds United that 'encourages us to be diplomatic in the press'. Great things are clearly afoot. But I pass on the politics of high finance and investigate the youth-team news.

This is much more like it: football. After beating Doncaster 6–0, they have been crowned champions of the Northern Intermediate League with two games still to play. Oh, there's a footnote: 'John Pemberton has today been given a free transfer and is listening to any offers but hopes to stay in the Premier League.'

Ah, dear 'Pembo'. The central defender, 32, recently recovered from a year-long injury, has a style best described as 'uncompromising' but it is one which has clearly left George Graham unimpressed. Leeds fans loved Pembo because he loved them. In fact, despite spells at Sheffield United and Crystal Palace, he always gave the impression that he was a Leeds fan who had climbed out of the Kop and pulled on a shirt. Trouble is, he plays a bit like that, too.

On the day of the Chelsea game, I discuss all this news over a pint with The Photographer outside the King's Road pub The Chelsea Potter. Worryingly, I hear myself discussing the source of the news with some enthusiasm. More worrying still, I can see from the crazed look in his eyes that he is immediately considering buying a modem to make Ceefax, Teletext, Skytext and Clubcall a thing of the past. I try to change the subject to something seen in the good old-fashioned newspapers: England's number one was once again in the England squad for the match against Georgia but was sent home from the training camp with suspected tonsillitis.

'Bloody typical, isn't it?' he sighs. Then there's a lull in the conversation and I just know he's thinking about going on-line.

We finish our drinks and wander down the King's Road. Our rendezvous pub is over a mile from Stamford Bridge, but the sun is shining, there are pretty girls everywhere and there is a Ruud Gullit garden gnome to laugh at in the World's End garden centre. Failing completely to hook up with The Biggest Yorkshireman In London, who today is swanning it in a box owned by the record company he works for, The Photographer and I go straight to the ground.

Stamford Bridge stadium is once again being rebuilt, the work this time at the southern end of the ground where in place of the old temporary seating rises a new stand which today, from the outside, looks like a block of flats. Inside it looks surprisingly small but perfectly maintains Chelsea's record of paying millions for grandstands that don't line up with those around them. This policy currently means that those sitting in a large portion of the north-east corner can't see all the pitch. But anything Chelsea get wrong is okay by me and I have to admit it hurts like hell to see so many of their fans buying flags and T-shirts for the FA Cup final in two weeks' time. At least this, and the fact that this is Chelsea's last home game of the season, seems to have put them in a good mood and the atmosphere is, uncommonly for a visit by Leeds United, remarkably convivial.

Although a handful boo, most Leeds fans are feeling convivial enough to applaud politely when Ruud Gullit walks out to make some presentations. Gianfranco Zola, who yesterday was named the Football Writers' Player of the Year, this afternoon picks up the trophy and another from Capital Radio to add to his recent award from the PFA. A final award goes not to Zola but to Mark Hughes, who runs out to applause from the Chelsea fans and convivial chants of 'Scum! Scum! Scum!' from the Leeds contingent. As he leaves the pitch and trots back towards the tunnel, he shows there's no hard feelings by smiling broadly and waving his trophy at his tormentors. Touched, we chant 'Useless! Useless! Useless!' in his honour – even though he isn't and scored a hat-trick in this fixture last season. Inspired, Leeds fans mix politics and sport by chanting 'He's on the dole, he's on the dole, Mellor's on the dole!' at the now ex-member of parliament who I hope is here to enjoy it. After which the teams run out and a 'Mo-lly! Mo-lly! Mo-lly!' earns a wave from Robert Molenaar, once again languishing with the substitutes.

At the kick-off the Leeds fans remain standing. But eventually the tedium becomes too much even for them, and after 15 minutes bums go back on seats like some perpendicular Mexican wave of apathy. I notice there seems to be no room in the dugout for the subs as Molenaar, Sharpe, Wallace and Beeney are all sitting with their backs to the advertising hoarding directly in front of the Leeds supporters. Laurent, mysteriously, sits elsewhere. Sitting down doesn't last long because those at the back – who surely have the worst view seated and therefore most to gain – strike up 'Stand up if you hate Man U' and so, dutifully, everyone does. Across the pitch in Chelsea's old West Stand, a single home supporter does the same.

On the pitch things are equally apathetic, but they get suddenly heated when Chelsea's big Norwegian defender Erland Johnsen, on a run forward, jumps for a ball with Wetherall and appears to use an elbow on the Leeds defender's head. Wetherall falls to the ground while Johnsen towers innocently over him, both immediately surrounded by a mob of yellow and blue shirts. Things threaten to get ugly until referee Jeff Winter steams in and manages to keep the peace.

The rest of the first half passes with stultifying dullness while the sun shines down. For Chelsea, everyone takes it easy, afraid of picking up an injury that will keep them out of the cup final. For Leeds, 'Dennis' Lilley alone gives it everything he's got, seemingly afraid that if he doesn't do so soon, he may never score. Watching a free header go wide, it's an opinion I'm beginning to share. Deane, in an effort to make him feel better, makes what might have been a shot go out for a throw-in.

The second half begins a little livelier, with Chelsea keeper Frode Grodas denying first Radebe then Deane in a frantic double strike, but it soon settles down into a goalless draw waiting to happen. Vialli moves around like a sulking schoolboy and even the normally tigerish Hughes can hardly be bothered to threaten. When Rush shoots pathetically after accidentally finding himself on a run that leaves him with no other option, I decide the final whistle can't come soon enough. There is a brief moment of amusement when a Deane shot cannons off a Chelsea defender and into Carlton Palmer's nethers, but I'm beginning to think of better ways to have spent the £20 I paid for the ticket. Lee Sharpe gets up and trots down the touchline but doesn't look for a minute like he believed Graham was about to bring him on.

Finally, it all becomes too much for the Leeds supporters who, in surprisingly tuneful desperation, begin to sing.

'All we are saying, is give us a goal.'

On the pitch, Leeds United do nothing of the sort. The supporters, entirely unsurprised, fall silent once more. As the final minutes approach Leeds perform something of a rally, but the ball has about as much chance of ending up in the net as John Major had of beating Tony Blair into number 10, yet from out of nowhere comes a bit of Dame Vera Lynn and the old Dunkirk spirit.

'We'll score again, don't know where, don't know when, but I know we'll score again some sunny day!'

It sounds good and is the most fun Leeds fans have had all day, so they sing it again. And again.

At the final whistle everyone breathes a sigh of relief and the longest-suffering supporters in the Premiership sing a bit more. Looking up I see the Chelsea chairman Ken Bates, at the front of the East Stand's upper tier, leaning over waving and applauding us as we turn and file out. Results on the electronic scoreboard show Forest are relegated but we are attempting to wash away our own misery, rejoicing in the booming acoustics underneath the stand to sing 'We'll score again' once more. With feeling . . .

Sunday, 4 May: Wolverhampton Wanderers vs. Portsmouth

In return for countless nights watching matches on Sky whilst slumped on his sofa, drinking his tea and laughing at his garden gnome painted in an old gold and black footie shirt, I agreed to drive The Wolves Fan to his team's final match of the season. For him it was meant to be a glorious celebration of promotion to the Premiership. For me it was meant to be a chance to see Leeds United's FA Cup conquerors put to the sword.

But football and life aren't like that. Wolves have instead finished in a play-off spot and spend the whole meaningless match treading gingerly, just as Chelsea did yesterday, lest they injure both their playing staff and their chances. Portsmouth, with nothing to prove, play almost as badly in a display which even Leeds could have bettered back on fifth-round day in February, then nick it at the end. Everyone goes home disappointed and I see in The Wolves Fan's weary face a painful misery I recognise well. It matters not which team you follow; in football, as in life, there are somehow always more losers than winners. So much for the lucky gnome . . .

Sunday, 11 May: home to Middlesbrough

Last day of the season. And so the nightmare ends. It's been a bad week. On Wednesday, the new Labour Chancellor Gordon Brown announced that he will allow the Bank of England to fix interest rates on its own, so that very night two Premiership managers, Roy Evans of Liverpool and Kenny Dalglish of Newcastle United, put their heads together and decide to fix Man United as Champions. Their teams lose 2–1 at Wimbledon and draw 0–0 at West Ham respectively. And don't tell me it's only Leeds fans who are upset about that.

Ceefax the next morning offered no relief in the form of 'top striker to join Leeds' transfer speculation, and when a small plastic bag falls out of the Rice Krispies box into my cereal bowl it contains not Wallace, Gromit or even 'Feathers' McGraw but Wendolene.

But today, things could be a lot worse – I could be a Middlesbrough fan. Nothing less than a win (or the restoration of the three points deducted for failing to play at Blackburn back in December) will keep them in the Premiership today and so they must score against one of the meanest defences in the league. This, though, is of no concern to me. I want them to be relegated.

Driving north in Little Andy's car, a sort of consensus emerges. We're stuck with losing Forest, so it's two from Middlesbrough, Sunderland and Coventry City. Middlesbrough are clear favourites. The idea amuses us and confirms that no matter how many expensive foreign imports you employ, you can't make a silk purse out of a sow's ear. Or arse, as Bryan Robson's team would more closely resemble if he left out the central triumvirate of Juninho, Emerson and Ravanelli. This reason alone is enough, but Middlesbrough's relegation would also save us one long drive next season and, of course, spare us ending this one with a defeat. Avoiding the long drive has The Photographer wavering over Sunderland, but with the promise of that new stadium to visit, in the end the third choice is simple: Coventry City. They are only in with a chance because Leeds were stupid enough to lose all six points to them this season, and only here at all because Leeds failed to score at Highfield Road on the final day of last season. Then there's the McAllister factor. Respect for our former hero has dwindled as the season has gone on to the point where the humiliation of relegation seems like justice. It's a perfectly horrible attitude and completely indefensible, but we adopt it anyway and motor on northwards.

We park and get to the West Stand just as the Middlesbrough team coach arrives. The players get off surrounded by dozens of people, most of them chanting 'You're going down! You're going down!', while a few visitors respond with 'We're staying up! We're staying up!'. Whether or not they really believe that is hard to tell, but without their Italian hero Ravanelli, who is on the bus but is not recovered from injury, it's going to be tough.

Inside the ground there's a palpable tension and it's set to be a big crowd. The players warm up in the sunshine. Mark Beeney, Gary Kelly and Rod Wallace come to the grandstands and sign autographs while the Middlesbrough fans chant their players' names. It's easy to sense nervousness in the South Stand but the players at least look calm. A steward chats to The Photographer and tells him they have been briefed to expect trouble should Middlesbrough not win. Around our seats behind the Sky camera — the match is to be broadcast live — the familiar faces assemble for the last time: The Man From Birmingham (who has somehow got tickets in row BB for him and The Copper), Kay From Blackpool, Ian The Moustache and Niki, Howard The Student and his father Ken. Only The Biggest Yorkshireman In London cannot make it and sits instead in front of Sky, chewing his lip.

Howard The Student is particularly excited because to his right sit two conspicuously attractive girls none of us have seen before. The man behind him reckons the blonde in the blue shorts is Lee Sharpe's girlfriend. The Sky cameraman hears this rumour and swings his camera around to get a shot. Both girls smile dutifully.

As kick-off approaches the atmosphere builds. The Kop taunts the 'Boro fans packed into the South Stand once more and they respond with 'Boring, boring Leeds!' to the tune not heard since Graham was manager at Arsenal. Presumably the 'Boro fans think they are telling the home crowd something it hasn't yet realised. Just before kick-off the blonde in the blue shorts whips off her shirt and runs topless on to the pitch to huge cheers. To Howard's right her friend sits giggling while two stewards chase and apprehend her. With an alertness that does not bode well, Brian Deane misses the whole thing while tying his boot-laces.

Sharpe is back in the starting line-up today, replacing Palmer, who isn't even on the bench. By six o'clock tonight, if tabloid rumours are to be trusted, both will have played their last game for Leeds United, as will Ian Rush, once again playing on the right of midfield. Contract negotiations continue to resecure the services of Deane and Dorigo, but the latter's future may be in serious doubt if another rumour circulating this afternoon — that Leeds are to buy the Glasgow Rangers left-back David Robertson — proves true.

None of this, though, seems relevant as the teams run out, Sharpe the last in line alongside the tiny figure of Juninho. The Leeds team run to the centre circle, form a line, then turn and wave to all four sides of the ground. The gesture revives a tradition invented by Don Revie that Leeds have since abandoned but so many other sides have adopted. If only Leeds could revive the Revie era tradition of winning things, Elland Road might be a much happier place.

As the whistle gets the game under way, however, happiness is all relative. The 'Boro fans roar encouragement but soon settle back nervously to relative quiet. Emerson is booed at every touch and Juninho struggles to get the better of Radebe, even though, I note with increasing anxiety, the South African is making no attempt to man-mark the Brazilian playmaker.

Lilley beats Clayton Blackmore but keeper Ben Roberts parries and there are two defenders there to clear when Lilley attempts to follow up. In a flash the ball is at the other end and Martyn has to stretch to parry a 25-yard Phil Stamp shot over the bar. More in relief than sound critical judgement, the Kop cries out, 'Bryan Robson is a wanker, is a wanker!' while the 'Boro manager stands watching, impassively, flanked by his assistants. Ravanelli, a spectator on the bench, looks on grimly.

Time passes. The Kop sings 'We'll score again' again, but no one is certain Leeds will. With the half almost gone a long ball from Radebe finds Deane on the wing. His cross reaches only a 'Boro head but the ball drops to Bowyer, who fires wide the best chance of the half.

Howard The Student has missed it, as he has yet again volunteered to get the coffees in. His tireless dedication to servitude is widely respected around rows BB and CC but tragically his absence in the first half's dying minutes has never once prompted Leeds to score and compound his misfortune. We live in hope for next season and turn to watch the half-times on the scoreboard. Damn – Man United are a goal up against West Ham! Good grief – Newcastle have put four past Forest! Groan – Coventry are 1–0 up at Tottenham! Shit – Sunderland are only 0–0 at Wimbledon. Which means currently Coventry are safe and 'Boro are doomed. The word is that the Coventry game kicked off 15 minutes late but no one can decide whether this makes any difference. Instead I pause to think how awful it must be to support Middlesbrough right now, knowing you have just 45 minutes to score or be relegated. I begin to feel a little sympathy for them but am easily distracted by the sight of the Leeds chairman Bill Fotherby emerging from the tunnel to present the youth team with the Northern Intermediate League Championship trophy. The youngsters do a lap of honour to much applause, including that of the 'Boro contingent – which is spectacularly sporting, given their current state of trauma.

The second half begins cautiously while the Kop does its Dame Vera Lynn bit again. After ten minutes Robson attempts to crank things up by bringing off Craig Hignett, but his worst problem is either striker Mikkel Beck, who is embarrassingly wasteful, or Emerson, almost an invisible man. Juninho, however, is looking better and better, chasing hard and running everywhere – still unmarked.

It's hard to tell whether the match is any better than those of late because of the sense of occasion. It's also hard to tell which I would prefer: to score or to keep a clean sheet. The latter would mean no team has scored against Leeds in the league at Elland Road since Coventry did on Boxing Day. Deane does his bit towards both causes by outrunning Emerson down the touchline but the Brazilian fouls him. From the free-kick the ball reaches Rush, who shoots high and wide (for the last time, please God) then appeals for a corner as if to shift the blame somewhere else. Referee Alan Wilkie is as unimpressed as the rest of us.

With a little over 20 minutes left, Bryan Robson is unimpressed enough to take off Emerson, still ambling around as if nothing at all depended on the game. On seeing his number held aloft and Chris Freestone ready to come on, Emerson doesn't head for the bench but storms straight down the tunnel. The Kop's chant of 'He's going home! He's going home!' follows him to the dressing-room. Good riddance.

Juninho seems to redouble his efforts and I am near frantic about the space he is being allowed, but despite his determination he is one man amongst ten boys this afternoon and the Premiership is slipping from his side's grasp.

In front of the Kop a ball by Bowyer falls to Lilley, who gathers and stabs it past Roberts, then turns and sprints to the halfway line in triumph. He gets almost all the way there before he becomes aware of what everyone else in the ground already knows: the lineman's flag is up for offside. At least when he finally scores his first goal he's already rehearsed the celebration. Two minutes later Rush, a man unlikely to be celebrating again, is replaced by Wallace and I begin to sense that Leeds will not be beaten. Wallace goes into the action almost immediately and, with two swift changes of direction away on the right, makes room to cross to Deane, whose flick header goes into the net by Roberts's right-hand post. Aware of what that goal means to the team in red, Deane celebrates sheepishly, but is instantly mobbed by all nine of his less subtle outfield team-mates.

For Middlesbrough it is now do or die, and predictably it is Juninho who two minutes later begins a darting run towards the Leeds goal. His path is blocked by Bowyer, who instinctively sticks out a boot when Juninho shoots. The ball clips that boot and the deflection sees the ball sail beyond Martyn's outstretched arms. Juninho merely waves his team-mates back for the restart to try to conjure one more in the 11 minutes of normal time that remain. Each one passes with agonising slowness as Middlesbrough's belated sense of urgency prompts some frantic Leeds defending followed by swift counter-attacking. There seem to be more shots on goal, at either end, in the last ten minutes than in the previous 80, but none of them count, and as Wilkie signals the end of the match after three minutes of injury time the cruel reality of football sinks home.

Even from my seat it's obvious that many of the 'Boro fans are in tears. On the pitch Juninho, Beck, Kinder and Fleming sit helpless on the grass. Juninho rests his head in his hands while cameramen train their lenses on his suffering. I'm relieved that Leeds have not lost, disappointed that they conceded a goal, but haunted by the sight of Juninho, an image that will surely be printed in every newspaper tomorrow.

Through the cordon of orange-vested security men fearing a pitch invasion that does not come, I see Halle and Lilley both walk past Juninho and pat him on the shoulder, but he does not, cannot, look up. Bryan Robson goes across to speak words of commiseration. The Kop sing 'You're going down!' but this hardly seems like a time for gloating. Martyn and Bowyer also try to console Juninho, while Deane puts a friendly arm around Robson. The scoreboard confirms that Sunderland have lost 1–0 at Wimbledon but even if Coventry surrender their 2–1 lead at Spurs, Middlesbrough are definitely down. Everyone in red on the pitch and in the stands looks numb.

When Juninho finally gets to his feet and walks towards the tunnel, Deane goes to him and puts an arm around his shoulder. Together they walk off the pitch and into separate dressing-rooms that must offer little joy for Leeds and no comfort at all for Middlesbrough . . .

Thursday, 15 May: away to Crystal Palace, FA Youth Cup final second leg

In the confusion of emotions at Elland Road on Sunday, it was easy to forget there was one last chance to see a Leeds United side take the field. It's tonight, and Leeds will start the game with a 2–1 advantage from the first leg.

The Biggest Yorkshireman In London meets me at Victoria along with his dad and Barbara, a small but enthusiastic party mysteriously completed by Slayer The Scouser, presumably along to see Leeds fail as miserably as his team Liverpool have done recently. Once again, no one can remember which three stations we have to choose from and so board the first train we think goes somewhere near. It takes us to Selhurst, the least familiar but ironically closest of the three, and we discover a more than half-decent pub already almost full with Leeds and Palace fans. There we discuss the first rumour of the season that has proved correct – Leeds' signing of Rangers' left-back David

Robertson – and whether sports minister Tony Banks ought to be allowed out unattended after suggesting this morning that foreign players in the Premiership should be allowed to play for England.

We reach the Arthur Wait Stand in good time for the 7.30 kick-off but have to walk halfway round the ground to join a disturbingly long queue at the main office because Selhurst Park will take no money at the turnstiles. We meet The Photographer in the street, but as he's been given a photo pass he can waltz right in. The rest of us have no choice but to miss the kick-off while waiting to buy our £3 tickets. When I get to the front, a Palace fan gives me £20 to get him a pair. The Biggest Yorkshireman In London says he'll get one for me so I swallow my pride and buy two for the Palace side of the ground. The Palace fan generously offers me a fiver for my trouble but I merely thank him and say we still owe Palace big time for selling us Nigel Martyn.

The stands behind both goals are closed, but looking around the Arthur Wait and at the main stand opposite there are clearly well over 4,000 people here tonight, despite the live Sky broadcast. Excruciatingly, an awful lot of these are schoolkids including four really annoying girls directly behind us whose screeching chant of 'Eagles! Eagles!' makes fingernails across a blackboard sound like Mozart. There are a lot of Leeds fans here, too, mixed in with the mostly young Palace supporters. The locals look shocked and confused when deep and mostly northern voices start bellowing 'Stand up if you hate Man U'.

On the pitch the young Palace are doing most of the attacking and are clearly a good side, with Clinton Morrison looking particularly menacing on the right, but Leeds are composed and look menacing whenever they win and distribute the ball. The Biggest Yorkshireman In London and his father, watching this team for the first time, are clearly impressed, and not for the first time the words 'better than the first team' hang in the air. Chances come and chances go but at half-time the score remains 0–0 and the big block of Leeds fans to my right are noisily confident.

'We are the champions! Champions of Europe!' seems madder than ever here, and judging by the looks of utter shock on the faces of the weenie Palace fans, the sight of a few coachloads of Yorkshiremen waving their shirts over their heads is quite unusual in SE25 too. I spot The Photographer taking pictures of them and so wander down to chat as two kids step forward to mug for him. They've both got their tickets by playing for one of Palace's youth development sides but neither seems keen to follow in the footsteps of the team they're here to support. 'No way, man! I'm going to play for Liverpool!' promises the taller of the two. Behind him, a gaggle of older Palace fans have taken up position in front of the bare-chested Leeds mob and are pointing and waving their colours while trying to outsing their visitors. Everyone is smiling. There's not a hint of malice. And given nights like this for foundation, the future of football is secure.

Leeds begin the second half the stronger of the teams and their sense of confidence is mirrored in their play. Palace are desperate to score but can't find a way through. Leeds are patient and Stephen McPhail, Lee Matthews and Matthew Jones all come close. 'Stand up if you're 2–1 up!' comes the chant.

The breakthrough seems to be edging ever nearer when with 25 minutes left coach Paul Hart substitutes Jones with Andy Wright. Every chance he gets, Wright, playing more than ever like Eddie Gray, dips his shoulder and goes for the byline, weaving his way through Palace defenders like they were cones on a training pitch. The home team's frustrations become apparent when their number seven, David Stevens, elbows Leeds captain Alan Maybury and is sent off. Ten minutes is all it takes Leeds to capitalise on their numerical advantage. Just as I was fearing yet another 0–0 draw, McPhail drifts into the Palace penalty area on the right and his sharply hit cross is turned neatly past keeper Gareth Ormshaw by Matthews to make it 1–0 on the night and 3–1 on aggregate.

As the celebrations die down, a proud chant rings out: 'Are you watching, Manchester?' If only it could have been this Leeds side that knocked them out instead of Watford in the fourth round . . .

To both teams' credit, neither side gives up trying to score again in the ten minutes that remain, but when the whistle goes it is Leeds who finish the stronger. For the last time this season I join in as the fans sing the supporters' anthem (technically the B-side of the 1972 squad's hit single) while the Palace fans file home and their young side wait unhappily to receive their runners-up medals in the centre of the pitch:

'Marching on together, we're gonna see you win. We are so proud, we're shouting out loud, we love you Leeds, Leeds, Leeds!'

The Leeds players are running out of team-mates, friends and club officials to hug and so trot over to the largest body of travelling supporters. As they get to the barrier, Matthews borrows a flag while others shake the hands of men perhaps twice their age, joining in as the chant goes up: 'We are the champions! Champions of Youth Cup!'

When the players return to the centre for the presentation of the trophy, I spot The Photographer muscling in among the newspapermen and the Sky TV cameramen. The cup is taken first by Maybury, then passed down the line to Damian Lynch, Matthews, McPhail, Robinson, Wright, Jonathon Woodgate, Kevin Dixon, Harry Kewell, Jones, Wesley Boyle and Tommy Knarvik. As I watch Matthews and McPhail trot off for a touchline Sky interview, I wonder how many of these names will go on to something greater in the years ahead. Interview completed, Matthews and McPhail rejoin the rest of the squad as they bring the trophy over towards the hundreds of Leeds fans still in the Arthur Wait.

I find myself hugging the Biggest Yorkshireman In London as the hairs on the back of my neck stand up and I try to savour this season's first moment of total triumph. Loving Leeds United has taken some doing over the last nine months. I have worked out that I have travelled the best part of 13,000 miles and spent more money than I dare to calculate. But only this team in front of me now, singing the same songs I sing, loving the same club I love, have made any real difference. For just about the first time since last August this love doesn't hurt, it actually makes me feel good. It's come a little late, but – as my dear departed dad would have said – all the best things in life are worth waiting for.

He would, however, have suggested I go to one or two fewer games next season . . .

Afterword

Leeds United finished in 11th place, having scored just 28 goals and been involved in nine goalless draws. They conceded just 38 goals, the fourth-lowest total in the Premiership, having kept 20 clean sheets. They didn't have enough players sent off to beat Arsenal to the top of the disciplinary points table.

England's number one, Nigel Martyn, won the player of the season vote by a landslide, scooping 75 per cent of the vote. He finally returned to the England team on Saturday 24 May in a friendly against South Africa at Old Trafford, which England won 2–1. He was still with the squad when they won the Tournoi de France in June.

Construction of a new West Stand and associated indoor arena was delayed a year and rescheduled to begin in May 1998.

Director of youth coaching Paul Hart left Leeds United for a job at Nottingham Forest in June 1997, saying, 'I find it astonishing that George Graham has only watched our youth team three times since he arrived . . .'

Appendix

Date	Match	League/Cup
Aug 10	Grimbsy Town vs. Leeds United	Friendly
Aug 17	Derby County vs. Leeds United	Premiership
Aug 20	Leeds United vs. Sheffield Wednesday	Premiership
Aug 26	Leeds United vs. Wimbledon	Premiership
Sep 4	Blackburn Rovers vs. Leeds United	Premiership
Sep 7	Leeds United vs. Manchester United	Premiership
Sep 14	Coventry City vs. Leeds United	Premiership
Sep 18	Leeds United vs. Darlington	Coca-Cola 2 (1)
Sep 21	Leeds United vs. Newcastle United	Premiership
Sep 25	Darlington vs. Leeds United	Coca-Cola 2 (2)
Sep 28	Leicester City vs. Leeds United	Premiership
Oct 5	Barnet vs. Torquay United	Division Three
Oct 12	Leeds United vs. Nottingham Forest	Premiership
Oct 19	Aston Villa vs. Leeds United	Premiership
Oct 23	Leeds United vs. Aston Villa	Coca-Cola 3
Oct 26	Arsenal vs. Leeds United	Premiership
Nov 2	Leeds United vs. Sunderland	Premiership
Nov 16	Leeds United vs. Liverpool	Premiership
Nov 23	Southampton vs. Leeds United	Premiership
Nov 27	Oldham Athletic vs. Leeds United	Pontin's Central
Dec 1	Leeds United vs. Chelsea	Premiership
Dec 7	Leeds United vs. Rotherham United	N. Intermediate
Dec 7	Middlesbrough vs. Leeds United	Premiership
Dec 14	Leeds United vs. Tottenham Hotspur	Premiership

Dec 21	Everton vs. Leeds United	Premiership
Dec 26	Leeds United vs. Coventry City	Premiership
Dec 28	Manchester United vs. Leeds United	Premiership
Jan 1	Newcastle United vs. Leeds United	Premiership
Jan 7	Manchester City vs. Leeds United	FA Youth Cup 3
Jan 11	Leeds United vs. Leicester City	Premiership
Jan 14	Crystal Palace vs. Leeds United	FA Cup 3
Jan 20	West Ham United vs. Leeds United	Premiership
Jan 25	Leeds United vs. Crystal Palace	FA Cup 3 (Replay)
Jan 29	Leeds United vs. Derby County	Premiership
Feb 1	Leeds United vs. Arsenal	Premiership
Feb 4	Arsenal vs. Leeds United	FA Cup 4
Feb 15	Leeds United vs. Portsmouth	FA Cup 5
Feb 19	Liverpool vs. Leeds United	Premiership
Feb 22	Leeds United vs. Scunthorpe United	N. Intermediate
Feb 22	Sunderland vs. Leeds United	Premiership
Mar 1	Leeds United vs. West Ham United	Premiership
Mar 8	Leeds United vs. Everton	Premiership
Mar 12	Leeds United vs. Southampton	Premiership
Mar 15	Tottenham Hotspur vs. Leeds United	Premiership
Mar 22	Sheffield Wednesday vs. Leeds United	Premiership
Apr 7	Leeds United vs. Blackburn Rovers	Premiership
Apr 9	Luton Town vs. Leeds United	FA Youth Cup semi-final (1)
Apr 16	Wimbledon vs. Leeds United	Premiership
Apr 19	Nottingham Forest vs. Leeds United	Premiership
Apr 22	Leeds United vs. Aston Villa	Premiership
May 3	Chelsea vs. Leeds United	Premiership
May 11	Leeds United vs. Middlesbrough	Premiership
May 15	Crystal Palace vs. Leeds United	FA Youth Cup final (2)